P9-BBQ-389

advertising directions | two

advertising

trends

in visual

advertising

directions | two

edited by

Arthur Hawkins

and

Edward Gottschall

published by

Art Directions Book Co.,

New York

contents

HOW DOES IT ADD UP?   **7**   *Edward M. Gottschall*

THE ARTIST, THE MARKET, AND TOMORROW   **9**   *John P. Cunningham*

FOUR CRITICS IN SEARCH OF AN ANSWER   **11**   *Russell Lynes*

ILLUSTRATION: THE SHOCK BECOMES COMMONPLACE   **17**   *Harry Carter*

ADVERTISING PHOTOGRAPHY   **25**   *Onofrio Paccione*

ADVERTISING TYPOGRAPHY   **33**   *George Guido*

DESIGN: A MEANS OF CORPORATE EXPRESSION   **43**   *James K. Fogleman*

ANNUAL REPORTS: MORE THAN FINANCIAL STATEMENTS   **55**   *Mahlon A. Cline*

THE EMPHASIS SHIFTS IN MAGAZINE PAGES   **63**   *Otto Storch*

APPLIANCES: FROM ADDY TO NEWSY TO CREATIVE   **79**   *Walter Glenn*

TRENDS IN FINANCIAL ADVERTISING   **87**   *Paul R. Smith*

TRENDS IN PHARMACEUTICAL ADVERTISING   **95**   *Ken Lavey*

GRAND ILLUSION: COSMETIC ADVERTISING   **103**   *Irving Trabich*

BEER ADVERTISING: MANY HEADS, FEW DIRECTIONS   **111**   *Howard Munce*

VISUAL DIRECTIONS IN AIRLINES ADVERTISING   **119**   *Andrew K. Nelson*

RETAIL ADVERTISING: A TREND IS NEEDED   **127**   *Arnold Varga*

TV TODAY AND TOMORROW   **131**   *William R. Duffy*

PACKAGE DESIGN TRENDS   **139**   *Donald R. Ruther*

designer: Arthur Hawkins

V.S.W.
12-10-81-

contents

TRENDS IN DIRECT MAIL   **147**   *Art Schlosser*

TRENDS IN OUTDOOR POSTERS   **155**   *Orville Sheldon*

IN POINT-OF-PURCHASE, DESIGN SELLS, OR ELSE   **163**   *David Flasterstein*

RECORD ALBUM DIRECTIONS   **171**   *Robert M. Jones*

FASHION GOES MIDDLE VOLUME   **177**   *Gene Federico*

TRENDS IN FOOD ADVERTISING   **180**   *Robert W. Wheeler*

TRENDS IN CIGARETTE ADVERTISING   **182**   *Robert West*

LIQUOR ADVERTISING'S NEW LOOK   **184**   *Fred Widlicka*

TRENDS IN AUTOMOBILE ADVERTISING   **186**   *George Lois*

THE TREND IS TOWARD CONFUSION   **188**   *Elwood Whitney*

IDEAS OF THE YEAR   **200**   *Edward M. Gottschall*

NEW TYPEFACES   **213**

WHAT'S NEW IN PRODUCTION   **215**

ART BUSINESS NEWS ROUNDUP   **223**

CLUB AND EXHIBIT DIRECTORY   **225**

NEW BOOKS   **227**

AUTHOR'S WHO'S WHO   **231**

INDEX TO ADVERTISERS   **236**

TRENDS INDEX   **255**

how does it add up?

by EDWARD GOTTSCHALL

The big trend is toward sophistication. There has always been sophistication but until recently it has been a class market attribute. Today it is in the supermarket.

As you thread through this book you will find many writers pointing toward increased sophistication in their markets and the products, packages, advertising and promotion material designed for them.

You'll find it in fashion advertising and luxury cars, as you would expect. And you'll find it in cosmetics distributed via variety stores, in TV commercials, in mass market packaging, in direct mail, in point-of-purchase material.

If sophistication is the big trend today, it is a natural companion to our still vital concern with believability, taste, images, symbology, creativity, communication-mindedness.

What is sophistication? Why is it a vital force right now? Where is it going? What can marketing men, ad men, visual communicators do about it?

Sophistication" has two meanings relevant to advertising's directions.

- *deprived of original simplicity . . . refined . . . subtilized . . .*
- *misrepresentation in argument . . . fallacious reasoning*

marginal product differences and boredom

In recent years many competitive products have very slight functional, appearance, price differences. Advertisers are reduced to saying the same thing about each, being factual and straight-faced, or to developing an unique image for the product or company. This image must give the product individuality that will help it prosper.

The need for images has brought about greater concern with visual symbology, with creativity, with communication-mindedness (a concern that the message be not merely subjectively fresh but clearly received). This interrelationship between all these trends and forces in recent years has brought about increasing use of sophisticated approaches. To avoid the boredom and lack of identity that could result from similar products with similar claims, we have added the new dimension of individual personality. Products may still be alike in character but they now differ in personality. And, since selling is more an emotional than a rational process, the building of product personality by visual communications has become the great direction in today's advertising.

Thus the selling statement became deprived of its original simplicity, refined, subtilized. We no longer say the obvious. We speak in tangents. The straight line is no longer the shortest distance between two communication points. We now carom our arguments off emotions and use predominantly visual rather than verbal persuasion to assure fast reception, to avoid negative rationalizations, to increase retention.

a moral question is involved

The sophisticated approach can be the deceptive approach. Sophistication, when Plato and Aristophanes fought it 2500 years ago, implied specious, false reasoning. It can mean these things today but need not.

Deception is not only the concern of the moralizers. It is the concern of the most hard-headed marketer who knows that he is in business for tomorrow as well as today and wants no backfires.

If today's big direction is toward more sophistication in advertising, today's and tomorrow's big challenge is to walk the tight-rope of creativity and sophistication without falling on the one side into clichés and boredom and indistinction or on the other into misrepresentation.

In this book is the work of many advertisers who have walked the rope successfully.

the artist, the market, and tomorrow...

how a blend of uninhibited ideating and disciplined thinking creates persuasive forces and advertising directions

by JOHN P. CUNNINGHAM

A strange thing is happening! The sensitive hand of the artist is becoming one of the so-called Pillars of the Free Enterprise System.

Every year it is reaching deeper and deeper into the factory.

Engineers are calling upon the artist to shape their ideas for product development.

Chemists are calling upon him to design the containers for their mixtures.

Marketing men are calling upon him to dream up shapes, pictures and packages that will move the product into the store and then move the hands of people toward the product.

More and more is the artist becoming involved in mercantile jargon—with such phrases as "share-of-mind," "share-of-shelf" and "share-of-market."

Why? Because a large section of America's industrial capacity has become dependent on the artist's brush or camera for business. Because one of the greatest needs in the country today is a more exciting and arresting visual interpretation of the things that America is making and selling.

Economists tell us we have become very proficient in mass production—that we must now become equally proficient in mass consumption.

They tell us that unless we people in commercial communications are able to increase the capacity of America to consume, our factories will be ejecting goods all over the landscape—with no takers.

In the last Presidential campaign, one of the few things that both candidates were agreed upon was that we must increase our industrial growth by 5 per cent every year to keep up America's strength and vigor.

But, unfortunately, the economists and politicians can't do this job. It has to be done by the salesmen of America, of whom the commercial artist is one of the most potent.

This is an assignment that will call for new selling techniques, new paths of persuasion. Men thinking new thoughts!

Such thoughts are always milling around in the mind of the true creative artist. Often these ideas seem to be nebulous, confused and half-formed—even to their possessors.

The greatest satisfaction, however, that a creative mind can have is in the disciplining of a capricious thought, or the conversion of a wild idea into a solid and usable persuasive force.

So I would like to raise an imaginary glass, in tribute to all the vagrant, half-formed and half-baked ideas now circulating in the minds of creative people everywhere. May many of them soon emerge into the national market-place as exciting new advertising trends.

many directions, many causes . . .

As Elwood Whitney points out, the many directions of advertising often add up to confusion. One source of our confusion as admen comes from our search for the great force in life. We are looking for what isn't. We read Dr. Dichter and find out it is to be found in the unconscious. We read Vance Packard and find it is the drive for status. Freud says it's sex; Marx economics. Huntington would have us believe that geography, weather, soil, climate, is the basic force. And deists ascribe everything to God. Each makes his point well, and you tend to believe the one read last. And if you read too much, you become confused.

Nearest to the truth was William James. His theory of pluralism explained that there are many forces, but no one force that determined all the others. In this spirit Advertising Directions notes not only many directions, but many reasons for them. John Cunningham has pointed to some of the economic influences on advertising. Russell Lynes focusses our attention on social and esthetic currents.

four critics in search of an answer

here advertising is dissected from the viewpoints of the social critic, the art critic, the social historian and the historian of taste

by RUSSELL LYNES

To the social critic advertising is likely to be anathema. To the art critic it is interesting more or less as folk art. To the social historian it is a booby-trap against which he must be constantly on his guard. To the historian of taste it is revealing, often confusing, sometimes amusing, but only partly reliable. As one who has dabbled in all four of these minor literary arts, my attitude toward what I see when I turn over the pages of old or new magazines and newspapers (I do it more often than most people, even more often than most writers) varies somewhat with the particular hat I happen to be wearing.

sour pusses and watch dogs

Let me explain. The social critic views advertising as one measure of the conflict between the moral concept of "the good life" and the commercial concept of it. He sees it as a tug of war between the values of industry on the one hand (economic values) and the values of the spirit (personal values) on the other. He sees claims, both physical and social, that he knows to be false or, if not false, then greatly exaggerated, which to him is the same thing. He sees seduction and he sees trickery. He sees snobbisms played upon, fears toyed with, aspirations for personal betterment put in false contexts, and trivialities made to seem important. He used to see advertisements which claimed that their products were ultimate, final, never to be improved upon. Now with planned obsolescence built into the style and manufacture of every sort of hard-goods, he finds these claims no longer. Now it's "we've never given it to you so good before . . ." but there are certainly no promises that it won't be better next year. There are, of course, many other aspects of advertising that the social critic finds distasteful. He deplores the billboards that he believes despoil our landscapes. He resents the imposition of commercials on what little patience he has with television, and most of all he shudders at what he believes the acceptance of advertising in every sort of medium reveals about the sheeplike quality of the public.

But then the social critic is a sour-puss; it is his function to be a sour-puss. He is a watch-dog and without watch-dogs, societies become slovenly. Indeed, they sometimes slip and slither in spite of their watch-dogs.

an echo of bigger voices What about the art critic? Presumably the strength of the art critic is as the strength of ten laymen looking at art because his heart is pure. He is interested in what he likes to think of as "the larger context," and he is interested in advertising as it reflects a new kind of patronage of the artist . . . corporate patronage as opposed to private, princely, public or ecclesiastical patronage . . . or as it is a shadow of the styles created by the fine artist. Now and then he discovers something new in advertising that he has not seen elsewhere, a new image like that of Toulouse Lautrec in his posters or more recently (but still quite a while ago) the work of Cassandre and E. McKnight Kauffer. But by and large advertising art is to him only the echo of more important voices, though he is entertained by the ways in which styles in architecture and painting find their ways into advertisements and are thus hurried into the public consciousness and become socially acceptable.

He looks, for example, at an advertisement for a Locomobile in *Harper's Weekly* of 1899, with its classical columns and nymphs in flowing robes, and he knows that if it had not been for the startling display of pseudo (or neo, if you prefer) classical architecture at the Columbian Exposition

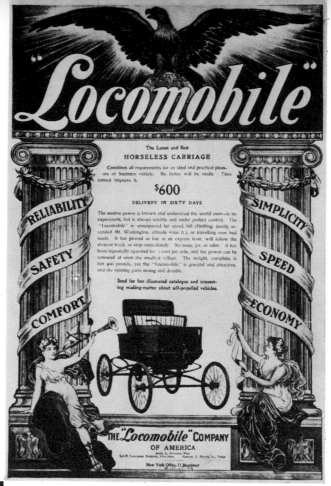

in Chicago in 1893 which dazzled millions of Americans, this style would not have occurred to the artist who drew the ad. Or he finds *Art Nouveau* in a Ford ad in the Saturday Evening Post in 1908 and a few decades later imitations of Dali in perfume ads, echoes of Chirico, of Pierre Roy, of any number of other so-called "serious" artists. He is amused, but he is not greatly impressed . . . not as impressed as he might be, in my estimation, by the quality of drawing, of layout, and of sensibility that is frequently the mark of good advertising. "Clever," he says, or, "facile."

The social historian's attitude is quite different. It is not primarily his function to pass moral or artistic judgments but to get as close as he can to finding out the truth of how a society leads its daily life. Advertisements tell him something he wants to know: what kinds of products did the public buy, what did they cost, how were they used, what needs did they fill, in what ways were they expected to make life more enjoyable? The social historian will spend a great deal of time pouring over advertisements in much the same way that he pours over diaries and letters looking for relevant detail. "Ah," he says to himself, "a lawn-mower." And then he goes thumbing back from the 1890s where he has first seen an advertisement for a lawnmower and tries to trace it to its first appearance. When, he wants to know, was the householder weaned away from cutting his lawn with a specially constructed scythe? The kinds of clothes people wear in an automobile ad tell him something about what people thought of "motoring" in Edith Wharton's day when it was considered a sport rather than a reliable means of transportation. He looks at the details of the interior of a room in a 1916 ad and he can tell from it something about how people entertained themselves. Is there a piano, a phonograph, a bookcase, magazines on the table, a collection of fancy plates on a plate-rail, a curio cabinet? What was culture? But he looks at such ads with skepticism. He knows that he cannot rely on them as primary sources of information and that they can be greatly misleading. They do not show life as it was but, rather, as most people would have liked to think it ought to be. Advertisements often bear about as much relation to life as the elongated and pin-headed fashion figure bears to the human body . . . nobody lives in either one. And so, for all the amusement and usefulness that advertising is to the social historian, he treats it warily.

To the historian of taste, advertising is meat and potatoes and baked-Alaska. Taste, as I have said elsewhere, is our "personal delight, our private dilemma, and our public facade," and it is the public facade and the private dilemma that emerge in advertising. It tells us what our taste ought to be which, as anyone knows who knows anything about changes in style, is what we are almost ready to accept. The advertisement, for example, which shows the family spick and span in the rumpus room, beer cans and glasses on the built-in bar, hunting prints on the knotty-pine walls and a golf trophy on the mantel may bear no relation to life as it is lived (nobody is that cheerful, that neat, or that vacuous) but it reflects the taste of a great many people— the kind of public facade that hosts of families presumably would like to present to the world. Advertising is always larger than life and cleaner. Taste is not necessarily what people have, it is what they think they ought to want. When the interior of an automobile, which is actually so small that to get in and out of it is like doing push-ups, is blown up in an advertisement to the spaciousness of a Pullman car, the historian of taste feels quite at home. False perspective is one of the oldest devices for making palaces out of paltry spaces. It is one of the oldest deceptions in the history of taste, but one of the most delightful to believe. The American dream is "a nice little house with a great big livingroom." How to be cozy on $75,000 a year, or how to be luxurious on $75.00 a week; it's all the same thing. Or so the advertisements seems to say to the historian of taste.

From advertising he can tell quite a lot about changing patterns in "good taste"—both visual taste and social taste. He can get less idea about social "bad taste," except in advertisements for books of etiquette. Visual and social (call it moral, if you prefer) taste are only slightly connected. It is quite conceivable, for example, to produce an advertisement that is visually in acceptable "good taste" and offensive to "good taste" in every other respect. You will remember a few years ago an advertisement for a television set that suggested that the ego of your child might be bruised for life if he had to go to the neighbors to watch TV. A howl went up when it appeared on full pages in the New York morning papers. "Dirty trick," people thought, and they said, "A low blow at those who can't afford a set and an insult to the intelligence of those who can." That was "bad taste" of one kind. Other kinds of bad taste are too numerous and too obvious to mention to anyone who knows advertising. The essential quality of bad taste is misjudgment of the audience to whom it is directed. There was no such thing as bad taste in the old *Police Gazette*.

But to the historian of taste, who isn't likely to be shocked by any sort of taste, there are nuances of taste in advertisements which he finds revealing. It is easy, for example, to trace from 1890 to the present the course of social informality, not only by what garments (or lack of garments) appear acceptable in ads, but in how close the male and female may be joined in embrace. The female nude from the back today is acceptable; the male is not. The breast, so long as the nipple is concealed, is acceptable now, though in some ads of the Victorian era the outline drawing of the female nude, nipples included, was evidently considered all right, though that was an era when a lady scarcely dared show her ankle in the parlor. Children can get away with saying things that adults for reasons of "good taste" cannot. "Mummy, they have a lovely house, but their bathroom paper hurts." That appeared in an ad some years ago. Nobody today, however, can say "toilet paper." It's not *toilet* that now is unacceptable, but *paper!* Tissue, however, is in "good taste." No one today would think of using the word "bowels" in an ad, but how to talk about their functions in glorious circumlocutions is a major intellectual challenge to the "creativity" of copy-writers. In the last century, the heyday of bottled panaceas for all the ills of the flesh, Lydia Pinkham would never have thought of saying "Because. . . ." [She said what she meant: "A sure cure for all FEMALE WEAKNESSES, including Leucorrhca, Irregular and Painful Menstruation, Inflamation and Ulceration of the Womb, Flooding, Prolapsus Uteri, etc."]

**LYDIA E. PINKHAM'S
VEGETABLE COMPOUND.**

A Sure Cure for all FEMALE WEAK-
NESSES, Including Leucorrhœn, Ir-
regular and Painful Menstruation,
Inflammation and Ulceration of
the Womb, Flooding, PRO-
LAPSUS UTERI, &c.

These are the sorts of switches in social acceptability that delight the historian of taste. How is it, he wonders, that as life becomes more informal, and "gentility" gives way to casualness in manners, as we discuss in the living room topics not so long ago taboo even in the bedroom, we devise the most elegant coynesses and euphenisms for these same topics in advertising? We laugh at our forebears for never using the word "legs"; even pianos had limbs a century ago; but while we expose and advertise and promote the female breast, we wouldn't think of calling it by its first name in public print. And yet, as we all know, "It's what's up front that counts."

Advertising, its foibles, its solemn rationale, its flights of fancy, and its concern with the manipulation of man's baser and nobler desires, is and will continue to be a moving target for the likes of me. It will be, as it has been in the past, a mirror, not entirely without its distorting characteristics, of what we are pleased to call our civilization. The social critic will read in it what he wants to find—a gold mine of psychological and economic dislocations and absurdities, but if he has any perspective, he will judge advertising no more harshly than the public values to which it appeals. The art critic will be tolerant because he believes that any form of visual expression that reflects the progress of the fine arts and sharpens the vision of the public is helpful to the understanding of the serious creator. (He will always be wryly amused at, but intolerant of, those people in advertising who insist on calling themselves the "creative" types. Creation, he believes, is the province of God and a handful of geniuses, and so do I.)

a muddle of contradictions

The social historian will continue to read advertisements the way a gypsy reads tea leaves or a psychologist reads Rorschach tests, trying to find in them clues to the personality and habits of a people, its past and its future. But the historian of taste will remain deliciously confused as always. He will go on trying to explain why one generation's "good taste" is so likely to be the next generation's "bad taste," why "good taste" has so little to do with the essential quality of the object to which it is applied and so much to do with the social morality and education of the person who is looking at it. He will go on puzzling about why taste is a muddle of contradictions.

That is not to say that the social critic, the art critic, the social historian, and the historian of taste do not depend on advertising. It is an occupational addiction with us; we couldn't give it up if we wanted to.

How are current social and economic forces applied to sell goods, services and ideas? When the potential customer sees an ad, a catalog, a package or the product itself he sees some combination of illustration, photography, typography, design.

Yesterday's commercial art may have been guilty of a single-minded concern with economic and business forces and so debased art esthetically.

Today's advertiser has both higher personal esthetic standards and a higher regard for the esthetic level of the mass market.

The result is illustration, photography, typography that is at once more effective and more pleasing.

Harry Carter shows current illustrations, best as communication and best as art.

illustration . . . *the shock becomes commonplace.*

Today's illustration blends expressionism with technical skill.

by HARRY CARTER

Great stylistic changes in the mainstream of illustration, both in editorial and advertising, come about slowly in cycles of ten to twenty years. Within this larger evolutionary framework, there occur transient fashions in illustration that shift in and out of focus, creating the illusion of much more rapid change in current tastes than actually takes place. Those who deserve it become part of the mainstream, altering the speed of its flow or changing its direction according to the degree of their talents. Others with less sustaining abilities remain briefly, creating temporary whirlpools and disappearing soon leaving little to remember.

At the present time, the artist is enjoying the greatest freedom of personal expression he has ever had. The American illustrator, long famous for his highly polished technical skill, has now joined it with a form of expressionism that is enjoying considerable acceptance. Public taste is conditioned to it, expects it and indeed, encourages it. Expressionism, as defined by Webster, is the free expression by objective means of the subjective feelings of the individual. The shocking qualities of expressionism in illustration when it appeared some dozen years ago was a startling innovation to the non-gallery going public. Today, it is even becoming commonplace.

For the artist, just the power to shock or surprise was not enough. Going beyond trickery and glossy techniques he demanded more of himself, intellectually and emotionally, and set it down in his work, with the result that much of his work today is near the level of serious and enduring art. Also, more frequently, the work of the fine artist is finding its way into illustration and the division between fine and applied art fades each year. The illustrator has benefitted by this trend. He is forced to extend himself in competition by absorbing the lessons of the easel-painting artist and applying it to his own assignments.

In the last few years there has appeared, both in advertising and editorial art, a formidable talent whose influences are now being felt in all facets of creative illustration. Twenty-six accompanying examples represent present-day illustration. They have been selected for their individual excellence, and to demonstrate, by falling into easily defined categories, the directions of current tastes.

2

1

3

The dominant group is the drawing-painting school. Although color is used importantly, the overwhelming factor is the superb drawing. The techniques of these seven artists is not unalike, yet each is of a personal nature.

The full color drawing-painting by Al Parker (1), which won an award in Illustrators '60, a national exhibition of illustration sponsored by the Society of Illustrators, is a marvellous specimen of the simplified statement that relies completely on its one surface, line drawing to create depth and form. Compare this with the Austin Briggs illustration (2). His drawing uses perspective combined with a stunning concentration of blacks and whites in the background to dramatize his story. In the Coby Whitmore illustration (4), also exhibited in Illustrators '60, the concept is based on simplified patterns with line and color equally sharing in its emotional success. Bob Peak is consistant in almost all of his work and the example illustrated (7) typifies his artistic statement. Strong, dramatic use of drawing enhanced by hot, flat areas of color. In the Henry Koehler (6) painting of a regatta, there is perhaps the closest approach to fine, easel painting yet done by an illustrator. One of a series commissioned by Sports Illustrated, it was selected because it is a fine example of the dominant drawing-painting group. In both the Harvey Schmidt (5) portrait of Roosevelt and the fashion drawing by Barbara Fox, drawing (3) conveys an intense emotional impression.

5

6

4

7

19

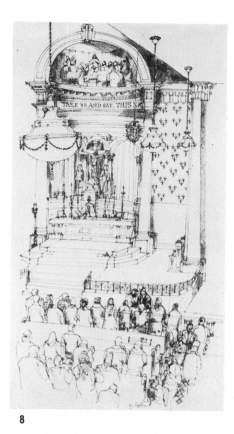

8

9

Not unrelated to this drawing-painting group but different and separate, are masterful pen drawings by Franklin McMahon (8) and Milton Glaser (9). Both are highly interpretive, have an absolute economy of drawing to state the artist's intentions.

Six examples illustrate today's varied uses of realism. With the exception of the Riley painting, all were commissioned for advertising. In the ultra-designed realism group, Robert Hallock (10), Leona Wood (11) and Dink Siegel (13) balance the factual realism of Ken Riley (14), Bernie Fuchs (15) and Stanley Meltzoff (12). In all six however, the color and design of pattern establish the illustration and communicate the artists' intentions precisely.

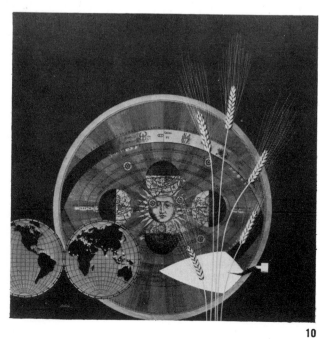

10   11

12

13

14

15

21

16

17

Another group, considered as fantasy illustration, includes the work of Ronald Bradford (16), Esta Nesbitt (17) and Domenico Gnoli (18). These show how this form of expression may be exploited to heighten emotional effects by works of imagination.

19

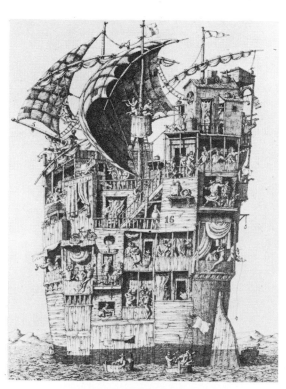

18

Decoratively designed, humorous illustration, when well-conceived has the impact and pungency of great satire. Edward Sorel (20) and Joseph Low (23) both understand this and use it with wit whereas Saul Mandel (22), Bud Simpson (21) and Tomi Ungerer (19) depend on gentle clownlike humor to make their point. In all cases the results are independently arrived at and no one would mistake one artists' work for another.

22

20

21

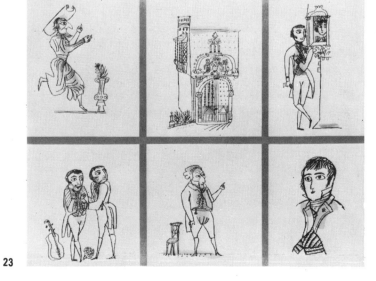

23

23

26

24

25

Stylistic manner using distortion, primitivism or naiveté to extend emotional content is gaining momentum. The three examples illustrated were commissioned for advertising and bear above all others the cachet of fine art direction. The Phil Hays illustration (24) shows a deft use of the manufacturer's product without once compromising the artist's highly individual style. The Earl Thollander illustration (25) for Morton Salt with its very sophisticated naiveté is another example of a very aware art director searching out the right artist for the right illustration. The Antonio Frasconi color woodcut again shows the influence of an imaginative art director who, desiring a primitive mediaeval style found it exactly in the work of Frasconi (26).

1 Art ● Al Parker
AD ● William Fink
Publication ● Ladies Home Journal

2 Art ● Austin Briggs
AD ● Elmer Pizzi
Agency ● Gray & Rogers
Client ● TV Guide

3 Art ● Barbara Fox
AD ● Peter Palazzo
Client ● Henri Bendel

4 Art ● Coby Whitmore
AD ● William Fink
Publication ● Ladies Home Journal

5 Art ● Harvey Schmidt
AD ● Robert Benton
Publication ● Esquire

6 Art ● Henry Koehler
AD ● Jerome Snyder
Publication ● Sports Illustrated

7 Art ● Bob Peak

8 Art ● Franklin McMahon
AD ● Edward Rice
Publication ● Jubilee

9 Art ● Milton Glaser
AD ● Janet Halversen
Client ● Harcourt Brace

10 Art ● Robert Hallock
AD ● Harry Payne
Agency ● BBD&O
Client ● First National City Bank

11 Art ● Leona Wood
AD ● Walter Reinsel
Agency ● N. W. Ayer & Sons
Client ● DeBeers

12 Art ● Stanley Meltzoff
AD ● Charles Evo
Agency ● Gray & Rogers
Client ● United Engineers

13 Art ● Leo Dink Siegel
AD ● Richard Hurd
Agency ● J. Walter Thompson Co.
Client ● Ford

14 Art ● Ken Riley
AD ● Ken Stuart
Publication ● Saturday Evening Post

15 Art ● Bernie Fuchs
AD ● Bill Conlon
Agency ● Kudner
Client ● International Hotels

16 Art ● Ronald Bradford
AD ● Richard Thompson
Publication ● Rogue

17 Art ● Esta Nesbitt

18 Art ● Domenico Gnoli
AD ● Irwin Glusker
Publication ● Horizon

19 Art ● Tomi Ungerer
AD ● Jack Steinau
Agency ● BBD&O
Client ● New York Times

20 Art ● Edward Sorel
AD ● Loring Eutemy
Client ● Columbia Records

21 Art ● Bernard Simpson
AD ● Robert Geissman, Joe Jacobson
Publication ● Men's Wear

22 Art ● Saul Mandel
AD ● Richard Weiner
Agency ● Leo Burnett Co.
Client ● Green Giant Co.

23 Art ● Joseph Low
AD ● Robert Jones
Client ● RCA-Victor Records

24 Art ● Phil Hays
AD ● Tony Mandarino
Agency ● BBD&O
Client ● Armstrong Floors

25 Art ● Earl Thollander
AD ● Tom Gorey
Agency ● Needham, Louis & Brorby
Client ● Morton Salt

26 Art ● Antonio Frasconi
AD ● Arnold Kushner
Agency ● Lynn Baker, Inc.
Client ● General Wine & Spirits Co.

. . . the trends in advertising photography are largely outgrowths of innovations in editorial pages. As Harry Carter noted in the preceding chapter and as George Guido reports in the story following this, the editorial pages also influenced trends in advertising illustration and typography. This was true in the 30's, 40's and 50's. To see if it is true today, take a look at McCall's. Here Onofrio Paccione traces ad photography trends by checking through 39 Art Directors Club annuals. He finds our "new" devices of out-of-focus pictures, side lighting, high or low camera angles, just recurrent fads, suggests that the one true trend is the use of photography for most effective communication regardless of whether the chosen technique is old, current, or never used before. . . .

advertising photography...

A desirable trend: less consciousness of fads in technique, more communication-mindedness

by ONOFRIO PACCIONE

Photography in advertising dates back to the 19th century with the introduction of the halftone process. Most advertisers at this time were not impressed with this new method of selling. First of all, they wanted their products to be visually exaggerated, not literally represented. And, if they could hire a famous illustrator to do a painting of their product, it was almost as important to them as having their portrait painted. Besides, there were few good photographers; technique was new and cumbersome, although the quality of 19th century halftones is acceptable by today's standards. Even though, throughout the late 1890's and early 1900's some good examples of photography appeared in food, fashion and automobile ads, advertisers were sold only on art work.

The rise of photography in advertising (see accompanying examples) can be traced through the Annuals of the New York Art Directors Club.

The first photos (mostly in fashion ads) appeared in the 2nd Annual in 1923, but in the 3rd Annual there were 37 including the first photographic auto ad and the first washing machine ad, and by 1926 even soap ads were using photography. The 1928 Annual carried two Steichen photographs and the following year a photograph won a medal for Ralph Steiner. Cigarette ads with photos showed up in the 9th Annual along with more auto ads. By 1933 there was greater diversity among products using photography, and Victor Keppler was shooting ads for Hoffman Ginger Ale. The 13th Annual in 1934 recorded a jump to 85 photographic ads including outdoor photography by Paul Hesse and Lucky Strike ads. The first action picture appeared in 1935.

1927

1908

Life spurs photography

By 1936 film and equipment developments had improved photographic quality and Life magazine was introduced, followed a year later by Look. From then on photography was increasingly used and new techniques were developed. The 16th Annual, for example, has examples of X-ray photography. In 1941 Four Roses showed up frozen in ice, by Anton Bruehl. Gjon Mili's strobe shots appeared in the 1943 Annual. One of the first uses of documentary photography in advertising was a medal winner in the 1950 book. And if it seems like yesterday, it was seven years ago when Irving Penn's Jello pictures, Bert Stern's man in the desert, and Hans Lownds' Commander Whitehead appeared.

Little by little advertisers recognized the success of editorial photography and began to use photographs to sell their products. This was the first and "true trend" . . . simply, the use of photography instead of art.

1940

1936

1935

1940

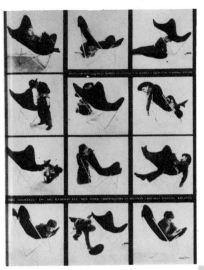

1950

1942

1952

trend vs. technique imitation

What we call trends today...the use of large or small cameras, in or out-of-focus backgrounds, fine grain or grainy shots, distant or extreme close-ups, etc., are merely "secondary trends." Trend is defined as "to have or take a particular direction." Unfortunately, the hidden meaning is conformity, dullness, repetition, lack of imagination... doing something "of today"...in the manner of the moment. The important thing is not being of today but being *right!*

the editorial pages show the way

Just using photography for photography's sake...without imagination...is like an ungifted, unschooled painter slapping a picture together. During the thirties and forties a handful of photographic Picassos and Matisses appeared with needed enthusiasm, imagination and greatness. Such

1953

1953

1954

1953

photographers were Robert Doisneau, Robert Frank, Henri Cartier Bresson, Ernie Haas, Alfred Eidenstaadt, Leslie Gill, Irving Penn, Richard Avedon, etc. Most of their experiments were first seem editorially in Life, Look, Vogue, Harper's Bazaar, and Art Annuals.

Advertisers in the thirties and forties accepted photography as a medium, and a desire to be different arose. To create an "identity" differing from their competitors, art directors picked up the "editorial look." They mimicked the inventions of the editorial photographers and found that readers not only accepted these photographic innovations, but *bought* as well. So the level of advertising was raised, and creative photography proved to be entertaining, informative and compelling. Leslie Gill started a still-life "look" and immediately advertisers copied it. The same happened with Penn's stark celebrity photos, and Avedon's innovation of the "live" fashion model. The present so-called "trend" of journalistic pictures for automobiles, liquor, insurance, etc.

1955

1956

1957

1957

stems from the work of photo journalists, Ernst Haas, Robert Frank, and Robert Doisneau.

Look back and see how all techniques and photographic solutions known today have been used before. Take for example, Penn's "Workmen." See how closely they resemble the occupation studies done in 1891 by Sigmund Kraus.

The end to following the technique fad of the day is near. More talented photographers are getting the opportunity to shoot exciting advertising pictures: such men as Penn, Stern, Kreiger, Dan Wynn, Derujinsky, Avedon, Gordon Parks, Saul Leiter, Art Kane, and W. Klein, just to mention a few, and they realize the need to break the chain of sameness staring up at us from every magazine and newspaper. Art Directors need to break with convention, too, by getting back to the "true trend" . . . that of using photography and using it *right* . . . using it to fit the problem, whether the technique is of the past, present or something never used before.

DANSK

1957

KRAUS

PENN

1958

. . . Typographic directions remind us of the man who got on his horse and galloped off in all directions. As George Guido notes, the variety of clients, media, products, message problems make for many cyclic trends, some contradictory, all ebbing and flowing so that it is almost impossible to tell which wave will make the biggest, and longest lasting, splash. The tide does seem to be moving toward fewer layout elements, more use of type for impact and more integration of type with picture, more visual onomatopoeia . . .

advertising typography . . .

follows editorial and direct mail leads toward word-picture fusing and visual simplification

by GEORGE GUIDO

There are two schools in today's typography; the formal and the informal. They have always been, and always will be, with us. They intertwine and alternate to make type trends almost imperceptible except to the most subjective eye. The current direction is toward typographic informality. In this, perhaps our use of type reflects the changing social structure. Lester Douglas has said, ". . . we obtain nothing but abject poverty of ideas and patterns . . . when we continually copy traditional forms. We cannot have typographic progress in this changing world unless we try new forms that may be expressive of today's living ideologies."

In the forefront of the move toward a more expressive type handling are magazine editorial pages and direct mail promotion pieces. A study of the advertising pages of the past few years indicates an inexorable, though slow, advance by advertisers, primarily the fashion industry, moving in the direction of the pacesetter magazines.

when you can spot a trend, it may be on the way out

It is the relentless search for new ways to frame ideas which starts trends, but when a technique or treatment is recognized as a trend, its demise is usually hastened. Today, a cacaphony of advertising claims battles to penetrate the defense barrier in the mind of the harassed consumer. Divergent, and sometimes diametrically opposed typographic means are used to produce the desired response. One has large dominant type forms swimming in white; another, 4673 characters of small size Caslon 540 in orderly columns. Which is best? The variety of content, circumstances and clients indicate there is room for both methods. In a roomful of chic females, the sole nude would get the attention. In a roomful of nudes, the one fully clothed would stand out. These examples parallel the diverse forms advertising takes as we seek new ways to communicate. The way we decide depends on many considerations, not the least of which is the designer's instinct.

type to startle

Type has become a new and vigorous means of expression. There is currently a tendency toward giving type the leading voice; of allowing it to startle and arouse the reader who formerly was attracted by elements such as the photo, art, color, etc.

Letters are fixed symbols and consequently formal. The better examples are beautiful in themselves. They fulfill the formal designer's need for expression. Other designers feel they represent restrictions to a free expression. So we find the compulsion to create, extending with ever greater frequency into this one time inviolate area.

attention value vs readership

Purists have said liberties should not be taken which might impair readability. In some cases these warnings prove to be well founded. But there are designers who have treated type with an energetic, but respectful flexibility. If legibility has been impaired, it has been more than compensated for by increased attention value. One still has to *hear* a voice before he can listen to it.

word-picture fusing One of the more interesting typographic developments is the "word-picture" advertisement, where the typography is the picture or a part of it. To eliminate extraneous elements things usually employed separately are combined. Words and picture are fused. The number of objects within are thereby reduced. The total effect becomes simpler; less for the eye to comprehend. Quicker. The psychological implications of the compounded elements are amplified into a unified striking force.

These graphic solutions grow out of the basic content. Designers tend toward subtraction rather than addition. This refining process reduces, or at least simplifies all compulsory elements while eliminating the extraneous ones. How much can be omitted without impairing the communication, rather than how much can be contained, is the question here. The simplest solutions always have the greatest appeal. Many examples of music have compositional weaknesses hidden by the noise of 100 instruments. The sound is loud and sometimes impressive, but is it good? Contrasted with this, the elementary Brahm's Lullaby is almost universal in its appeal.

Art Direction Magazine, reporting on the most recent Type Directors Club Show, has well noted that "it is becoming increasingly difficult to distinguish the head from the illustration, the text or the signature yet it is easier to get the message in an instant." When the designer integrates type, pictures, text and logo, the result is roughly akin to Wagner's blend of words and music. Many parts occupy the same time and space but are interwoven into *one* powerful idea.

Other manifestations of today's type directions may be seen in the illustrations. Each of these examples delineates a small pattern to be sure, but as a whole they reflect a general relaxing of the typographic ground rules used in the past.

type-picture fusing . . .

The author's hypothetical rough (1) shows the congestion that results when an attempt is made to relate three kinds of fruit to the product in a **conventional** layout. The poster as it appeared (2) says the same thing more simply and is a delightful solution.

The Goebel rough (3), again typical of a less inventive layout, has to rely on an added element to convey its message. The loss of the negative space results in a more crowded and harder-to-read caption. The poster actually used (4) is better. The original cover sketch for the proposed Detroit AD Annual (5), currently being designed by the author, has since been refined and simplified. The more complete embodiment of this same idea is still retained, and plussed, in the approved design (6).

1

2

3

4

6   5

Contemporary designers of advertising and promotional material have long found the News Gothic series one of the most valuable in the whole Composing Room catalog. Ever since it was made available for machine composition in both the regular and condensed versions (and most notably when the "odd sizes" of 7, 9 and 11 pt. were added) the scope of its use has greatly widened. Recently our acquisition of small caps in all sizes of the regular News Gothic has made it even more flexible in its use. In this handbook we show sample paragraphs, complete alphabets and type calculation data on the two series: the News Gothic teamed with the Bold and the News Gothic Condensed with the Alternate Gothic No. 2. We include, too, the display sizes of the News Gothic Condensed on the Ludlow. We hope that this compact showing will prove to be a helpful working tool for designers, art directors, type directors and production men. The Composing Room, Inc.

7

dynamic borders . . .

Here we have the absence of the white border which is traditionally equal on four sides. Advantage is taken of the resulting negative areas. This assymetrical placement of type within the frame imparts an active quality to the page. In some cases the type completely negates the border on one or more sides and sometimes portions of letter forms are bled. This does not seem to hinder the legibility.

BIRTH PANGS OF A GIANT

Text by PETER RITNER   Photographed by KEN HEYMAN

8

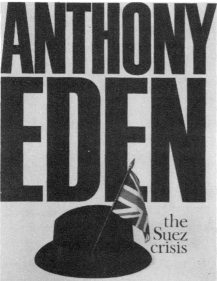

9

10

something old + something new . . .
The mixing of varied and sundry type faces, the
old with the new, produces a lively effect reminis-
cent of the handbills of the gay 90's.

11

12

13

visual onomatopoeia...

The imaginative juxtaposition and/or unusual rendering of these headlines augments the idea, making both words and picture more effective than they would otherwise be. In proof 14 the word "GO" is placed in the exhaust pipe. This is the only place in the ad where the position of a word reinforces its meaning.

GO
FOR MORE CORVETTE SALES WITH YOUR PROSPECTING PLANS FOR 1959

14

allergic **itch**

Dimetane works!

15

TONNAGE

16

If advertising isn't memorable, it doesn't sell!

17

non-integrated type ...

Here, the copy is treated as a unit, and placed at the extreme limits of the ad in relation to the pictorial elements. Whether this is a positive typographic pattern or a negative one resulting from a positive positioning of the illustration is hard to say.

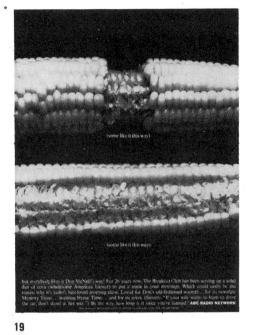

18   19   20

fun with type ...

Some of these defy categorizing, but all indicate that the designer just had plain "fun" with his type, and at no sacrifice to legibility. Further proof of today's less inhibited typography.

21

22

23

minor surgery...

Small liberties have been taken here. Lower case is mixed with caps apparently to retain an alignment of stacked multiple lines. Different size letters are employed in the word. Complete words are tucked into spaces made by the use of smaller letters. Without regard for syllabification, words are divided into two lines. Parts of the letter forms join to others, making new shapes. The impression is fresh and communicates despite the surgery.

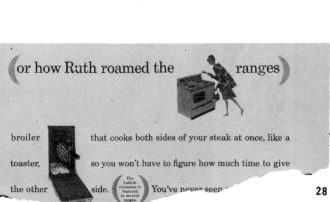

. . . Jim Fogleman reminds us that every company has an image, suggests it might as well be a good one. Here he explains how design helps convey the correct image, how it is an adjunct of sales, how it must derive from the nature of the company and its product or service rather than be created on the outside, and how it serves as a unifying element for many divisions, products, and markets, building cumulative impact regardless of product, market or medium. Alongside the big trend toward sophistication in advertising is the slow trend to make every ad sell both company and product. Jim Fogleman suggests that in the long run, what with rapid product turnover in many fields, the company sell may be the most important . . .

design: a means of corporate expression

the best images grow naturally from the company or product and are not invented or superficially imposed.

by JAMES K. FOGLEMAN

The recent awareness of the importance of the corporate image has brought serious consideration by many firms of their design programs. Many businesses have long regarded such a business principle—the principle of corporate imagery. Some called it "reputation," but more often it was considered without a name.

CI is not new Along with the current popularity of the term Corporate Image, many believe it a new business wrinkle. Together with serious consideration it has also been looked at suspiciously, and little wonder when you consider its misuse. It has been used as an excuse for anything for which a more specific reason couldn't be given. It has been a sales device, a fad, and grossly misunderstood.

Through this misunderstanding, the concept of Corporate Image has been treated superficially. Result, disappointment. To correctly understand corporate imagery, regard it in its proper perspective. It is not an entity nor can it be treated so. Painting an old house may create an illusion of newness and solidarity. But if the timbers are rotten the truth will soon come through. Similarly, concern with imagery must go down to products, markets and business practices. Corporate imagery is a form of corporate self-expression and alone cannot cure ailing sales.

Every company has an image. Making it work is good business sense. Every move from the products produced to letterheads contributes to the total impression.

Current forces make the corporate impression extremely important. Self-service marketing places the purchase decision entirely in the consumer's hands. Brand names once meant a great deal, but mean little when launching new products, as so many companies are doing at a record pace. We have seen a revolution in this form of merchandising in the last decade with considerable importance placed upon corporate identity as a decisive element.

What can a program of consciously guiding and controlling the image and impression achieve? It can support product lines in the face of new competition and work as a catalyst for the numerous products and many diversified markets of a large corporation—to say nothing of important employee relations and recruiting. Only recently corporations were disguising their holdings in the face of anti-trust and monopoly suits. But because of consumer buying and stock market changes many corporations are reversing their position. Some have found this extremely difficult. One major firm is trying to tie together some twenty-seven divisions which had been treated as separate entities. This meant renaming the divisions and undertaking an extensive program to bring forth something that always

existed but had been impossible for the public and customers to recognize. This was made necessary by a stock situation and new consumer markets. A self appraisal by another corporation revealed that it was regarded as old-fashioned although it was actually one of our most progressive companies. They instituted a program to show their true character.

As one engaged in visually communicating spirit and personality of an industrial firm, the principles which I apply are set by the corporation legal, financial, research, production, marketing and general administration officers. The principles and disciplines together form what I call a CORPORATE PURPOSE. This dictates the kind of products we produce and market and the markets in which we will operate.

It is the design director's responsibility, along with others in the many aspects of communications, to express this PURPOSE clearly, accurately and effectively. It is *not* my duty to create or invent an image. Its basic ingredients are there, it is my duty to recognize them and bring them forth in their true light.

I often face the question, "What is the image that my company wishes to present?" I could say that we wish to be considered progressive, imaginative, backed by years of tradition and integrity, a company that develops and manufactures products of quality and dependability. A lot of other companies will say the same thing. The thing that sets each of us apart is an individual attitude or spirit.

In our early physiology days we learned of our involuntary and voluntary muscular system. One can find a direct analogy here for there is both an involuntary and voluntary aspect in a corporation's expression. The involuntary being the very nature of its business field as well as the development and manufacture of its products.

The voluntary aspect is the broad area of communication, which includes advertising, public relations, promotion, packaging, trucks and vehicles, exhibitions, publications, office forms, trademark, signs and symbols, architecture, interiors, etc. All of these areas are entirely controllable by the corporation. Policies and controls can be instituted to ascertain that these many avenues of expression are headed in the right, and same, direction, and toward a common purpose.

To realize more worth from the promotional dollar, and glean the utmost benefit from every action, consider every action as having at least two functions. In the instance of a product advertisement, its primary function is to sell a product, but its secondary function should be to sell the company. Products come and go. In the long run selling the company may be the most important. It is cumulative— the foundation, the reputation, the image, if you will.

As for company spirit, consider CIBA. We enjoy a rich heritage of achievement and prestige throughout the world, qualities we try to reflect in every way. This endowment often reduces the problem to a refining, organizing, adjusting and strengthening of our visual expression. Our image is based on the application of values and standards and does not result in a tailored uniform—which, I feel, is more often a veneer or synthetic image. By adhering to a strong, basic family philosophy, each country and division can express itself in its own manner, depending on nationality and markets. This demands a flexible program, close cooperation, understanding and guidance. Our only standard element, worldwide, is our trademark.

I have read advertisements from leading design firms heralding themselves as expert creators of CORPORATE IMAGES. It seemed that here was something to be bought off a rack as you might buy a suit. My regard for these firms dropped immensely.

There are times when visually exposing the corporate purpose or image may be dangerous. Reconstruction of many aspects may be necessary before a concerted program can be gotten under way. Here the designer and public relations expert can offer valuable counsel. Or, perhaps the basic purpose would never bear revealing. It is in this latter case that the firms who are expert at creating corporate images should be called in. Perhaps an artificial image, or a synthetic veneer, will get them by, though I doubt it.

An eastern railway always comes to mind when I think of corporate images. An outstanding program was inaugurated via the redesign of all their rolling stock, stations, printed matter, trademark, etc. It received wide acclaim. But the corporate purpose did not parallel the projected images. Product performance, in this case service, kept declining. It is shockingly low if you poll the commuters. No designer, no p. r. genius, could rescue it. Product performance is paramount for a favorable image.

Here are examples of companies which have taken an interest in their visual expression to increase sales by effectively communicating strong corporate identities. Each example applies very high standards, standards they must demand of their research, production and other departments. Good design has been considered by each of them to be an asset to sales, or they would not have taken the trouble to set up the controls which they obviously have. None show design for design's sake. They do show how good design can clarify, amplify and effectively present the written word and project meaning that defies verbal description.

Rather than illustrate the complete design program of one company, sections of the programs of nine companies show different phases of CI graphics as well as calling attention to companies whose work in this area is outstanding.

45

ANSUL

Ansul is a comparatively small chemical company. Design has been used extensively to get recognition despite the larger programs of competitors. Ansul makes chemical products which are not basically consumer items, nevertheless the company has one of the most completely integrated design programs. The accompanying illustrations show only a small part of the area where Ansul has applied design. The program reaches product design, packaging, vehicles, advertising, uniforms, signs, symbols, technical literature, virtually every place where a visual impression can be made.

GENERAL DYNAMICS

General Dynamics successfully expresses an image of being generally dynamic. All that is done is unique and with a sense of the future.

They use outstanding artists, designers, photographers. Although there is no effort to make everything look alike, all seems to blend through the application of the highest standards and highest quality of thought.

This conveys the image of a progressive organization.

Even as this book is being published, General Dynamics is changing the corporate symbol. The new symbol is planned first for corporate stationery and will soon appear on trucks, packages, other divisional nomenclature—further evidence that this corporation is progressive and not only recognizes but acts upon the need for change.

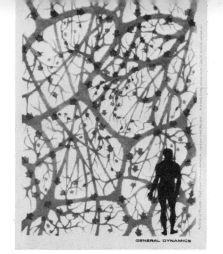

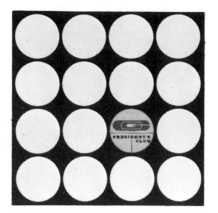

CONNECTICUT GENERAL

Connecticut General, selling assurance, faces a problem quite different than those with more tangible products. Product performance may not be tested for many years. Therefore it is the establishment of an image of dependability and integrity that an insurance company seeks to express.

Connecticut General has done a superb job in this respect. First of all, it expresses its personality largely through its salesmen, but after the point of sale further contact with the company on the part of the policy holder is almost entirely through printed matter. As one can see by the examples, CG has paid considerable attention to this medium. Along with salesmen and printed matter, architecture is a major means of expression and here too Connecticut General has made some remarkable achievements.

Their national advertising is unique and outstanding. The printing matter is straight-forward, modern in concept, all of which contribute to expressing themselves as modern and progressive.

a place to begin in 1960

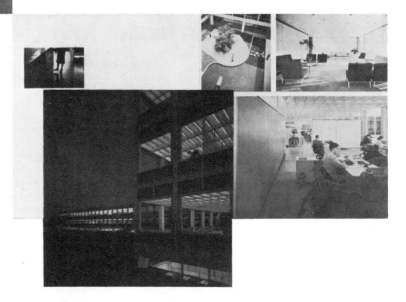

B.E.U. helps your best people put roots down.

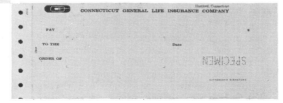

CONNECTICUT GENERAL LIFE INSURANCE COMPANY

NEIMAN-MARCUS

It has been said that, "NEIMAN-MARCUS is not just a business, it's a state of mind." NEIMAN-MARCUS has been so successful at creating an image in customers' minds that they impart in each and every label a particular quality of choiceness that causes people to prefer their garments to others. According to Mr. Marcus, this has been an accumulation of many things over a period of many years.

The image with which they are dealing is complex for they try to be a number of things to a number of people, but not everything to all people.

Here are some of the things they have tried to establish—friendliness, sophistication, urbanity, internationalism, selectivity, taste, authority, dependability, quality, civic mindedness and integrity.

Mr. Marcus has stated that in his opinion every company creates an image, sometimes accidentally and sometimes intentionally. He says, "It is surprising to me that so few companies recognize this fact and go along creating an image in sheer ignorance of what they are doing. The most successful companies are those who have knowingly set out to create a given image and have used all the devices within their power to achieve that objective." He credits this as being one of the major factors in the success of his institution.

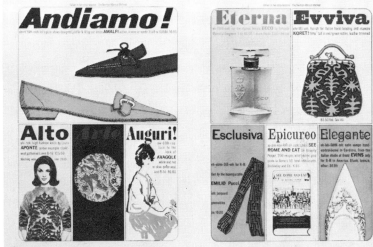

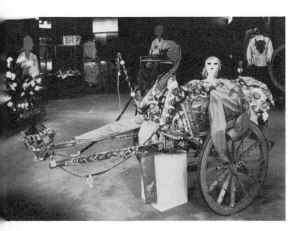

SWISSAIR

Of all the world airlines SWISSAIR holds the front rank in well integrated and effective corporate identity. SWISSAIR expresses its own national spirit.

The illustrations show the program's solidarity and thoroughness, from trademark to interior design, of vehicles and the nature of its service. All are strongly working toward a common purpose, applying some of the best Swiss advertising. Meticulousness and precision are effectively projected and who could ask more when choosing an airline.

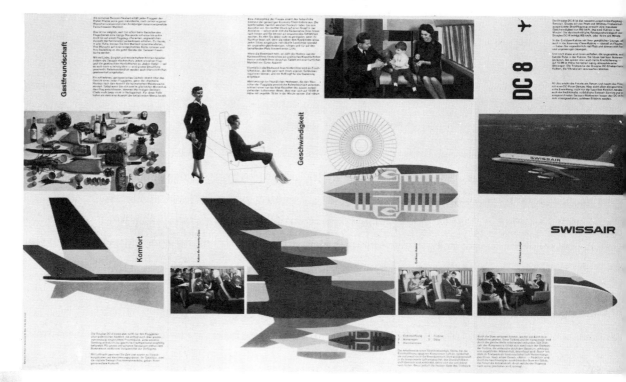

TORRINGTON

TORRINGTON MANUFACTURING COMPANY, operating in a hard industrial environment, has had a great deal of success with a controlled corporate design program.

Its purpose is to portray leadership and a contemporary approach. As they say, "The real value of our products is in their sophistication of functional design and the desire of our customer to use this sophistication for his own problems."

Corporate design has been integrated through all aspects of the company—from letterhead to exhibitions.

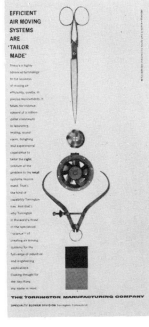

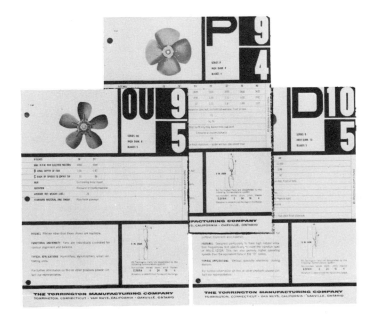

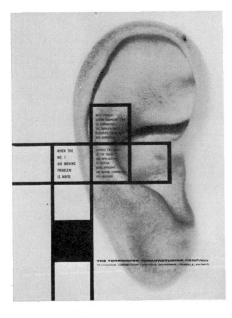

VOLKSWAGEN

The distinct functionalism of the VOLKSWAGEN is further expressed through their advertising. There seems to be an unusual product pride expressed compared to other advertising that usually hides their products behind beautiful women or attempts to strike other associations.

The simple direct statement of their advertising and other literature is as forthright as their product. One can certainly say that the same principles have been applied.

In one ad the headline questions, "Do you think the Volkswagen is homely?" They are squarely facing an apparent criticism. They say, "The Volkswagen was designed from the inside out— Every line is a result of function...." The copy also describes their ads and literature which is a further extension of the VOLKSWAGEN image. The VOLKSWAGEN approach is a good lesson for any company when one considers their image. Every corporate program must be developed from the inside out.

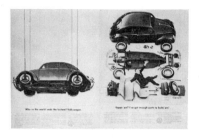

Why is a Volkswagen like no other car on the road?

Do you think the Volkswagen is homely?

What year car do the Jones drive?

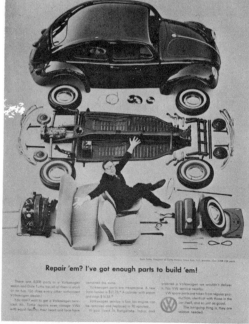

Repair 'em? I've got enough parts to build 'em!

PAN AMERICAN

PAN AM is a major U. S. airline which has undergone a comprehensive change-over. "The new PAN AM look" includes official renaming of the organization from the old initials PAA to PAN AM, a name long familiar to employees and the traveling public. This is part of an effort to establish a strong image of the company in the public mind and eliminate confusion with other airlines.

In the beginning PAN AM employed dark blue as their identifying color. The current light blue replaces it. It is interesting to note how important one aspect—color—can be in the over-all problem. Color alone can influence attitude. One airline is greatly handicapped today because of its use of a dingy, depressing color. I am sure they will soon change based on the experience of PAN AM and with whom they compete.

Although the "new look" has been in effect for a couple of years, it is still being integrated throughout the world.

BRAUN

BRAUN

A superb example of good design application.
Apparently drastic changes took place in 1951.

Convinced that the manufacturer has a high responsibility, in the age of mass produced products, as an influence on the taste of many, Braun conforms with the highest standards, not only in technical performance, but in design as well.

Clear, uncluttered design exposes the technical character of the products. German consumers associate the trademark BRAUN with a modern progressive firm.

Many innovations in marketing have been explored. For example, housewives—usually labeled as conservative—were considered to be capable of being convinced that well designed appliances would function best, thus be easily accepted in the kitchens.

In the radio industry, before BRAUN started its new line, there was no modern looking radio set in spite of the industry being technologically advanced.

Quality has been paramount in all of their thinking and is successfully expressed in whatever they have done, whether it be product design, advertising, technical literature or exhibits.

Although this company's enlightened spirit comes directly from the owners, the road has not been easy. Many things had to be changed, such as re-orientation of sales staff, realignment of its dealer system and a re-appraisal of its advertising. In the case of advertising, BRAUN realized that they were speaking to an entirely new line of customers who were individualists and could not be attracted by conventional advertising. Persuasion and superlatives could not reach them. The answer was to reduce their advertising copy to straight information, describing as thoroughly as possible the quality of their products. Straight copy plus clean design worked. The changes in advertising influenced all forms of company communication, through the style of lettering, quality of paper, layout and printing.

Heute
neu in allen
Fachgeschäften

Braun SM 3
ein neuer
Maßstab für
das Rasieren

. . . As corporate image programs slowly but surely increase their use of contemporary design and art, so does the annual report. Just as James Fogleman has shown, in the preceding pages, how companies are now using graphics to express their personality and to establish a continuity of identity, here Mahlon Cline shows corporations changing their annual reports from merely informative financial statements to persuasive and highly visual statements of company purpose. . . .

annual reports are more than mere financial statements

trend is toward modernity and use of symbols to convey product and corporate personality

by MAHLON A. CLINE

And why be surprised? Look at almost any well-conceived corporate annual report. Invariably the last major section is devoted to financial statements.

That's not so incongruous. The function of an annual report today is as much *persuasive* as it is informative. It provides a sense of corporate purpose, of corporate identity, of corporate philosophy.

In the past, reports were meager black and white unillustrated documents. They contained a short stodgy letter by the president, financial statements, a list of Directors and Officers, an accountant's letter and the address of the company. The letter and statement, at the last minute, was sent to a printer who set all the material overnight and delivered proofs the next morning. There was little room for any design or page layout.

Then, too, many companies were afraid that stockholders would become suspicious of a new and fresh approach, so they did the same thing year after year. Today, however, business finds that better organized and designed reports strengthen their financial structure.

Hence, the problem of designing a corporate brochure is more complex and challenging than a mere presentation of financial condition.

The designer must graphically express a company's personality in terms of its products, its activities and personnel. He must incorporate many diverse elements into a cohesive report which must reflect unity of concept, continuity of thought and design.

This checklist of elements indicates the scope and gives direction to the design problem.

KIND OF REPORT (design direction)
  A. Conservative format
  B. Modern format
  1. straight text treatment
  2. straight text with occasional pen and ink or spot sketches
  3. generous use of pictorial charts and graphs
  4. generous use of photographs
  5. generous use of art (2 or 4 colors)

SHOULD THE REPORT INCLUDE ANY OF THESE ELEMENTS?
  1. pictures of company's products
  2. drawings of employees at work
  3. drawings of machines at work
  4. drawing showing main steps in the manufacture of product
  5. diagrammatic chart showing organization of departments
  6. diagrammatic chart of method utilizing by-products
  7. map showing location of raw materials in relation to plants
  8. charts of progress of corporate financing
  9. charts of corporation taxes
  10. charts of increase in purchasing capacity
  11. charts of improvement in working conditions (i.e. hours of work and wages)
  12. photographs of all plants
  13. photographs of trip to one plant
  14. photographs of some finished articles in use by important customers
  15. photographs of officers and/or directors

16. photographs of typical employees, research men, salesmen
17. reprints of advertising
18. company-owned trade marks
19. map sales offices and show rooms

The treatment and organization of these diverse elements will vary with the purpose of the annual report. Precisely because annual reports are not merely handsomely printed financial statements, the designer must first determine what mood or character management wants to convey before he attempts to translate elements into visual form. Conservative, the report may be bookish. Merchandising, the report may call for photographs, artwork, advertisements. Far out, it may be pure design.

Once the basic purpose has been determined, then the designer selects his materials accordingly—typography, artwork, colors, paper, method of printing. This is not to suggest that there are formulas for approaches—there aren't. Rather, different purposes require different techniques. How well those techniques are used is the measure of the designer. As the purpose and scope of the annual report has grown, the format, the treatment, the very conception of the annual report has also changed. From the staid, tried and true has evolved a clean modernity which is now developing into symbolic representation of company, product or personality.

It is a healthy trend for design to be used intelligently and top management, as a result of exposure to good design, to recognize pure design as a valuable element in corporate representation.

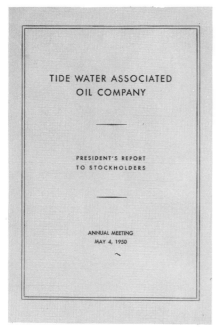

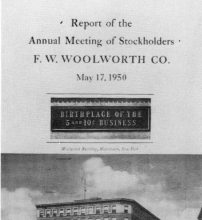

Early Efforts — Ten years ago simple folders gave financial data. These are typical of many produced during the 1940's and early 50's.

Progress of Cover for One Company — Concept of cover design change from one year to another depicts in a general way the all-over operation of the company. A dignified, simple type treatment can give a solid effect . . . on the other hand a forward up-to-date look using abstract art might fit the need . . . the company with diversification often needs to show a wide range of products thus a fully illustrated cover . . . diversification of activities can be indicated with pure type design.

Symbols for Cover Design — The turn to symbolic form has been successful both in art and photographic treatments — parts and pieces come together to identify the the company. Simplicity in handling the elements is vital.

ABBOTT LABORATORIES   1959 ANNUAL REPORT

DIRECTIONS FOR THE SIXTIES

PSI-COLA COMPANY **ANNUAL REPORT 1959**

IBM Annual Report 195

NORTH AMERICAN AVIATION, INC., 1959 ANNUAL REPORT

ANNUAL REPORT / 1959

NEW JERSEY
BELL TELEPHONE
COMPANY

REYNOLDS METALS COMPANY

ANSUL

1959 ANNUAL REPORT · TENNESSEE GAS TRANSMISSION COMPANY

BANGOR AND AROOSTOOK RAILROAD COMPANY

DEF 3
ABC 2
1
JKL 5
MNO 6
BELL SYSTEM
0 OPERATOR
8 TUV
9 WXY

"...a high point in 10 years of steady progress.

The Trend to Pure Illustration — Today's illustration, photographic or art, is generally of better quality. The illustration might be abstract, realistic or contemporary. These are some of the best.

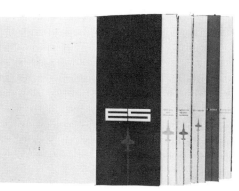

General Make-up — Many new ideas in the general make-up of the report have been developed: short pages using index methods — half pages to contain a full story in itself — and financial sections printed on colored stock as a wrap around the general review of the company.

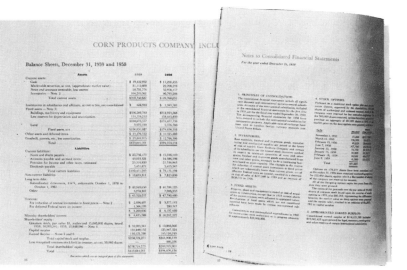

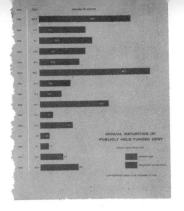

The Chart Trend — Pictographs as chart illustration have been replaced with simple bar charts — either in color or black and white. Simplicity and easy readability is the main objective.

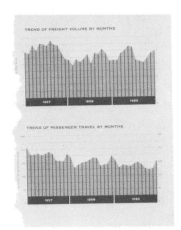

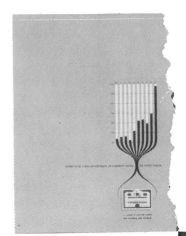

Outstanding Type Treatment — Not only has type found its place on the cover, there are many reports using type continuity of treatment on the inside pages. Typographic design is as important as illustration in effectively telling the corporate story and establishing the desired attitude.

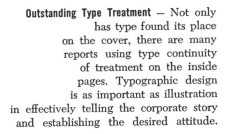

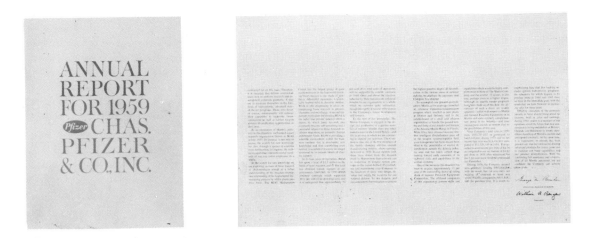

Are magazine's seeds, advertising's flowers?

The togetherness of esthetics and communication effectiveness has been dramatically demonstrated in the editorial pages of some of our leading magazines. The emphasis this year may be on visual drama, but magazine art directors are blending power with beauty.

What the leading magazine ADs, illustrators, and photographers do is often a forerunner of what advertisers will do. This was shown in the depth visual-analysis made by Suren Ermoyan in the first edition of Advertising Directions. Here Otto Storch has asked the ADs of several of our creatively distinguished magazines to show what they have done this year. Perhaps in their work are the seeds of more dynamic, more effective advertising directions for tomorrow.

the emphasis shifts in magazine pages...

from esthetics to communication effectiveness; 8 ADs discuss this approach in their magazines

by OTTO STORCH

I don't really believe in trends common to all magazines but in solutions to each magazine's individual problems. It is necessary to create an image that is just right for a particular audience.

This is the day of the thinking Art Director who no longer designs for the sake of design alone. The trend is away from doing things chiefly for artistic reasons. The Art Director is expected to produce creative ideas to inform and entertain. The only trend I see is basic: the Art Director solves his own problems with good visually communicative ideas. This is the only sound and lasting direction in which we are going.

In addition, presentation is important. Excellent presentation will put across a sound idea, but if the idea itself is not good the best presentation will not save it. We must produce pictures, through photographers and artists, that strongly express the message. Typography must be legible and integrate with the picture into an arrangement that puts the whole idea across.

If there is currently a trend, it is in the basic approach to a problem and should not be in the solution itself. There are always a few innovators whose thinking is so strong and original that it influences others and imitation is mistaken for a trend. Imitation is never long enduring. Each Magazine Art Director has his own audience and problems and must create his own unique direction. Following are representative pages from magazines with notes from their Art Directors. They tell us their problems, their solutions, and the visual direction they are planning for their magazines.

1. Integration of picture and typography. Action ideas of this kind get reader participation. Photographer Diane & Allan Arbus

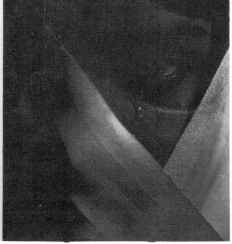

2. For a special section on parables it was necessary to get the essence of each parable in one revealing photograph. Each was carefully planned and staged. This one illustrated a mother's grief for her child. Photographer: Art Kane

McCALL'S... *integration, drama, sensitivity, scale*
by OTTO STORCH, WILLIAM CADGE

ON THE COB OR OFF: YOU CAN'T BEAT GOOD SWEET HOT OLD-FASHIONED CORN

...e Indians loved it. The Pilgrims loved it. Everybody loves ...Plump, tender corn, well buttered, salted and peppered, ...without a doubt, a favorite American vegetable. Boil it, ...st it, scrape it, pickle it, eat it straight, or combine it with ...er foods—it's wonderful, no matter how... only, get it from ...den to pot as rapidly as possible, to preserve that heavenly ...art-of-summer taste. If you think that corn is best boiled ...d buttered (and most people would agree with you), cook ...n a tightly covered skillet instead of a deep kettle. Lay the ...s flat in three fourths inch of boiling water, and boil hard ...six to eight minutes, for really tender, memorable corn.

Do you recall wistfully the taste of corn roasted outdoors? If you'll forgo starry skies and the smell of smoke, we'll tell you how to get nearly the same taste indoors: Dot husked ears with butter; sprinkle with salt, seasoned salt; wrap each ear in aluminum foil. Roast on the rack of a 400-degree oven until tender—about half an hour. It's just plain marvelous! And for delicious corn off the cob, combine four cups of kernels, a cup of heavy cream, a teaspoon of sugar, half teaspoon of salt, dash of pepper, and a quarter cup of butter or margarine, and simmer ten minutes in a covered saucepan. This serves six. For more ways with corn, see page 172.

3. Dramatic scale eliminates non-essentials. The entire impression is of the mouth-watering goodness of corn. The melting action of butter was caught at just the right moment. Photographer: Paul Dome

5. A headline of monumental scale for a monumental subject. The blurb and text also have a serious look. The Homburg Hat and British Flag give it the diplomatic, political flavor. Photographer: Elbert Budin

These, we believe, are the bare essentials

Stripped down to its fashion fundamentals, the bathing-suit picture is bold and bright. Most revealing new trends are: The skin-tight maillot, looking for all the world as though it were painted on. The maillot, we say, knows no rigid age limits but requires a notably slender figure. The audacious bikini, the number-one conversation maker, should be worn, we believe, by the blood-young, supershapely, coolly confident only. Newest version has an adjustment feature that allows more or a little less exposure. The cut-down back, the cut-out waistline give a feeling of bareness to more conservative swimsuits.

The indispensable coverup: A next-to-nothing bathing suit, we maintain, is for the water's edge only. If you're venturing even as far as the hot-dog stand, you'll need a topper or jacket, often made to match the suit. The siren colors: Our favorite shades of the season are the elegant acid greens and yellows, the immodest violets, and, for the subtlest mermaids, the taupe-to-brown range. The native prints: Fruit and flower and leaf patterns, Hawaii- and South-Sea-inspired, give minimal suits an erotically feminine feeling. We like these particularly when the suit has a suggestion of a sarong drape. The head-to-foot look: We enthusiastically underwrite the color-coordinated bathing costume, with coverup, cap, beach shoes geared to the suit itself. The captivating cap: Precious-little suits demand precious-little millinery — and the choice today is wider than ever. The prettiest versions are covered with flowers; highest new fashion, the peaked, pointed-head cap.

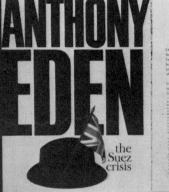

ANTHONY EDEN

the Suez crisis

4. The fun and playfulness of being in water, shown as simply as possible, also shows bathing suits to full advantage. The idea was to entertain our reader and have her participate in our idea. Photographer: Jerry Schatzberg

6. Children's fashions photographed as nostalgic portraits and presented as every mother would want her little girl to look. The idea to photograph the children this way originated with the old fashioned look of the clothes. Photographer: Bert Stern

She's Sleeping Beauty in a romantic rose-garden gown, waiting patiently for her prince   She's a latter-day Jane Eyre, proper and proud, in the decorous dress of the past cen...

AMERICAN HOME... *simple, straightforward, exciting*
by WILLIAM R. BOWMAN

It becomes more apparent as we study our concepts of design and layout in the pages of The American Home that the problems presented to us always seem to narrow down to one rather obvious answer; in effect to find a simple, straightforward, honest approach to the problem no matter what the subject; to make it as visually exciting and attractive to read as all the talent at our command can muster.

This would seem to be a rather easy approach and one to which many people would say "sure, of course, that's an obvious approach." But to execute a page or pages in this manner is not easy. To use these "obvious devices" consistently and to make it mandatory is sometimes grueling but always rewarding in its completion.

1. PROBLEM: A definite merchandise directed editorial idea. Seven blenders had to be used as well as the "cooling results" of their use.

SOLUTION: A close grouping of the blenders was done to overcome the possibility of their complete visual dominance of the layout. Their **confinement** to the center of the spread **and the** placement of the drinks in **the fore**ground in elegant glassware made a satisfactory working relationship between appliance and its use. (ADs William Bowman and Alvin Grossman; designer, William Grossman; photographer, Irwin Horowitz)

2. PROBLEM: To show a new rose called "The American Home Rose."

SOLUTION: Displayed one rose in a very special manner so that it was the only red object in the photograph, making everything else secondary by keeping the other colors muted. The rose appeared as just cut from the garden for arrangement in the case. (AD/designer, William Bowman; photographer, Irwin Horowitz)

6. PROBLEM: To show hot chocolate recipes from different countries.

SOLUTION: An old fireplace was used to convey warmth and a comfortable family, traditional feeling. Cups were chosen to suggest the countries from which recipes originated. (AD/designer, William Bowman; photographer, Stan Young)

3. PROBLEM: To show the variety available today in household gloves.

SOLUTION: Show objects held by animated gloves indicating typical household duties. Choose the gloves best suited to these duties. Use real hand for realism of animation. (AD/designer, William Bowman; photographer, Peter Dimitri)

4. PROBLEM: To combine a food piece with a collection (bread and butter molds) and achieve a pictorial relationship.

SOLUTION: Bread-box and cabinet (to display the collection) were used to their fullest typographically, resulting in a balance between the editorial concept and visual presentation. (AD/designer, Alvin Grossman; photographer, Irwin Horowitz)

5. PROBLEM: To design a single page opener for a large gardening section that would reflect the complete package.

SOLUTION: A daisy was used symbolically to represent flowers and the body copy and title were typographically worked out as a flower pot shape for the daisy. Basically, the text and headline were utilized to carry the weight of the design. (AD/designer, Alvin Grossman; Photographer, Irwin Horowitz)

PLAYBOY... *urbanity for the ins*
by ARTHUR PAUL

The range of material we present makes necessary thinking and experimenting in many different directions. Also, the audience Playboy appeals to, and its function for that audience, adds another dimension to the breadth of creative thinking required for it. Our reader is a young man who is, or would like to be, "in." It is important to him to know about the newest and "smartest" developments in entertainment, fashion, food, travel, music, literature, and art. Playboy acts also, in a sense, as the young man's manual of savoir faire, and must accordingly fill him in on cars, special sporting events, and personalities. It is natural then that the approach, both editorial and visual, reflect this feeling of urbanity for which the reader, himself, is striving. This demands a fresh, sophisticated visual approach.

The temptation, although great, to design each spread to the hilt must be avoided so that a kind of visual rhythm can be maintained throughout a single issue. The technical requirements of story placement and importance must be balanced by a sense of timing developed from page to page by color, division of space, size, illustration technique, amount of copy, and size and style of display type. Using these elements to visually differentiate the stories presented, we must at the same time maintain a family resemblance among the components of each issue.

This brings to mind the other aspect of pacing—pacing in time. Because we run such diverse material, we try to avoid repetition in the visual presentation of the same type of material from issue to issue. For example, we may use a photo for fiction in one issue and a drawing in the next.

Both food spreads presented here have recipes in the text, yet each, while very much to the point, represents a different point of view. Hors d'oeuvres ran in a holiday issue. Through the use of the calendar for the month of January, the food itself was integrated with the timeliness of the story. In the "Eat Great, Lose Weight" spread no food was shown. Instead we used a black and white photo of an obviously slim hand poking into the title with a fork...as if it were something to be eaten. The only color on the spread was used in the title for emphasis and "appetite appeal."

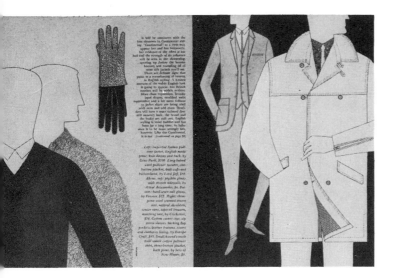

Fashion is an important service feature for our readers. I think in terms of strong direct approaches, whether done with photography or art. The above spread was done on a special paper and printed in two colors. The color of the paper on the right-hand page is the actual color of the clothes illustrated.

Fiction spreads afford a great deal of experimental visual expression. Here the gamut is run, because the stories themselves are diverse and often intense. Since we seldom run picture captions with the illustrations, the picture alone must often project the feeling of a story. They are specific enough to relate directly to the text, yet vague enough to leave room for psychological play. THE TASTE OF FEAR was solved with a photograph and type treatment. THE RUNAWAY was a three-color etching.

the chronicle of a man and his genius
By CHARLES BEAUMONT

The Chaplin head was a page introducing a three-page article about Chaplin's genius. The tricky use of his name to form his mustache is related to the comedy of the man himself, and so a visual gimmick becomes a forceful part of the editorial statement.

LOOK... *design as an editorial force*
by ALLEN F. HURLBURT

The highly concentrated competition for reader time and reader interest in the 1960s is placing new demands on the magazine art director. These demands are in turn leading to new directions and new trends in magazine design, new approaches in typography, and new attitudes toward picture selection and picture use.

Perhaps the most significant trend in magazines is the growing importance of design as an editorial force. The traditional role of the layout as an assembly point for existing material has gradually given way to a realization that design thinking belongs in every phase of magazine creation.

trends in page design

To satisfy the need for freshness and excitement in modern magazines the art director must approach the printed page with a new freedom and flexibility. Fixed format, prescribed margins and rigid typographical style are being replaced by a treatment of the page or spread unit as a special entity. Within this framework editorial and visual elements are freely interpreted with the editorial function dictating the final form of the design.

Visual and typographic elements are receiving bolder treatment. Pictures are larger and frequently cropped to extract the maximum dramatic effect. Type elements are stronger and varied in selection and use.

trends in typography

The display or selling lines of magazine features and covers were once written to fit format specifications or to match dummy type the art director had pasted into a layout. Today the headline often directs the layout and on many occasions the words become the primary design element.

Behind this reassertion of typography is the growing importance of ideas in magazine success. These ideas may be conveyed in words, in pictures, or more perfectly in an absolute unity of both these elements. This means that the magazine art director today must be increasingly aware of editorial thinking.

For many years photography has been placing more and more emphasis on naturalism...the documentary realism of a moment arrested in time and its revealing insight into people's lives. Today there is growing evidence of a counter-trend toward the controlled, as against the candid approach. Studio lighting, planned situations, and the 8 x 10 camera are again taking an important place in creative photography.

Today man is exposed to a virtual treadmill of visual impressions. Projected and printed images pass before his eyes until most of them become blurred and meaningless. Repetition and imitation swiftly reduce yesterday's new idea to tomorrow's cliché. If the art director is to successfully serve the modern magazine, he must constantly adjust his creative approach to meet the challenge of this changing visual climate.

land of conflict
land of contrast
land of hope

1. In modern magazine typography the headline need not occupy its traditional place at the head of the column nor does the text fall in a pre-specified box. The type is Peignot. (Photographer: John Vachon)

2. A near perfect unity between typographic and visual elements is achieved as the word "California" becomes the shore line in the photograph. (Photographer: Cal Bernstein)

4. The interplay of three pictures captures the emotional essence of the story in a way that no single photo could. (Photographer:: Paul Fusco)

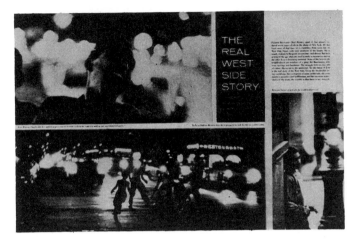

3. Typography becomes the dominant element of the design and the idea is made more forceful and direct by the subordination of the illustration.

5. Little more than a quarter of an inch of negative extracted from a mediocre photograph makes an exciting and revealing statement when blown up across an editorial spread. (Photographer: La Tesse)

6. Small photographs used in a modified "rebus" style permit a variety of statements without loss of impact and with complete harmony of words and pictures. (Photographer: Cal Bernstein)

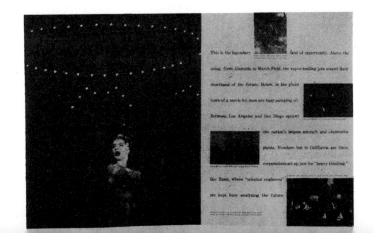

NUGGET...*decoration, frivolous or purposeful*
by BILL PAGE

At the moment I believe there is a trend toward frivolous decoration. It should be perfectly obvious that only the trend makers will deal with the complexities of ornamentation so as to make it flexible, understandable and beautiful. I hope that before we have filigree around each boy-girl illustration someone will question the validity of the indiscriminate use of this kind of illustration. And before William DeKooning is assigned an illustration, question the reasonability of his painting as illustration *...and when it's right, use it!*

The value of the art director and those he chooses to work for him lies in their ability to clearly interpret and express the message of each article in harmony with the editorial direction of the magazine.

Art ● Cliff Condak

Photo ● Larry Shustak

Photo ● Bill Page

Art • Jerome Martin

Art • Arno Sternglass

Art • Cliff Condak

ESQUIRE...*when solutions are too far in, they're out*
by ROBERT BENTON

Saul Leiter said once, when asked about photographic data, "I saw them, I had a camera, I took the picture." I think this is true with anybody—you see a problem, you solve it as well as you can and it works or it doesn't work. When you do find a solution that works you are constantly tempted to fall back on it. But once a problem and its solution become familiar you must look either for new solutions or new problems.

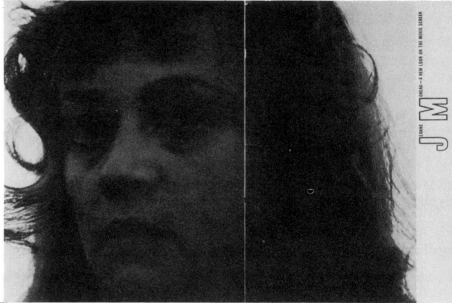

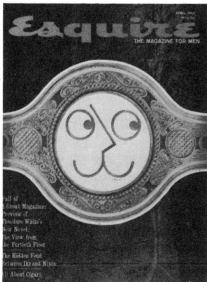

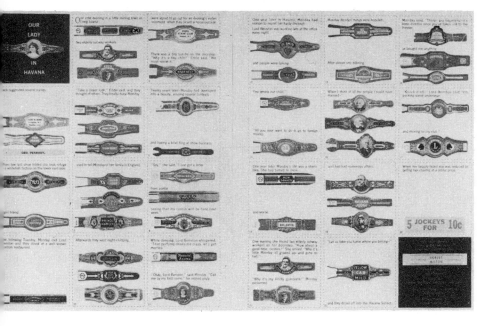

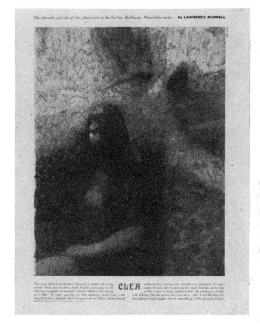

Art: Tom Allen

25

Robert Benton and Harvey Schmidt's   Or Things That Should Be Done In 1960

1. Refilm PORGY AND BESS. 2. An LP record of
YOUR GUN. 3. A new line of Piper Cubs designed
regular radio show called ART RADIO with
MYSTERY. 5. A book of Diane Varsi poems. 6. A
and billboards. 7. A Museum of Modern Art retro-
SURPLUS. 8. Find Clare Boothe Luce a job. 9. An
BLACK AND WHITE PHOTOGRAPHS OF
Ingrid Bergman and Ingemar Johansson in a new
the life story of Gustav Klimt. 12. An LP album of
Somebody do something good with Jane Fonda
paint Jayne Mansfield in the nude. 15. Larry
dance marathon on TV. 17. A comic strip by Jasper
Tuesday Weld and Fabian. 19. Build a Nigeria
married on BRIDE AND GROOM. 21. An LP
22. COKE TIME with Lotte Lenya. 23. Geraldine
Hyer in THE FLEUR COWLES STORY. 25. Hugh
AND HARVEY SCHMIDT STORY.

the Judy Garland sound track for ANNIE GET
to look like WORLD WAR I fighter planes. 4. A
old shows like VIC AND SADE and I LOVE A
Museum of Modern Art show of old movie posters
spective show of TWENTY YEARS OF ARMY
expensive book by Richard Avedon of FIFTY
JULIA ORYNSKI. 10. Ingmar Bergman directing
movie. 11. Orson Welles directing and starring in
GREAT THEMES FROM LOONEY TUNES. 13.
before she gets too big. 14. Norman Rockwell to
Rivers to paint Norman Rockwell in the nude. 16. A
Johns. 18. Re-make HITLER'S CHILDREN with
Hilton. 20. A book of photos of each couple ever
record where you can sing along with Maria Callas.
Page in THE BETTE DAVIS STORY. 24. Martha
Downs and Jose Melis in THE ROBERT BENTON

GENTLEMEN'S QUARTERLY... *boy-girl realism*
by AL GREENBERG

A man's fashion magazine is a strange animal. The art director has a set of problems that never face the women's fashion books —how to make avant garde merchandise look masculine. You can't pose a man in a Continental suit in front of an Italian cheese store, an angelic smile on his lips, his arms gracefully curved upwards. We must glamorize clothes but never look chichi. We pick models who convey masculinity, watching their poses to avoid hands on hips, crossed legs or a gingerly way of holding a cigarette. We pick backgrounds that are interesting, but masculine. Finally, we create realistic situations using a girl model as often as possible and on-the-spot local color and/or people when available.

Occasionally we have used a photographic process—grainy color, replolith line, etc.—to vary the pages, but only certain merchandise lends itself to these techniques in the generally subtle men's apparel field. Closely cropped blowups are still another layout approach, but for the most part, we stay with boy-girl realistic situations.

The realistic approach, Havana, 1959 before Castro became a problem. The models were two **barbados**, bearded soldiers who posed gladly. (Chadd Hall, photographer)

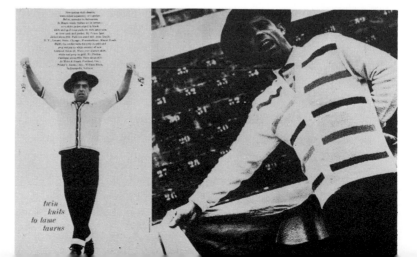

Realism in Portugal. A real bull fighter posed in high-fashion sweaters in a Portuguese bull ring. (Photographer, Chad Hall)

We took high-fashion sweaters down to Greenwich Village. The locations were scouted beforehand to get all the local flavor possible, and the models were authentic beatniks hired through an agency that rents them out for private parties. The girl beatnik is actually a secretary at Gentlemen's Quarterly who let her hair down and her hips out for the occasion. (Emma Gene Hall, photographer)

HARPER'S BAZAAR... *excitement within standards*
by HENRY WOLF

1. The big problem of a high-fashion magazine is to find a way to be exciting and still conform to its standards of elegance. This cover achieves a contemporary, clean design without gimmickry, the enemy of elegance. Photographer, Avedon

2. The reason for this spread is lateness for a deadline. I combined a picture I had bought some time before (for possible future use) with a drawing made with the lipsticks directly on the layout paper. Elapsed time, 1 hour

3. Photographer, Ernst Haas.

4. This spread is the result of an afternoon in Mr. Steinberg's studio. We spoke about pictorial features generally and he showed me a diary in which he had experimented with rubber stamps.

5. This Paris Collection was a 25 page variation on a theme of Bruno Caruso's paintings. Photographer, Avedon

1

3

2

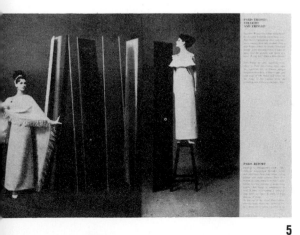

5

4.

. . . In appliance advertising there is little sophistication, little visual creativity, but, Walter Glenn reports, the trend is toward "more sound, more original, more sophisticated thinking."

The exciting layouts noted by Otto Storch in the previous chapter are encouraging advertising ADs to add visual flair to their layouts, encouraging clients to accept them. But one of the areas slow to follow is the hard-headed appliance field. Walter Glenn traces the past 15 years of appliance ads from the post-war device-y ads through the newsier ads of current ad leaders, predicts a visual breakthrough. . . .

appliances: from addy to newsy to creative...

ad leaders break away from the restrictions of product similarity and the appliance syndrome

by WALTER GLENN

During the war years, January 1942 to December 1945, there were 6,414,000 marriages in the United States. In this same period only a trickle of appliances reached the consumer market to satisfy the needs of these new families—not to mention the needs of the older families whose appliances had worn out,

Millions of people needed and were eager to buy appliances in the early postwar years. The annual retail business in household appliances in this country jumped from a one-billion dollar pre-war average to four-billion post-war.

It would be great if the advertising business could take the credit for this rise, but all an ad had to say in order to perform well then was, "Here is an appliance; here's what it looks like; here's what it will do for you."

Look through the issues of Life Magazine starting in 1946 when the appliance assembly lines were rolling again and you will find that most of the appliance ads were addy and device-y. Ads #1 through #7, all of which appeared in LIFE in the spring of 1948, are typical.

One exception was General Electric. G.E. had settled on a modified editorial format which delivered as much news and information as possible about their appliances, and did it in a direct manner. Ads #8 and #9, which appeared in 1948, illustrate this.

2. Westinghouse used circular illustrations for continuity

If you look through some more LIFE's that came out after the "Korean conflict" had come and gone, you'll notice that while most of the appliance ads in the mid 50's continued to be addy, device-y, and promotional, a fast-growing minority were swinging over to the newsy, editorial approach. This is evident in the copy, illustrations, design and typography, as well as in the overall concept of ads #10, 11, 12 and 13, clipped from LIFE in 1955.

Headlines and copy are not just bare-faced boasts or contrived phrases; the claims are there, but basically these ads are reporting facts.

The illustrations are better than the 1948 versions. The art directors have cleaned up the layouts; they have thrown out the jazzy lettering and settled down to readable editorial typography.

1. similarity

The people who create the appliance ads often have, like the admakers in several other fields, a very serious problem because of the similarity of the features being advertised. (When a manufacturer is the sole advertiser of a particular appliance, as in Ads #14 and 15, he does not have to worry about brand confusion in the mind of the reader. But these cases are exceptional.)

Manufacturers of the staples of the appliance business who are on the ball have a pretty good idea of what the competition is up to, so that several companies are likely to come up with similar product features at about the same time. This applies to refrigerators, stoves, home laundry equipment, etc., the products which have reached a high saturation figure. (98% of all U.S. families own a refrigerator, 98% own stoves, 93% own automatic washers.)

From the advertising agency's standpoint, the problem is— how does a manufacturer say "my refrigerator-freezer needs

1. Philco ads used Alice in Wonderland in the post-war years

3. Kelvinator was less cluttered than most of its competitors

4. Norge had a strongly promotional flavor

5. Ads like Thor's are "hard-working"

6. RCA Victor's ads (not really appliances) busy but classy

no defrosting either in the freezer or in the refrigerator" and make *his* product stand out from all the others? (See Ads #16, 17, 18 and 19, all of which ran in 1960, all based on the same selling theme.) The similarity at this point becomes epidemic.

Expecting the agency to solve this is expecting a lot. The right cure for the disease begins in the manufacturer's Product Development Department.

In 1954 there was built into the General Electric Automatic Washer a filter which removed lint from the wash water—an exclusive, saleable benefit. That year and for a number of succeeding years the advertising was built around this feature. Because of this difference in the product the G. E. washer advertising stood out. (Ad #20.)

The same principle gave the agency the same kind of opportunity to talk about an exclusive feature in 1954 when G. E. put revolving shelves into their refrigerator. (Ad #21.) Two years ago Tappan introduced a new configuration in their "400" range. (Ad #22.) This gave Tappan an exclusive advantage in the range business.

Westinghouse's introduction of the center-drawer refrigerator in 1960 is another example of an opportunity to build advertising around an exclusive development. (Ad #23.)

An exclusive product feature which promises the buyer a real benefit is the first step towards the solution of the problem of making a particular brand stand out from the competition.

2. progress

The second thing you notice when you review appliance advertising is that many ads today are suffering from bad habits carried over from the not-too-distant past. If you put these ills all together they add up to what we might call the appliance syndrome:

- most have too many elements in them
- they try to emphasize too many things
- typographically, most shout instead of speaking
- they are likely to include (usually at the insistence of someone at the plant) bits of trade jargon
- they frequently suffer from sloganitis, simple or multiple
- the illustrations are trite, unimaginative in concept and journeyman in technique

But the trend among the leaders in the business is away

Now A New Era Of Complete
HOTPOINT...World's

THE REFRIGERATOR THAT DARED TO BE DIFFERENT

7. Hotpoint has favored spreads with black or red backgrounds

GENERAL ⊕ ELECTRIC

8. 1948 G. E. Refrigerator ad concentrated on news and facts

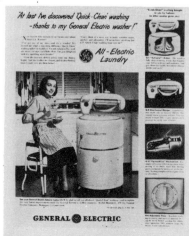

GENERAL ⊕ ELECTRIC

9. G. E. Laundry copy is less direct but has some basic concept

from these faults, as illustrated by our 1955 examples and some of our 1960 examples.

I am sure this trend will continue and will broaden.
I do not think the General Electric Refrigerator people are quite ready to okay an ad which shows a picture of their product with the word "lemon" under it—as the Volkswagen people did. Or that the Westinghouse Refrigerator people would okay an ad with no copy, no logotype, just a picture of a woman with the words, "Westinghouse Refrigerators because," under it.

(Maybe I'm underestimating the audacity of these two giants of the appliance business. After all, both of them were bold enough to get into the rocket business in the days when you and I still thought of rockets as a Fourth-of-July diversion.)

But if the trend towards more sound, more original, more sophisticated thinking continues, they will come up with ads that will be just as original, arresting and effective as the Volkswagen and Modess ads. This development is due in the very near future.

Certainly the near future promises plenty of excitement as far as the products to be advertised are concerned. You have probably read or heard that we can expect in the '60s the broad-scale marketing of many electronic, ultrasonic and thermoelectric appliances—electronic ovens, ultrasonic dishwashers, portable refrigerators, etc. (Maybe you've read about the daddy of them all; you put a week's supply of frozen foods into one end, spin dials, push buttons,—and out the other end come three meals a day all week long.) The alert manufacturers know that those appliances which are to flourish will need new ideas superimposed on their purely utilitarian images so that they can compete with the fun, glamor and other benefits offered by swimming pools, outboards and trips to Rome. As the Young & Rubicam house ads say, "People buy ideas."

In the '60s the challenge to the advertising agencies will be to find—and sell to the manufacturers—ways of advertising these ideas which will be as new and exciting as the wares they advertise.

10. RCA used LIFE-like story, pictures, layout and typography

11. By 1955 the Westinghouse circular illustrations are no more

12. Maytag has neat layout, exploits
picture, caption technique

13. Whirlpool has editorial look,
achieves individual identity

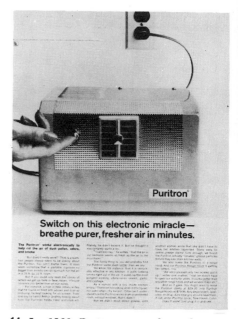

14. In 1960 Puritron was the only big air-purifier advertiser

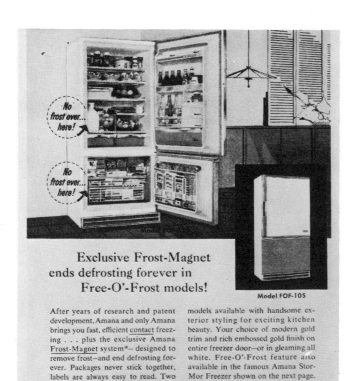

Exclusive Frost-Magnet
ends defrosting forever in
Free-O'-Frost models!

After years of research and patent development, Amana and only Amana brings you fast, efficient <u>contact</u> freezing . . . plus the exclusive Amana <u>Frost-Magnet</u> system*– designed to remove frost—and end defrosting forever. Packages never stick together, labels are always easy to read. Two models available with handsome exterior styling for exciting kitchen beauty. Your choice of modern gold trim and rich embossed gold finish on entire freezer door—or in gleaming all white. Free-O'-Frost feature also available in the famous Amana Stor-Mor Freezer shown on the next page.

*Patented

Model FOF-105

Backed by a century-old tradition of fine craftsmanship

16. One page clipped from a multi-page, multi-product Amana ad

17. Norge departs from usual photo of one model with refrigerator

New General Electric Partio Cart has 5 big wheels
(One is you)

An electric range on one side, a charcoal barbecue on the other, a serving bar on top and both sides.

Entertaining new idea from General Electric! Watch your guests turn green with envy while the roast turns brown with succulence on a Partio Cart.*

Big charcoal grill sizzles steaks, chops, burgers, franks, you name it. Or roast a whole turkey or ham on electrically driven spits.

Meanwhile, back on the range (by General Electric) cook all your side dishes. There's a large oven, too, for roasting, baking and broiling.

Don't risk losing your "man who has everything" status. Be the first in your crowd to own a Partio Cart. See it at your General Electric dealer's. If he's not with it, write Partio Cart, General Electric Co., Louisville 1, Ky. *Trademark of General Electric Co.

Progress Is Our Most Important Product

GENERAL ELECTRIC

15. G. E. was alone in featuring this
kind of appliance in 1960

18. So does Frigidaire

NO MORE DEFROSTING—EVEN IN THE FREEZER!

General Electric Frost-Guard System prevents frost from forming anywhere in this big new Refrigerator-Freezer! Adjustable Swing-Out Shelves bring all foods out front!

Progress Is Our Most Important Product

GENERAL ELECTRIC

General Electric Company, Household Refrigerator Dept., Louisville 1, Ky.

Three Adjustable Swing-Out Shelves bring even the food in back right out front! You can adjust shelves up or down even when loaded with food—to fit in a large ham or a pie. Cleaning the refrigerator is so easy, too. The shelves lift out completely.

Handy Freeze-N-Store Ice Service. Simply flip trays over to eject cubes; refill with water right in the freezer! Container stores up to 6 trays of cubes. Freeze-N-Store Ice Service and Frost-Guard are available in both the 13 and 15-cubic-foot models.

Straight-Line Design and Big Roll-Out Freezer. 1. Fits flush with walls—no coils in back to accumulate dirt. 2. No waste space at side for door clearance. 3. Front lines up with base cabinets. 4. Roll-Out Freezer holds up to 4 huge supermarket bags of frozen foods!

19. G. E. uses posterized, reportorial
presentation, plus device

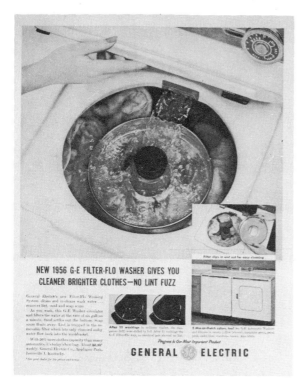

20. G. E. "Filter-Flo," introduced in
1954, still going strong

21. Typical G. E. use of pictures
and captions to get copy read

22. No one else had a "400," so no
one else had ads like Tappan's

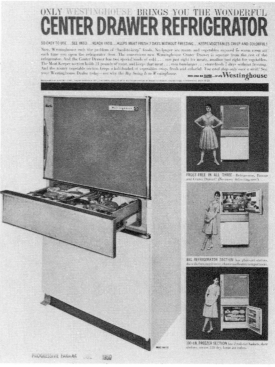

23. Exclusive feature, tidy format
make Westinghouse stand out

Financial advertising presents a strong contrast to appliance advertising. If the air conditioner, TV set, freezer comes in new models, with color and fashion appeal, and represents a one-shot expense for a tangible boost in living comfort, the bank offers a variety of intangible services, even more like those of its competitors than is true of many products. And there is no lure of fashion, glamour, immediate benefit.

If graphics are increasingly sophisticated, there is evidence not only among the design leaders but among the trends toward the contemporary look in conservative areas such as retail and financial advertising.

trends in financial advertising . . .

much plastic surgery fails to hide old stone faces; but in a few places informality and lively graphics are showing the way

by PAUL R. SMITH

Financial advertising, since the early days of the business, has been the object of much censorious comment. "Tombstone" copy—"Marble Pillar" layouts—the "Rigor Mortis" school of English prose—are some of the phrases directed at financial advertisers. Indicated is the suspicion that much of such advertising was directed at the advertiser's own board of directors.

The truth is that financial advertising has come a long way. There has been contemporary movement in layout, typography and illustration. There has been an attempt to limber up. Many institutions use such mass media as radio and television. There has been a trend toward humor to readers, and toward an intelligent use of human interest as a leavening agent in an otherwise indigestible fare.

new facade not enough   But a sizeable file of contemporary financial advertising indicates that in many cases these devices, while an improvement, have been only plastic surgery—that underneath the new facade is the same old stone face. Even though many well known and well proven readership devices are used to snare the customer, the copy often is in financial jargon. Let me quote a couple of examples:

"We value highly the confidence that has been placed in us, since it is only through this confidence that we have been able to become one of the largest non-bank trust companies in the industry."

"The bank which has always held fast to sound principles of dependable progressive service—the bank that looks to the future with confidence and faith in our patrons, our community and our nation."

These are fairly formidable, but they illustrate the point. There still is a tendency to be general rather than specific— to patronize the community rather than participate in it —and to talk in terms of what the company likes about its services rather than what the folks want to know. Too much financial advertising talks to itself.

The financial community has a crying need for communication with the public. Few businesses come into such intimate daily contact with all kinds of people—are so vital to them—and are so misunderstood.

People are intimidated by financial experts. They mistrust those whom they think are smarter than they are, especially where it concerns money. Behind this prejudice is a semantic problem. Most of the words in finance are semantically "bad" . . . mortgage, note, loan, trust fund, co-signer, financial, collateral, credit, trustee, escrow, banker. People feel uneasy because they don't understand the words and they associate them with things that may end to their own disadvantage.

Yet, many people want to know, but are too embarassed to ask.

1. An example of high readership techniques brought to a long and complicated story. The indirect (yet direct) headline leads into copy presented in dramatic dialogue to maintain readership. This advertisement had high Starch readership scores and high coupon response, much of which was converted into the sale of securities.

a need for information

There is clearly a need for plain, easy-to-understand explanations. Some financial advertisers have learned this, and their attitude has been reflected in the copy approach and in the visual presentation. Humor in their advertising demonstrates that, after all, bankers and brokers are people. Their copy calls spade a spade and their layouts are clean without being so sanitary that customers are afraid to read them. There has been an upsurge of modern art, a strong movement toward human interest, in many cases following the lead of insurance advertising. One format which appears again and again demonstrates that the institution's services are world-wide. There has been a strong tendency to humanize the financial institution and to talk to people as though they are people and not dollar signs in an annual report.

humanized facts

Case in point is the advertising of the New York Stock Exchange and of Merrill Lynch Pierce Fenner & Smith. Well-written, informative, interestingly presented information of these advertisers has been rewarded by high readership figures. For the Stock Exchange, the candid explanation of its services, accompanied by realistic warnings, have won unusually large audiences. Their recent announcement of a sixteen-page advertisement in Reader's Digest is an example of the aggressive financial institution's desire to be informative and of real service to its readers, rather than to flex its institutional muscles.

All in all, the trends in financial advertising are in the direction of informality, lively graphic presentation, and away from the formal, stuffed-shirt attitude of the past.

For a better way to take care of your nest egg
talk to the people at Chase Manhattan

THE
CHASE
MANHATTAN
BANK

2. This advertisement is typical of a series which had widespread comment for its arresting visual idea. It is one of a few campaigns which have been consistently maintained, with consequent high scores in memorability and sponsor identification. Some might think this series a little too cute.

A banker makes a decision

financial leader first, your banker is likewise a man of community affairs

UMPIRING a close one on Saturday helps many a banker make wiser decisions on Monday. That's because taking part in things close to the community's heart is a sure way for a banker to better know the people and their financial needs.

In that way, a banker can have both the understanding and the insight to evaluate an individual's financial problem, counsel local businessmen, work wisely and profitably.

In a nutshell, a banker has to be a civic doer as well as a financial counsellor. By taking on community responsibility and learning what makes his neighbors tick, a banker makes his bank more useful every day.

When all's said and done, it's usefulness that makes commercial banking so important to the nation's economy and the American way of life.

THE
CHASE
MANHATTAN
BANK
CHARTERED IN 1799
Head Office: New York 15, N. Y.
MEMBER FEDERAL DEPOSIT INSURANCE CORPORATION

3. An unusually clean and professional presentation of a good idea. This series showed American scenes and identified the advertiser's interest with the public's

Protect your castle! In chess—or in protecting and preserving an estate—long-range strategy is of the greatest importance. Every possible move must be carefully considered—and far in advance. • Here's where Bank of America can lend you a hand. Our Trust Department will help you plan the management of your estate—safeguard the interests of your family, now and in the future. • Why don't you and your attorney come in and talk it over? **BANK OF AMERICA**

4. The basically good idea here is handicapped by a somewhat banal pictorial device, although the twist of a house on the chess piece goes a long way to rescue it.

Man-on-the-spot...in London. Need a quick credit check in Mayfair? He'll be on his way before Big Ben strikes the hour. Market reports from Brazil? See our man in Rio. In California, across the nation, around the world, **BANK OF AMERICA** can provide you with first-hand banking assistance—save you time, effort and money. If you need the services of a man-on-the-spot, see Bank of America—first in banking.

5. An advertisement typical of a series dramatizing world wide banking services. This version professionally presented a favorite financial theme.

90

6. Many bank advertisers — particularly savings and loan companies—have taken a leaf from the book of the insurance companies. This probably had excellent readership.

7. This typographic example was very effective. The bands between the lines of type were in different bright colors.

8. Many banks appeal to specific industrial and technical audiences, feeling a "vertical" approach establishes their competence in specific areas and qualifies them in general. This advertiser is located close to the aircraft industry.

9. This advertiser has adopted a highly decorative modern photo-montage, or a photographic presentation of unrelated elements. The series gives favorable impression of modernism of outlook. Another "vertical" approach.
Query: Will it get readers?

10. This obviously tries to correct the impression that bankers are formidable and unsympathetic. Professionally executed, it still raises the question: Do people really believe that New York bankers have the hometown touch?

Some day some bank will run an ad saying: "All our vice presidents have **two** glass eyes."

Meet the New York Banker | with the hometown touch

Chemical Bank
New York Trust Company

A Bank for the Space Age

CHEMICAL BANK
NEW YORK
TRUST COMPANY
Founded 1824

11. This seems to claim too easy a victory by tying in with the highly fashionable space age. The fault is not restricted to banks. Many advertisers whose contribution was probably no more important than providing paper towels for the wash- rooms at Cape Canaveral have claimed credit for orbiting Discoverer XVII.

VIA **BANK OF AMERICA**
TRAVELERS CHEQUES
money only you can spend
KNOWN AND ACCEPTED THROUGHOUT THE WORLD

12. One of a long, continuing two color series. Excellent poster visibility, but one wonders whether it might not be mistaken for a travel ad.

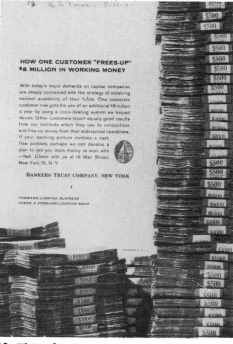

HOW ONE CUSTOMER "FREES-UP"
$8 MILLION IN WORKING MONEY

BANKERS TRUST COMPANY, NEW YORK

FORWARD LOOKING BUSINESS
NEEDS A FORWARD-LOOKING BANK

13. This advertisement assumes that everyone is interested in money—even just to look at it. Actually, the theme of "freeing-up" money would interest bank customers who have a cash flow problem.

Make His Steps Easier—with a

GOLD MEDAL
SAVINGS ACCOUNT

College for your children...a new home—a new car—a trip abroad...whatever you save for will be yours faster, easier when you save *regularly* in a Gold Medal Savings Account at Chemical Bank New York Trust Company. 3% annual interest is compounded and credited every calendar quarter. Deposit by mail—or at any of our more than 100 convenient offices. All this, plus Gold Medal Service—prompt, courteous, efficient.

CHEMICAL BANK
NEW YORK
TRUST COMPANY
Founded 1824

DEPOSITS MADE ON OR BEFORE
JANUARY 8 EARN INTEREST FROM JANUARY 1.

MEMBER FEDERAL DEPOSIT INSURANCE CORPORATION

14. A savings account advertisement which follows the techniques of insurance companies, showing the emotional rewards of thrift.

Fixin' up....?

Remodeling?
Repairing?
Plumbing?
Painting?
Landscaping?
Air-Conditioning?

NEED MONEY TO REPAIR OR IMPROVE YOUR HOME
OR BUSINESS PROPERTY? Arrange a low-cost loan at this bank.
up to 5 YEARS TO PAY!
NO DOWN PAYMENT • NO ENDORSERS

Phone, Write or Visit the Office Nearest You

INDUSTRIAL
BANK OF COMMERCE
The Bank that Pioneered Consumer Credit in the United States
Main Office: 56 East 42nd Street, New York

Authorized ◆ Member

INDUSTRIAL BANK OF COMMERCE
Please send me information on
MODERNIZATION LOAN

Amt. $_____ _____Years

Name_____

Address_____

City_____

MANHATTAN
56 East 42nd St.—MU 2-5000 *
100 Church St.—CO 7-3000 *
462 Seventh Ave.—LA 4-9550 *
5 Union Square—AL 5-6139
126 Delancey St.—OR 4-8000
110 East 125th St.—LE 4-0024

JAMAICA, L. I.
89-05 165th St.—OL 7-7200

BROOKLYN
26 Court St.—MA 4-6500
1668 Pitkin Ave.—DI 2-0115

BRONX
391 E. 149th St.—MO 5-3100
2460 Grand Concourse—LU 4-4600

YONKERS
26 South B'way—YO 8-5400

* OPEN DAILY AT 8:30 A.M.

15. This newspaper ad offers loans. The check list of projects is changed to fit the seasons.

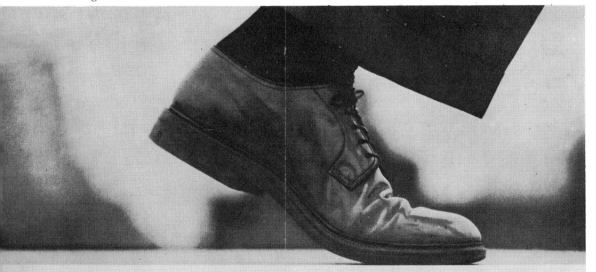

His shoeleather keeps   your money one step ahead

Shoeleather, as we use it, takes in more than the miles we travel in your behalf.

Our kind of shoeleather wraps up the brief effort that brings Chemical New York's brand of banking service to your office.

Starts in the Heart of the Money Market
"The New York Banker with the hometown touch" starts working for you right in our own New York offices. Here he covers the money market with the thorough skill you expect from a dedicated man whose home base is the financial capital of the world.

He knows how to set up a better cash flow to speed receipts and free your money for more profitable use. He can streamline a regional collection plan, with simplified controls—such as lock box and wire service—to cut down your handling time and costs. And he knows best of all how to work with you and your local banker to design a tight over-all financial plan for your company.

Gets the Local Point of View
As a traveling financial consultant, he calls on companies in your region only. That's

why he can bring you behind-the-scene knowledge of your business community as well as the money market.

The man from Chemical New York can walk this storehouse of information right into your office. He can put it to work to solve an immediate problem, and he can help you plan a sound financial future for your company. Just let us know where and when. Chemical Bank New York Trust Company, New York 15.

Member Federal Deposit Insurance Corporation

Chemical Bank
New York Trust Company

THE NEW YORK BANKER
THE HOMETOWN TOUCH

16. A good, human, commonplace idea, well presented, that should go a long way toward building a good image for the sponsor.

BIG WHEEL! Because, together with 1,200,000 other school children, he has $55,000,000 on deposit in the Savings Banks of New York State.

Who else but your Savings Banks start our school-agers out on the ways of saving—make thrift a habit that sticks throughout the grown-up years?

Somehow this is the sort of vision you expect from your Savings Bank. For this is a special breed of bank.

Your Savings Bank works only for its depositors. All earnings, after providing for expenses and reserves to protect the savings, come back to depositors in generous interest dividends. Savings Banks have no stockholders. This is why Savings Banks are called "mutual" banks.

Yes, a special breed of bank is your Savings Bank.

Q. How do Savings Banks differ from "checking account" banks?

A. Your Savings Bank specializes in savings, with all its efforts devoted to the growth of your savings. There are no stockholders—only you, the depositor, share in its earnings.

A few other statistics further prove it!

Savings Banks finance more New York homes than any other financial institution! Some 4,375,000 New Yorkers, more than one quarter of the State's population, live in these homes.

There are 50 billion dollars on deposit in New York State Savings Banks—most of it invested right here in the state. These savings create jobs and prosperity at home.

No other financial institution serves the individual saver and the community like the Savings Banks of New York State. Your Savings Bank—a very special breed of bank, indeed!

THE SAVINGS BANKS ASSOCIATION OF THE STATE OF NEW YORK

...the banks where your money works only for you

Member Federal Deposit Insurance Corporation   The Savings Banks Association of the State of New York, 110 East 42nd Street, New York 17, N. Y.

17. An association advertisement which successfully humanizes the institution of banking and invites junior depositors.

18. The Chase Manhattan Bank's symbol, created to cut through the confusing multiple bank names.

...new symbol for an old friend....

THE CHASE MANHATTAN BANK

Starting today, you will begin to see this new symbol wherever the name of The Chase Manhattan Bank appears. We hope it will come to stand for all the things we mean when we say: "You have a friend at Chase Manhattan."

MORE THAN ONE HUNDRED OFFICES THROUGHOUT METROPOLITAN NEW YORK
Member Federal Deposit Insurance Corporation

HOW TO INVEST
for Growing Income and Family Security

An investment guide inserted in the Reader's Digest as a special advertisement by **THE NEW YORK STOCK EXCHANGE**

	Page
America Unlimited	2
What Investing can Mean to You	3
Rules for Wise Investors	3
What Stocks do Institutions Own?	4
Just What are Stocks and Bonds?	5
Five Easy Steps to Investing	6
Four Successful Shareowners	7
About Federal Taxes	8
How to Own Stocks for $3.08 a Week	9
How to Choose Your Broker	10
How Much do Brokers Charge?	11
Who are The Weals, The Modots, The Wigs?	11
Ten Do's and Don'ts	12
Longest Records of Regular Dividends	12
For Women Only	13
A Growing Gift for a Growing Child	13
What Makes Stock Prices Go Up and Down	14
How to Read Newspaper Stock Tables	14

19. The New York Stock Exchange used Reader's Digest's large circulation for the mass distribution of this informative 16-page booklet. An example of financial advertisers' increasing tendency to be of service to their prospects.

. . . Pharmaceutical advertising is still an adolescent compared to advertising for many other products and services. But it was born sophisticated. From the outset in the early '40s it showed the way with contemporary design and typographic innovations. But the trend of the past two decades has been toward increasing competition, more campaign rather than single-ad mindedness. As we started through the '60s a 20% decline in prescription sales and Senate investigations of drug prices and profits put still further pressure on advertising to help produce sales. Here Kenneth Lavey shows how pharmaceutical advertising is changing its face to meet this challenge. . . .

trends in pharmaceutical advertising...

less photography, greater use of drawing and painting, more imaginative typography

by KEN LAVEY

Why does pharmaceutical advertising have a reputation for exceptional design and consistently imaginative graphic work?

Following discovery of the antibiotics in the late thirties and early forties, pharmaceuticals became a major industry. It was only natural for this vital, young industry to be receptive to the new directions in graphic design. The Bauhaus and other European schools, and many young American designers, had created a new visual language. The pharmaceutical industry produced commodities that lent themselves to symbolism and abstraction. Its products were presented to the doctor on an intellectual level considerably higher than many other advertisers dared to use.

Great skill in balancing many elements of design was characteristic of pharmaceutical advertising in this period. Symbols, lines, and other graphic devices were frequently employed. The human figure and product-related symbols were combined, often bringing to mind surrealism and other fine art forms of the time. Type was elegant, restrained, and often subordinated to the stronger graphic element which gave this kind of advertising a "clinical" or "pharmaceutical" look.

In the fifties pharmaceutical advertising was influenced by two factors that brought about harsh changes graphically. First, the market became more competitive. With the development of many new drugs, a highly accelerated advertising program emphasizing the campaign rather than the single piece was demanded. The pharmaceutical industry and consumer industry have more in common now than they had in the past.

Unique to this field is the short life of most drugs—many reach "old age" 18 months to three years after they are first marketed. Even pharmaceuticals of comparative lon-

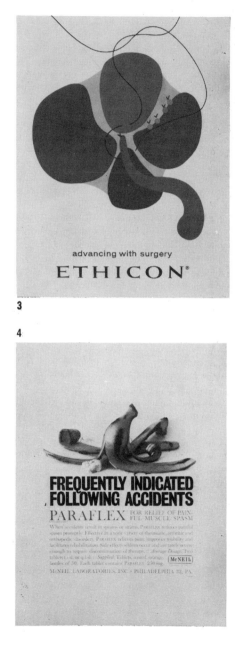

3

4

1

2

The pharmaceutical look characteristic of the forties (above) utilizing various graphic devices has given way (right) to greater boldness and directness in recent years.

gevity—on sale eight to ten years—presented problems. They are advertised to keep their names before the doctor, but, unlike many consumer products, they cannot be dressed up in new colors or refurbished with a new chrome trim! Another design challenge stemmed from the use of clinical data and instructional material, such as service items and aids to the doctor, as vehicles for promoting pharmaceuticals and achieving sales goals. Even frequency mailers and journal ads carry instructional and clinical data about the product.

Another influence in the fifties were the trends in other areas of advertising. As the decade advanced, the pharmaceutical look became less apparent. The formula—squared layout, blocked type, big type, stacked type—became the look for other advertising as well.

Perhaps the most characteristic graphic device of this period was the photograph. The reportorial photograph was the solution for almost any situation. The experimental photograph became common! The candid miniature camera solved innumerable problems! Photo still-lifes, simple and big, plus strong typography, was another characteristic. Drawing, painting, and graphic arts were utilized more in the pharmaceutical industry than in most other areas.

quiet scratching fingers in chickenpox and measles
Chlor-Trimeton Syrup

6

5

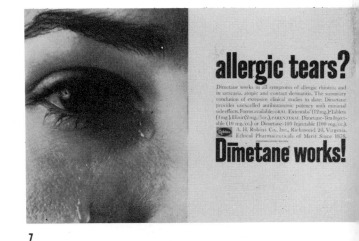

allergic tears?

Dimetane works!

Type becoming a dominant graphic element in recent years, for visual competition, especially in trade journals, required a more forceful and succinct message. Bold photography and poster-like art has characterized the visual image.

7

8

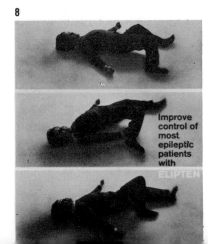

Improve control of most epileptic patients with

What are the trends of the early sixties? There seems to be a movement away from photography and an increased interest in drawing, painting, and graphic arts. Type is undergoing provocative changes. We are still blocking it, perhaps with even more determination than before, but now there is a playfulness and an imaginative trend that was lacking previously. Great influence undoubtedly will be exerted by the drugs now being developed, when they are ready to be marketed. This much is already evident—journal advertising is reaching an all time high and direct mail is undergoing many changes to increase its attention value to the doctor. More than ever before, a high quality of graphic design will be essential if the pharmaceutical advertiser's product is to stand out. New media *may* become increasingly more important but the *designer* will have to set the pace. If this industry's philosophy of advertising continues to encourage creativeness as in the past, its future trends will continue to pace the advertising industry.

9

10   11

The editorial type spread has been a challenge for the designer in this field. It has been used in informational material, doctors' aids, and clinical data supplied to the doctor.

12

13

New trends in art illustration have been stimulated by the diverse product demands, and the variety of media such as direct mail, house organs, institutional data, and journal advertisements.

14

15

16

17

In current journal promotion the strong product image has prevailed and the use of co-ordinated campaign themes, in all media, is the trend. The goal is to bring basic facts, quickly, to the physician and to act as reminder advertising. Except for their technical nature most of these reflect many of the better trends in consumer advertising.

18

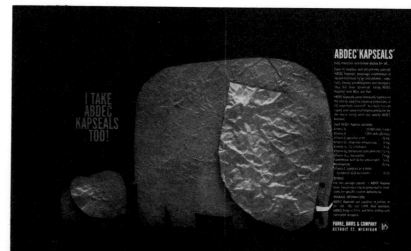

CHOO!

19

NEW
LIBRIUM
A MAJOR ADVANCE IN THE TREATMENT
OF COMMON ANXIETIES AND TENSION

20

21

22

VERT THE SHATTERING
MPACT OF DEPRESSION

Marplan

for good health in later years
GERIPLEX KAPSEALS
geriatric vitamin-mineral formula

Specially compounded for the middle-aged and elderly patient, GERIPLEX Kapseals provide a vitamin-
mineral supplement that helps to insure the adequate nutrition needed for good health in later years.

Each GERIPLEX kapseal contains:

Biotin .... 25 mg.	Vitamin C (ascorbic acid) .... 50 mg.
Choline dihydrogen citrate .... 20 mg.	Nicotinamide (niacinamide) .... 15 mg.
Vitamin B₂ (G) (riboflavin) .... 5 mg.	Taka-Diastase (aspergillus oryzae enzymes) .. 1 gr.
Vitamin B₁₂ crystalline .... 2 mcg.	Ferrous sulfate .... 30 mg.
Vitamin E (supplied as d-alpha-tocopheryl	Copper sulfate .... 4 mg.
acid succinate) .... 5 I.U.	Manganese sulfate (monohydrate) .... 4 mg.
Vitamin A .... 5000 Units	Zinc sulfate .... 2 mg.
Vitamin B₁ (thiamine mononitrate) ..... 5 mg.	Dicalcium phosphate (anhydrous) .... 200 mg.

PARKE, DAVIS & COMPANY • DETROIT 32, MICHIGAN, U.S.A.   PARKE-DAVIS

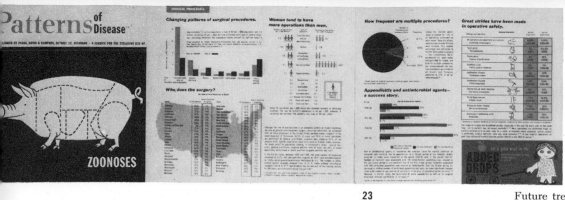

Future trends in this field are impossible to predict, but it is a good guess that promotion in general and direct mail in particular will have an even larger proportion of educational material and doctors' aids. The pharmaceutical industry communicates with the doctor in many ways and this diversity is where the future can hold a great challenge for the designer.

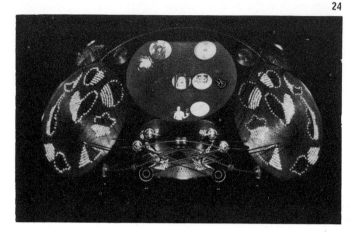

SCHERING'S CHILDREN'S EYE CHART

NOTICE: THIS CHART SHOULD BE VIEWED AT 15 FEET.

1. AD art • Lester Beall
Client • The Upjohn Co. (1947)

2. AD art • Alexander Ross
Client • White Laboratories

3. AD • Kenneth Lavey
Art • Eliott Herman
Agency • L. W. Frohlich

4. AD • Charles Attebery
Design • Richard Bergeron
Photo • Eugene Moses
Agency • L. W. Frohlich

5. AD • Jerry Andreozzi
Photo • Irv Bahrt
Agency • McAdams

6. AD • Kenneth Lavey
Design art • Eric Carle
Agency • L. W. Frohlich

7. Design • Herb Lubalin
Photo • Carl Fischer
Agency • Sudley & Hennessey

8. AD • Philip Swift
Design • Dick Jones
Photo • Jay Maisel
Agency • Sudler & Hennessey

9. AD • Carl Regehr
Art • Franklin McMahon
Client • Abbott Laboratories

10. AD • Kenneth Lavey
Design • Richard Bergeron
Photo • Gary Winogrand
Agency • L. W. Frohlich

11. AD design • Kenneth Lavey
Art • Donald Murray
Agency • L. W. Frohlich

12. AD • Kenneth Lavey
Design art • Norman Gorbaty
Agency • Intercontinental Marketing

13. AD • Carl Regehr
Art • Jerome Martin
Client • Abbott Laboratories

14. AD art • Eric Carle
Agency • Intercontinental Marketing
Client • Parke-Davis

15. AD • Charles Attebery
Design art • Lou DiPaolo
Agency • L. W. Frohlich

16. AD • Charles Attebery
Design • Robert Greco
Art • Jeannine Apostal
Agency • L. W. Frohlich

17. AD • Kenneth Lavey
Design • George D'Amato
Agency • L. W. Frohlich

18. AD • Charles Attebery
Design • Richard Matson
Art • Robert Saffir
Agency • L. W. Frohlich

19. AD • Robert Fiore
Photo • Mark Slade
Agency • Sudler & Hennessey

20. AD • Gerald Philips
Photo • Scott Hyde
Agency • William Douglas McAdams

21. AD • Gerald Philips
Photo • Phillip Leonian
Agency • William Douglas McAdams

22. AD • Charles Attebery
Design • Richard Bergeron
Photo • Francis Duval
Agency • L. W. Frohlich

23. Monthly coverage of disease patterns sent out by Parke-Davis. Designer, Henri Boots; Agency, L. W. Frohlich.

24. Model of brain created for the Upjohn Co. as an institutional exhibit for the medical profession. Designer, Will Burtin.

25. Eye chart designed for Schering to distribute to medical profession. Designer, Norman Gorbaty; AD, Kenneth Lavey; Agency, L. W. Frohlich.

. . . Sophistication in Mass Markets . . .

It is no news that pharmaceutical advertising is what it is because it is addressed to doctors who are well-educated and therefore, presumably, highly sophisticated. In fact there are some counter directions indicating they are too sophisticated to succumb to such an obvious approach, and are increasingly demanding direct, factual, helpful material.

On the other hand, the teen-ager who drops into a variety store in a small city or town is wooed by increasingly sophisticated ads, packages, product designs, displays as she buys a new — or perhaps her first — lipstick.

Irving Trabich tells about the grand illusion and its range of appeals.

grand illusion... *cosmetic advertising's variety of appeals range from utility to elegance*

by IRVING TRABICH

The American woman may be moving away from the conspicuous "car" symbol but she is digging her way deeper into the ultra-feminine world of cosmetics. If Detroit, in 1961, is catering to her sense of realism and reason, cosmetic manufacturers are encouraging her into excesses of self-indulgence; the fashion magazines and newspaper beauty editors are ever reminding her of her special responsibility to keep her youth from fading—her loveliness enduring.

And women are accepting each new trend in cosmetics as fast as laboratories, marketing men and advertising agencies dream them up. Just a decade or two ago, when manufacturers introduced home hair coloring, the products couldn't get off the ground. Hair coloring sales are now over $45 million and are still going up—just a small item in the $1.5 billion beauty industry!

As each new cosmetic trend exerts its authority and influence over more and more women the conventional shackles, the neurotic inhibitions, the prudishness recede along with household drudgery, provincialism and matronly silhouettes.

Any analysis of the American woman must remain curiously elusive. Among other things, she combines two seemingly incompatible elements: *first*, her simplicity and sensible approach to life, her natural desire for conformity, her basic separateness, her personalizing of her emotions, her female arithmetic, her honesty and realism; *and second*, her imaginative life and the world of love, beauty and extravagance, her desire to be smart and desirable and to build a more exciting life around herself, her goal of togetherness, her search for never-ending novelty, her willingness to believe.

don't fuss,
do fuss

Throughout the last decade cosmetic ads have served one or the other elements of this duality. They've said in effect —"cosmetics are a utilitarian need—don't fuss, don't primp, —see how easy it is to look lovely." Other ads have been flippant and elegant, have offered the promise of treats instead of treatments and the exultations of moon and moods. And, of course, many combined both sweetness and light.

In addition to the varying appeals, cosmetic advertising of necessity has had to correlate the personality of the product with distribution patterns, pricing, and packaging. The Elizabeth Arden image, for example, has had to be conceived in a marketing stature of franchised dealers and department stores—a relatively limited distribution—priced

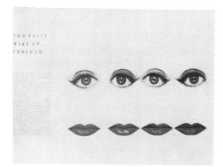

1. *Vogue Editorial* spread of 1950 shows rare use of abstract design for powerful poster effect in cosmetic visualization. Photo by Blumenfeld.

2. One of a series of brilliantly designed pages in *McCalls* utilizing strong simple beautiful photos. Photo by Herbert Matter.

3. Ben Rose's juxtaposition of two heads reveals the vigorous, inventive approach to cosmetic illustration found most often in editorial pages. This from *Harpers Bazaar*.

in the $2 and up category, luxurious simplicity of packaging, and the paid cosmetician behind the counter. The Cutex personality, on the other hand, has to be understood in relation to variety store and super market mass distribution, the under $1 pricing and self-selling packaging.

Art directors have had a hard time with it—Venus de Milo's arms twisted, but not broken—women being ever ready to fulfill the image created for her.

the basic
symbols

Although images of individual advertisers keep changing, art directors have kept to the basic symbols: women pictured in new fashions, luxury and social prestige; occasional bits of daring and decolletage to satisfy woman's need to shock and be different; the sultry, seductive model who promises intrigue and excitement, the haughty sophisticated model, the mature model to appeal to the woman of 35 and over who feels the loss of youth and can now revel in cosmetics; clear-eyed, smiling gals and guys in teasing situations—having the time of their lives.

Techniques are predominantly photographic. Photographic illustrators have created stunning, stirring photos that have spoken the language of seduction—have stopped women dead in their routine tracks—have deadened their senses

4. *Breck ad* . . . when advertising effectiveness is discussed, Breck and its stoical approach gives one pause. Perhaps, in a fleeting world, some women feel the need of solidity and worth reflected consistently by Breck advertising.

5. *Coty ad* . . . the draftsmanship and genius of Eric left his mark on cosmetic advertising, is still being felt today. Economy of line, simplicity of color, elegance and freshness! Note rendering of packages that unifies with spirit of the main drawing.

6. *Elizabeth Arden and Bouché* . . . a wonderful marriage for many years. Bold, daring drawing, perfect for perfume.

sufficiently to have them believe that here, at last, is the "fountain of youth."

The editorial style—the service angle—has been used effectively by many advertisers—the beauty ritual is as important as any to many women. Recently, there is evidence of a return to the whimsy of cartoon and illustration.

There are increasing uses of inserts—"Beauty Books," gold foil and even a personalized letter insert by Revlon. There is, too, that old hard sell stand by, before and after photos.

the future　　The future? As products tend to become more and more similar in formula and design, and promises tend to overlap and become indistinct, art directors will become increasingly important in the mechanics of persuasion. The art director's basic visual mindedness, his creativity and design, his sense of drama are complements to the estheticism of woman, her eternal sensuousness, her constant desire to renew herself. The art director provides the taste and skill necessary to the marriage of product and promise to company image. Communication becomes persuasion.

7. *Red Roses After Bath Freshener by Yardley* . . . red roses, ice cubes and a bee add whimsy to this graceful ad. For the woman who wants to *feel* lovely.

8. *Angel Face by Ponds* . . . consistent high level of glamorous photography combined with smaller, problem skin photos, done with taste and polish.

9. *Outline — Dorothy Gray* . . . resourceful design, modern and effective to illustrate both the main copy point and emphasize the name of the product.

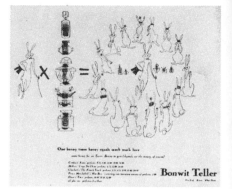

Uncovers Your Beauty Overnight Here it is at last, the way to beauty in a single jar. So incredible is its performance that Elizabeth Arden calls her newest preparation Creme Extraordinaire. No other cream—not even any of Miss Arden's does ever helped the skin in so many different ways: smoothing, moisturizing, neutralizing and conditions. Blended with a new and exclusive ingredient, Creme Extraordinaire smooths away the waste tissue that is being constantly used off, leaving the skin fresh and lovely. Use Creme Extraordinaire tonight. Look at your face in the morning. See how glowing and vital it has left your skin. See how this truly extraordinary cream has made the years seem fewer, how it has helped your skin to look young and radiant. Creme Extraordinaire, 10.00, 18.50, 27.50. All prices plus tax.

Elizabeth Arden

11. *Creme Extraordinaire by Elizabeth Arden* — the height of snob appeal combined with the promise of youth. The woman who will spend $27.50 for the elegant jar will have no difficulty identifying herself with this ad.

12. *Bonwit Teller ad* . . . art directors of department stores seem to have the most fun! Another ad with the strong feminine appeal of a greeting card. This is beautifully designed in the decorative cartoon manner.

10. *Tussy Eye Cream* . . . as playful, whimsical and to the point as a greeting card — an art form no woman can resist — a gentle reminder that cosmetics can be fun. Illustrated by Morrow.

13. *Juliette Marglen* . . . shall we say, "very low pressure?" . . . a presentation not an ad. For the lady of distinction in the mink and diamonds tradition with a knowing subtlety. Photo by Gerald Hochman.

14. *Parfums Christian Dior* . . . in the French tradition — the name is enough. Enhanced by the elegant simplicity of the layout and jewel-like photograph of the bottle.

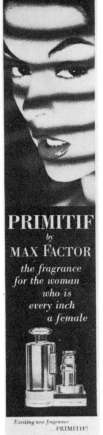

PRIMITIF
by
MAX FACTOR
*the fragrance
for the woman
who is
every inch
a female*

*Exciting new fragrance
...PRIMITIF!*

A bit bold perhaps...but why *not*
let your perfume say the things you
wouldn't dare to? Primitif in perfume, parfum cologne, dusting
powder. From $1.50 to $18.00 plus
tax. Try it...if you dare!

15. *Primitif by Max
Factor . . . a single
column ad that
captures the mys-
tery, sultryness and
allure of fragrance.*

16. *Intoxication by D'Orsay . . . gos-
samer and lace — a symbol of femininity full of meaning to women.
Stunning, simple design.*

someone lovely has just passed by!

Intoxication
BY
D'ORSAY
GIVE THE CELEBRATED
FRENCH FRAGRANCE THAT WHISPERS
"SOMEONE LOVELY HAS JUST PASSED BY"

Does she...or doesn't she?

Hair color so natural only her hairdresser knows for sure!

MISS CLAIROL HAIR COLOR BATH

17. *Does she . . . or Doesn't she? . . . Clairol . . . only
shady women dared change their hair color in the past.
Now respectable women, even mothers, do it and keep
their secret.*

19. *How Female Hormones Help you Look Younger
. . . Helena Rubenstein . . . editorial in style, classic,
authoritative, combined with an insert, on the new cosmetic science, that women will read.*

Is it
true...
blondes
have more
fun?

NEW INSTANT WHIP **Lady Clairol** Creme Hair Lightener

18. *Is it true . . . blondes have
more fun? . . . Lady Clairol . . .
the secret's out — but who cares?
"A man responds to blondes." This
campaign aimed at more glamorous women is almost at the oppo-
site end of "Does she . . . or
doesn't she?"*

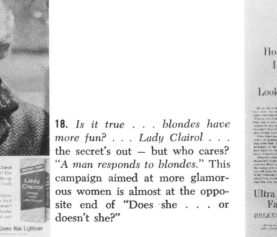

How Female
Hormones
Help You
Look Younger

Ultra Feminine
Face Cream
HELENA RUBINSTEIN

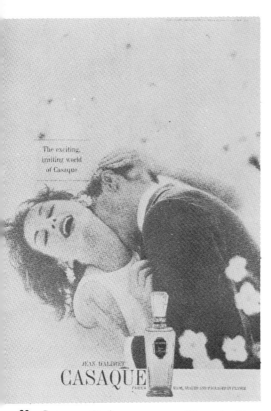

20. *Casaque Parfum* . . . exciting, igniting *real* photograph. Does this obviously sexual approach appeal to women? Yes!

21. *Hazel Bishop Ultra-Matic Compact* . . . "A mailed fist in a velvet glove." Elegance with hard sell.

22. *Quelques Fleurs* . . . *Houbigant* . . . flowers and femininity. Old fashioned in feeling — but, for women, never really dated. A busy design delicately conceived.

23. *"Pango Peach"* . . . *Revlon* . . . one of a long line of impressive Revlon shade promotions. Holds the promise of adventure with a lipstick and a bottle of nail enamel.

they'll go mad over you when they **"SEE RED"**

a hot-tempered new red in
MAX Factor's Color-fast lipstick

25. *"See-Red . . . Max Factor . . .* it's all about Eve. Memorable, bold layout with a humorous touch. An ADC medal winner for Bob Gage, Photo by William Helburn.

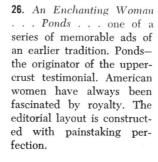

AVON'S HI-LIGHT SHAMPOO now for three hair types!

Avon's Hi-Light Shampoo is now available in three formulas for dry, normal and oily hair. It leaves your hair dazzling clean yet easy to manage. And those high lights!

Avon Hair Cosmetics are brought to you only by your Avon Representative. Welcome her when she calls with exciting new Hi-Light Shampoo in the type right for you.

TAKE TIME OFF FOR BEAUTY WHEN YOUR AVON REPRESENTATIVE CALLS TO OFFER YOU AN AVON TRY-ON

24. *Avon Cosmetics . . .* Typical, fresh looking ad by largest cosmetic company in U.S. Directed towards creating acceptance for house to house representatives rather than stimulating demand.

26. *An Enchanting Woman . . . Ponds . . .* one of a series of memorable ads of an earlier tradition. Ponds— the originator of the upper-crust testimonial. American women have always been fascinated by royalty. The editorial layout is constructed with painstaking perfection.

27. *It's the Fashion . . . Charles of the Ritz . . .* a trenchant, stunning cosmetic ad. This is obviously the conception of an art director — beautifully conceived and executed. AD, Ched Vuckovic. Photo by Don Briggs.

variety within limits . . .

Beer advertisers, all 208 of them, have quite a job trying to make you remember their beer, to distinguish it from all the others. If ever there was a need for product personality building, it's at the top of the glass with the head on it. You can't tell the heads apart even when not blindfolded.

Cosmetics come in a wide range of products, packages, colors, with many purposes. They even seem to change the product before the Starch ratings are in. But beer makes little news. Howard Munce tells how some of the leaders meet this challenge. . . .

many heads, few directions... *beer advertising*

calls for image building within narrow confines

by HOWARD MUNCE

Apart from the handful of rules concerning liquor laws that one learns the second day, there is no difference in doing beer ads than there is in any other product. I think it's important that different art people constantly get a crack at laying out beer ads. Because after a couple of years, you feel that there can't *possibly* be another fresh way of showing a can, bottle, glass or stein. And until someone starts a trend of drinking through his ear, there will remain little novelty in showing a beer being consumed. Take Rheingold, for example.

From Jinx Falkenberg to Emily Banks with 18 sisters in between Miss Rheingold has been the Rheingold image since 1940. Even the photographer (Paul Hesse) hasn't changed. Until 1960 Miss R. smiled prettily at the people and said, "My Beer is Rheingold, the Dry Beer." — and millions of consumers burped and said "Me too."

This year, through a combination of a change from the ancient One-Shot camera to the good fortune of having a lively athletic girl elected, to the equally good luck of going to a bleed page with no body copy, Rheingold ads now have a spirited bouncy look. Concurrent with the girl and her capers, Rheingold has long been a leader in the use of Hollywood and Broadway endorsers.

To see what's new in this field, let's look at a cross section of *contemporary* beer ads.

The "before and after" difference between old and current ads is mostly in technique. Photography, of course, dominates today; though it's interesting to see that every now and then out of sheer desperation, someone goes back to art to try to bust out of the sameness that photography produces in such a limited field. Note Bob Peak's recent paintings for Narragansett.

Most beer pages are limited to the following working props. Happy people (not *too* happy!), frosty beer—interesting vessels — food and fun (good clean fun). This brief list breaks down in many ways. People range from snooty socialites to gay young moderns to middle class "folks" with an occasional rugged fellow to represent the *real* beer drinker. The vessels range from antique Bavarian steins to the most modern 17 dollar numbers from Steuben. Food runs the gamut from the banquet table to the pizza parlor. And the fun gets frolicked from State occasions to beach barbeques.

With ads constantly being ground out for 208 breweries across the country it's easy to see how the cliché heads up this foamy field.

I dream of the day I can show a fat guy in his union-suit sitting on his front porch in Jersey City with his bare feet on the stoop railing, guzzling from a bucket to his heart's content.

No article on beer advertising — or *any other* advertising would be complete even at this late date without a comment on Bert and Harry Piel. I have heard this wonderful pair praised and damned since they first appeared. Always it is asked, "Yeah, but do they sell beer?" Happily, that's someone else's problem. I don't know. I *do* know that they were lionhearted fellows who looked a lot of formidable German gentlemen in the eye and said "Handle Brand X as you will — this is *our* way."

The first years

Special full page to take advantage of news break

The middle years

The new format — Miss R romps at last

ALL DESIGNED TO DO A DIFFERENT JOB IN A DIFFERENT PLACE

For Negro market

For Spanish market

Celebrity endorser

1. Falstaff uses "gay young moderns" cavorting in an untroubled world. Only in our business are people so joyous and carefree. The large figure is a painting.

2. A small-spacer for Carlsberg. Little sizes are mostly used by the imported beers.

3. A marvelously clever series for Utica Club. A free lunch goes to anyone who doesn't wish *he'd* done it.

4. Full page newspaper for Carlsberg. Here's the *different* beer ad. Reams of copy, no pretty girls or boys, no bottles nor glasses — just good reading, excellent drawings and a handsome page over all.

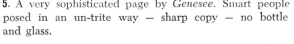

It's an ice-breaker. It's a fun-maker. It's the light, bright brew that was born for a party because it's naturally more refreshing: Genesee Beer!

GENESEE *Beer*

The Genesee Brewing Company, Inc., Rochester, N. Y.

5. A very sophisticated page by *Genesee*. Smart people posed in an un-trite way — sharp copy — no bottle and glass.

6. A typical Budweiser ad. Bleed, a modicum of copy and a lively picture.

The Holsten Knight and his Noble Brew

Hamburg is Germany's oldest brewing center, dating back to the 13th century. The Knight of Holsten-Schauenburger then gave to the town of Hammaburg (now Hamburg) the most important privilege of brewing beer and Hamburg's beer was shipped to all the northern areas, including England, Holland and Scandinavia. Over the centuries, Hamburg's brewing fame spread throughout the world. Today, this tradition is in every glass of Holsten beer. True German flavor, Hearty taste. Satisfying to those who appreciate a truly fine beer.

Imported by Holsten Import Corp., N. Y.

7. Holsten—Lager — another import. This is a black and white campaign. The gent in the tin suit is the resident character. His boyish-bob goes Commander Whitehead one better.

WHEREVER GOOD FOOD, GOOD LIVING and good companions meet, they produce what Germans call "gemütlichkeit." Define it? You cannot. But you can experience it, and in many ways.

One of the best — shared the world over — starts with Munich Löwenbräu, imported German beer, in bottles or on draft.

Take a frosty-cool, foil-capped bottle and your favorite glass. Pry off the cap . . . pour. Winking golden bubbles, a snow-white foamy collar, a pleasing aroma that bespeaks the finest hops. Then taste the golden goodness that is Löwenbräu.

Here, indeed, is a unique beer with character and zest. Your palate tells you this full-bodied flavor comes from long months of aging in casks cloaked in cool darkness . . . born through masterful blending of perfect ingredients.

And, as the last drop disappears from your glass, you'll know what "gemütlichkeit" means . . . and why so many people tell us there are but three kinds of beer — domestic, imported and best of all, Löwenbräu.

Munich Löwenbräu is not only the largest selling imported beer in the United States—but also the most popular beer in Munich. Brewed Since 1383. Imported by: Hans Holterbosch, Inc., New York 51, N. Y.

8. One of the many imported beers currently advertised. Lowenbräu sets a tone-y table for their bottle and glass act. This is a b/w photograph, rare for beer in magazines.

Reach, sir! It's something special!
...from the land of sky blue waters.

You'll discover the subtle bit of difference in flavor that has made Hamm's the most popular beer of all in the broad area where it is sold. You'll discover a wonderfully crisp, clean-cut taste—captured in the enchanted land of sky blue waters. Why wait a minute longer? Enjoy this special refreshment now. Reach for the one and only Hamm's Beer—refreshingly yours!

Always the same refreshing flavor . . . glass after glass after glass!

Theo. Hamm Brewing Co., St. Paul, Minn., San Francisco and Los Angeles, Calif.

9. Hamm's format is still based on its "sky blue waters" line. The beer is habitually pine shaded, dew dappled or snow bound. Art work throughout.

"My Family Has Brewed Fine Beer For 200 Years
...Today's **Hampden** is The Finest Yet!"

says Karl B. Bissell, Sr., Chairman of the Board

"Here—and in the old country—my family has been brewing superb beer for generations. And today's Hampden Beer is the lightest, tastiest, most refreshing we've ever brewed. That's because we take a number of extra-special steps in the brewing process. For example, ordinary beers come out of the pasteurizer while still very warm—almost hot. This is why you sometimes notice a bitter afternoon bite. But our Hampden Beer has no bitter afternoon, even, because it goes right from the pasteurizer through a special Frost Chamber which gradually cools it to the right temperature and preserves its delicate flavor. So—may I respectfully suggest you try Hampden Beer soon at your package store or tavern?"

Hampden Beer NEW ENGLAND'S FINEST BEER AT NEW ENGLAND'S FAIREST PRICE

Hampden-Harvard Breweries, Inc., Willimansett, Mass.

11. A fine old trusty device by *Hampden:* the elderly Gent who tells the "several generations of fine brewing" story.

12. Miller continues to pour its beer in a setting of lush food and highly styled backgrounds. >

People try it... and they like it

Had a tough day? Just drop into a nice big easy chair and pour yourself a tall glass of cold beer—Carling Black Label Beer, that is. You'll like it. Most people *do* like Black Label. That explains Carling's swift rise to first place in the brewing industry. Next time you're thirsty, try popular-priced Black Label, America's fastest growing beer. Just say, in that friendly, cheerful way, *"Mabel, Black Label"!*

CARLING

Black Label
BEER

SEE THE BIG PHIL SILVERS CARLING SPECTACULAR CBS-TV—10: P.M. EDT, SATURDAY, JUNE 30TH
National Beer Wholesalers' Assn. figures

CARLING BREWING CO., INC., ALSO BREWERS OF RED CAP ALE *The Best Brews in the World come from Carling*
CLEVELAND, O. ATLANTA, GA. BELLEVILLE, ILL. FRANKENMUTH, MICH. NATICK, MASS. TACOMA, WASH.

10. A fresh use of the bottle and glass technique. Carling shows an interesting pouring shot and a collection of unusual beer glasses.

Put the finest label ...on your table

Miller HIGH LIFE

The Champagne of Bottle Beer

"Fresh-Poured" flavor all the way down because today's Piels has a longer lasting head!

As any beer drinker knows, that first long, satisfying swallow of a just-poured beer is really something pretty special.

But today's Piels gives you that "fresh-poured" flavor each and every swallow, right down to the bottom of the glass.

That's because tests prove Piels longer lasting, natural head captures and holds the "true beer essence"—prevents it from escaping.

Prove it for yourself at home. Match today's Piels longer lasting head against any beer you choose. See how Piels gives you "fresh-poured" flavor right down to the last golden drop in the glass.

These glasses of beer were poured at the same time, photographed two minutes later. Note how today's Piels Beer has retained its head while the others have begun to turn clear.

Piels LIGHT BEER

"The beer-drinkers' beer"

13. Dear old Bert and Harry, the T.V. Stars, seldom get their pictures in the paper for Piels. Here is a rare instance.

What d'ya hear in the best of circles? *Schaefer all around!*

Schaefer sits well with you. The pleasure doesn't fade after a glass or two . . . Schaefer is brewed to be savored through an evening. Your last glass is as rewarding as your first. Bright. Smooth round flavor. All the pleasure of the first beer—every beer through. Settle for good on Schaefer . . . your cue to

14. Schaefer has been off on a happy spree of circles and round objects. A good example of a clever copy line opening endless picture possibilities.

BACK IN THE DAYS—THE GOOD OLD DAYS . . . WHEN BEER WAS REALLY BEER!

No one can bring back the good old days, but Pabst has brought back the taste—the Original Pabst Blue Ribbon! There were many great beers in those days. That's why it was such an honor when Pabst was acclaimed America's finest at the 1893 World's Fair. And the Pabst you buy today is brewed the same way as that old-time favorite. So if you've ever wondered how a truly great old-time beer tasted, just ask for Original Pabst Blue Ribbon. We think you'll keep on asking for it!

Pabst Blue Ribbon

15. Pabst's current kick pictures the "good old days" of the Gay 90's — a customer's delight.

Wherever you go in all America you'll never find a better beer

Try any of America's finest beers . . . from Natchez to Nashua. You'll find none finer than refreshing Narragansett Lager Beer. It's light, but not too light.

Light as you like it. Never bitter . . . because 'Gansett's better brewed with expensive seedless hops. So go right . . . to the light side. Hi, Neighbor—have a 'Gansett!

Narragansett LAGER BEER

16. Narragansett is currently trying many things. This Bob Peak painting uses a contemporary art technique as a change from the sameness of photography.

17. Ballantine print takes its cue from the straight portion of their T.V. commercials. A beer with a nature background. This series combines a stylized rendered glass with a photographic background. >

Ballantine LIGHT LAGER **beer** the crisp refresher . . .

the light beer with true *lager* flavor!

No wonder Ballantine is the largest-selling beer in the East.

18. A new look of Ruppert. New name (the second time around) new label, new format. Ruppert people have no cares either.

19. Schlitz is back to art work with this campaign which combines their product with the kinds of food that go with beer.

1 Agency ● Dancer-Fitzgerald-Sample Inc.
Art Director ● Robert Shaw
Photographer ● Tom Kelley
Artist ● Livoti

2 Agency ● Wexton Co., Inc.
Art Director ● William Spewak
Artist ● Chwast

3 Agency ● Doyle, Dane, Bernach, Inc.
Art Director ● William Taubin
Photographer ● Wingate Paine

4 Agency ● Wexton Co., Inc.
Art Director ● William Spewak
Artist ● Chwast

5 Agency ● McCann Marschalk Co.
Art Director ● Arthur Hawkins III
Photographer ● Horn-Griner

6 Agency ● D'Arcy Adv. Co.
Art Director ● Gene Kowall
Photographer ● Pagano Inc. ● Jacques Simson

7 Agency ● Ellington & Co., Inc.
Art Director ● John Stoehrer
Photographer ● Florian de Narde

8 Agency ● Fuller & Smith & Ross Inc.
Art Director ● James Woodward
Photographer ● Tony Venti

9 Agency ● Campbell-Mithun, Inc.
Art Director ● Pat Nolan
Artist ● Carl Paulson

10 Agency ● Lang, Fisher & Stashower, Inc.
Art Director ● Edmund Kagy
Photographer ● Tony Venti

11 Agency ● Cohen, Dowd & Aleshire Inc.
Art Director ● David Smiton
Photographer ● Marty Bauman

12 Agency ● Mathisson and Associates Inc.
Art Director ● C. A. Mathisson
Photographer ● Frances McGlaughin Gill

13 Agency ● Young & Rubicam Inc.
Art Director ● Tom Melahn
Artist ● Chris Ishii

14 Agency ● Batten, Barton, Durstine & Osborn, Inc.
Art Director ● George Sanders
Photographer ● Robert Monroe

15 Agency ● Kenyon & Eckhardt Inc.
Art Director ● Luther Johnson
Photographer ● Paul Hesse Studios

16 Agency ● Doherty, Clifford, Steers & Shenfield Inc.
Art Director ● Bill McCaffery
Artist ● Bob Peak

17 Agency ● William Esty Co., Inc.
Art Director ● Gene Hooker
Artist ● Jack Damron
Photographer ● Jos. Muench

18 Agency ● Norman, Craig & Kummel Inc.
Art Director ● Henry Scheck
Photographer ● Richard Avedon

19 Agency ● J. Walter Thompson Co.
Art Director ● Robert J. Taylor
Artist ● Harriet Pertchik

... How do you tell the same story differently? Beers may look alike, even taste alike; appliances may perform alike in comparable price categories; but product or package design gives each brand its own personality. What can an airline AD do when competitors offer the same services, the same prices, the same planes? Andrew Nelson shows how leading airline ADs are meeting this challenge, explains the trend away from the lure picture to the picture of the big jet and why ADs now concentrate on the small competitive advantages that identify their line ...

visual directions in airline advertising . . .

similarity of competitors' equipment, fares, destinations and services test the art directors' ingenuity.

by ANDREW K. NELSON

Fortunate indeed is the art director who works on an airline account with built-in inspirational qualities of romance, adventure and excitement. Even more important, the art director helps advertise a service which enriches men's lives. Those "far-away places with strange sounding names" are now within the reach of all. It's pretty exciting to think that tomorrow could find you on a secluded beach in the South Seas, far away from deadlines.

getting back to reality If working on an airline account can be exciting, what are some of the problems the art director faces? Problems often force him into solutions that are brilliant in communicating the message.

As things stand, this is our number one problem: How do you advertise "your" airline when:

1. virtually every major competitor flies the same type of aircraft—either Boeing 707's or Douglas DC-8's?

2. when all fares are exactly the same?

3. when most of your competition flies to the same destinations in the same amount of time?

4. when the "in-flight" service of competition is generally of a high-standard?

It would seem that there is little difference between airlines other than the paint job on the fuselage and tail. However, there are differences, large and small, seen and unseen. They must be brought before the general public in a meaningful, honest and imaginative manner. If these differences are not discovered and aggressively exploited, the advertising will lose much of its effectiveness.

One of the best ways to discover these differences is to get your nose out of the layout pad and spend a few days conducting personal research.

Go out and find what makes your airline "tick"—learn first hand about its equipment, reservations system, communications, crew training, maintenance and all the things that go on behind the scenes. Talk to passengers—find out what they like and don't like. If possible, a writer should accompany the art director since an exciting interplay of thoughts and ideas could result. Dig hard enough and you might find a gold mine of ideas.

Ideally, airline advertising should graphically reflect a feeling of fun, adventure and excitement yet maintain a balance between these qualities and a feeling of safety and assurance. Although most of us realize that it's safer to fly in a jet than to drive our own car on a crowded highway, most people still feel uneasy about flying.

The art director must be discreet, making sure not to frighten, but to convey a feeling of well being.

For a dozen years after the second World War airlines concentrated on developing the market for overseas and domestic vacation travel. Most ads consisted of the large lure picture with not too much emphasis on the aircraft.

With the introduction of the jets, there was an abrupt change. In place of the lure picture was one of the big jet coupled with a big, black headline. As each airline got delivery of its first jet a sort of "follow-the-leader" pattern developed resulting in a deadly sameness.

The last 2 hours are the longest

—and those are the 2 hours you save, right now, when you fly El Al jet-powered Britannia to Europe.

EL AL jet-prop Britannia

El Al ad approaches story of speed in a fresh and intriguing manner. Design had great stopping power in the newspapers. Art Director, Bill Taubin. Agency, Doyle Dane Bernbach.

This trend is now coming to an end. Since all airlines have the same jet equipment, and competition is becoming keener day by day the airlines are now taking a hard look at what causes a passenger to favor one carrier over another. The big plane photo will go. There will be little emphasis on the lure picture since the expansion of the market will continue satisfactorily from the momentum already gained (except for South America which is still a relatively new vacation land). The airlines will concentrate on advertising their own competitive advantages and the art director had better go out and find out what they are and how to portray them.

Double spread introducing Panagra jet service to South America uses strong graphic treatment to convey idea of speed in reaching new and exciting vacationland. Art Director, Andrew Nelson. Agency, J. Walter Thompson Co.

Panagra
DC-8
Jets to
South America
cut your
travel time
in half!

You'll find a hundred different ways to use the many hours you'll save when you fly Panagra jets to leisurely South America . . .

Picture yourself, off Peru's Cabo Blanco, bringing a 1500-pound marlin to gaff, or bargaining, in the Andes, with descendants of the Incas for a handcrafted rug. Hotels in the great tradition rub shoulders with ancient ruins, and luxury is the keynote of your trip from the moment you step aboard your custom-built Panagra DC-8 jet. En route you get a preview of the fine food and good living you'll find in this friendly continent.

Make reservations now. You'll fly without change of plane over the short-cut, scenic routes of National, Pan Am, and Panagra. Savings up to 35% now available. See why experienced travellers say: "You haven't seen anything until you've seen South America." Call your travel agent or Pan American.

PANAGRA
WORLD'S FRIENDLIEST AIRLINE

Send 25¢ to Don Wilson, Room 4497, Chrysler Building, New York City 17, for a 130-page book: "How to Get the Most Out of Your Trip to South America."

KEY TO JET TAIL SILHOUETTE
1. Argentine gauchos, cowboys to you, are equally at home in folk songs or pursuing wild ostrich
2. Trout are so plentiful in Chile's lake district they fight to take a hook
3. Peru has many miles of beaches. This one is near Lima
4. Trece Monedas (13 Coins), one of Lima's fine restaurants, is set in an old colonial home

Why do well-traveled people travel Sabena? Haute cuisine six miles high is only part of it. People who know Europe know Sabena shows it off best: with the world's only 3-speed fleet of Boeing "Intercontinental" jets, Caravelle "Continental" jets and Sikorsky helicopters; with a special savoir-faire that extends to and through Europe, Africa and the Middle East. Next trip . . . fly Sabena. Le service Belgique—c'est magnifique!

Sabena uses a sophisticated poster approach that emphasizes the continental touch in air travel. Art Director, Bob Miller. Agency, McCann-Marshalk.

48 Pan Am Jet Flights each week to Bermuda Nassau and all the Caribbean

More than all other airlines combined

You're in U.S. hands all the way!
You fly serene, with the comforting knowledge that you're aboard the world's most experienced airline—in the hands of U.S. crews trained to uncompromising U.S. standards. Every Pan Am officer is a specialist in the fine art of flying.

Only Pan Am flies Jets to all 6 of these paradise islands: Bermuda, Nassau, Jamaica, Dominican Republic, Puerto Rico and Trinidad. Choose from 48 Jet Clipper* flights weekly . . . more often than the tides to the Caribbean.

In only 1¾ hours from New York, you can be

relaxing in Bermuda. And Pan Am Jets are *fastest* to Nassau. Fly first-class *President* service or tourist-class *Rainbow* to all the Caribbean. Call your travel Agent or Pan Am—
*Trade-Mark, Reg. U. S. Pat. Off.

WORLD'S MOST EXPERIENCED AIRLINE

Pan Am stresses exclusive claim in headline. Convincing picture of captain coupled with picture of the Caribbean tells you that "you're in good hands all the way." Art Director, Andrew Nelson. Agency, J. Walter Thompson Co.

Air France sells their services in a light-hearted manner using decorative art which reflects a feeling of French joie de vivre. Art Director, Martin Stevens. Agency, BBDO.

Pan American uses a bold, straightforward approach in announcing a new fare. Photo of huge aircraft tail reflects feeling of stature of the airline. Art Director, Andrew Nelson. Agency, J. Walter Thompson Co.

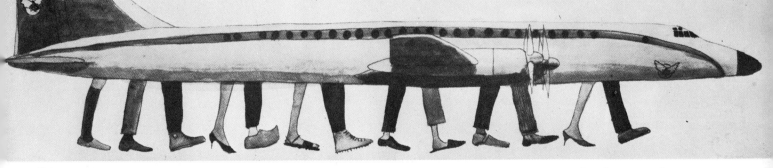

What has 13 extra legs, and flies?

Answer: An El Al round trip ticket to Rome! You can, if you wish, drop in on any (or all) of these 13 cities, and stay as long as you like at no extra cost: London, Paris, Geneva, Nice, Milan, Venice, Vienna, Munich, Zurich, Frankfort, Cologne, Amsterdam, Brussels! And if it's more convenient for you to fly another airline on any particular leg, let's say from Nice to Milan, we'll book you that way at no extra cost. Wonderful way to get around Europe, isn't it? Tickets are valid for one year. Generous stop-over plans are also available on El Al tickets to London or Paris, or Athens, or Tel Aviv. You fly the famous El Al jet-prop Britannia—non-stop from New York to London or Paris, and one-stop to Rome or Athens or Tel Aviv, if you choose to get there direct. And you pay the new low fares: $108 less round trip than a pure jet, first class; $36 less round trip than a pure jet, economy class. See your travel agent or El Al Israel Airlines, 610 Fifth Avenue, New York, PLaza 1-7500.

Another El Al stopper. This un-conventional solution at first amuses then teases you into reading every word of the copy. Art Director, Bill Taubin. Agency, Doyle Dane Bernbach.

Direct flights to Rome

El Al jet-prop Britannias fly one-stop to Rome without a change of planes. Or you can take advantage of El Al's free stop-over privileges coming or going: visiting any of these cities and staying as long as you like: London, Paris, Geneva, Nice, Milan, Venice, Vienna, Munich, Zurich, Frankfurt, Cologne, Amsterdam, Brussels. De luxe, First Class, Economy. Phone your travel agent or PL 1-7500. **EL AL**

Direct flights to Athens

People are surprised to discover that El Al flies one-stop to Athens, and without a change of planes. (But if you *want* to stop over, you can visit many extra cities in Europe at no extra cost, and stay as long as you like.) El Al jet-prop Britannias also fly non-stop to London, non-stop to Paris, and one-stop to Rome or Tel Aviv. De luxe, First Class, Economy accommodations. Phone your travel agent or PL 1-7500. **EL AL**

Direct flights to Paris

First stop, Orly Airport. And you feel fresh and relaxed when you step off an El Al Britannia, because of the smoothly-spinning turbine engines. El Al Britannias also fly non-stop to London, and one-stop to Rome, Athens or Tel Aviv without a change of planes. De luxe, First Class, Economy. Free stop-over privileges. Phone your travel agent or PL 1-7500. **EL AL**

Every airline must run destination advertising. This excellent series by El Al does it in a simple manner and rewards the reader with a warm chuckle. Art Director, Bill Taubin. Agency, Doyle Dane Bernbach.

How do you do something new with a map? Pan Am advertises its new exclusive route to Tokyo by superimposing it on a Japanese fan. The result is at the same time informative and colorful. Art Director, Dave Blossom. Agency, J. Walter Thompson Co.

124

Only PAN AM JETS fly the Great Circle Route
CALIFORNIA TO TOKYO — FASTEST, SHORTEST

And the only Jets from California to Manila, Saigon, Singapore and Djakarta

great Caesar, what luxury!

All this and non-stop flights to Paris, Milan, Rome, or London.

Inside story

on the calm
beauty of
Japan Air Lines'
new jets

Inside Japan Air Lines' new
DC-8 Jet Couriers are the fabrics and furnishings, the taste
and simplicity that beautifully
anticipate the calm beauty of
Japan. The atmosphere of
Japan is all around you . . . in
the pine-bough pattern of a
seat fabric and the symmetry
of a shoji screen, in the tatami
carpeting of the lounge and
the chrysanthemum motif on
the drapes. Here is the rest-
fulness of Japan, its serenity,
as you fly high above the Paci-
fic. Here is the calm beauty of
Japan at almost the speed of
sound.

Japan Air Lines' DC-8 Jet Courier service from San Francisco
to Tokyo starts August 12. Very
soon after that, jets will begin
serving all the trans-Pacific
routes of Japan Air Lines.
Serving them swiftly and luxur-
iously, and in a manner that's
so delightfully Japanese. Flying
you to the Orient in little more
than half a day. Carrying you
amid

JAPAN AIR LINES
DC-8 JET COURIER

Repetition of an image
works hard to create a
strong visual statement
for Qantas. Art Director,
John Flack. Agency, Cun-
ningham & Walsh, S.F.

Japan Air Lines whispers
its sales message very
softly and with exquisite
taste. Agency, Botsford,
Constantine & Gardner.

ere again we see a foreign flag carrier emphasizing
xury aloft in the true Roman tradition. Art Direc-
r, Joseph Del Sorbo. Agency, Cohen, Dowd &
eshire.

int Panagra and Pan Am ad uses collage to create
ree-dimensional effect in illustration which points
t an exclusive route structure to South America.
t Director, Andrew Nelson. Agency, J. Walter
ompson Co.

THE ONLY
JET
SERVICE
'ROUND
SOUTH
AMERICA

Now the Pan American Airways System
brings you Jet service down both coasts
of South America to Buenos Aires.

Your fastest way from California starts
with Pan Am's DC-7C express service
to Panama or Caracas. From these
cities it's big Jets to Buenos Aires via
either coast of South America. You can
go one way, return the other with the
U. S. airline system that has 33 years
of experience in South America.

The cost? Special new fares bring it
way down. For example, 45-day
tourist excursion by Jet from Los
Angeles to Buenos Aires and back
is only $696, a saving of 30%. Big
savings on first-class service, too.

The carefree way to go?
Preplanned holidays save you
time and money. One 21-day
tour visits 7 cities and includes
tourist flights, hotels, sightseeing
for only $975.

Map shows heavy lines for Jet routes,
thin lines for piston routes. On the east
coast of South America you're on the
routes of Pan American—on the
west coast, Panagra.

Make your plans now. Call your Travel
agent or the nearest Pan American office.

PANAGRA · PAN AMERICAN
PAN AMERICAN AIRWAYS SYSTEM

125

Highly appealing human interest picture in American Airlines institutional ad conveys a feeling of the warm friendly service of the airline. Art Director, Bob Wall. Agency, Young & Rubicam

Don't you owe your son this unforgettable experience?

AMERICAN AIRLINES · America's Leading Airline

If you're lucky enough to be going to San Francisco...

hurry there on American Airlines 707 Jet Flagships. Starting November 1st, American inaugurates non-stop jet service to San Francisco with two flights daily. You can leave at 8:45 AM and arrive at 11:55 AM...or you can leave at 7:00 PM and arrive at 10:10 PM. Take your choice of either deluxe Mercury or economical Royal Coachman service. Just ask your Travel Agent or call American now. It's LOngacre 4-2000 in New York, Mitchell 2-8570 in Newark. **AMERICAN AIRLINES** The Jet Airline

A different approach to destination advertising. The picture makes its point in pleasing and imaginative manner. Art Director, Kevin McNally. Agency, Young & Rubicam.

Only **one** trans-Atlantic airliner can fly high enough to ride the smooth currents of the jet stream **regularly**: the jet-prop Britannia! You fly high above the weather – as high as 36,000 feet, more than 10,000 feet higher than any other airliner! You cross the Atlantic 2¼ hours faster. Fly the new El Al jet-prop Britannias to London, Paris, Rome, Brussels and Tel Aviv. **EL AL** ISRAEL AIRLINES

El Al uses abstract symbolism to sell an equipment advantage. Art Director, Bill Taubin. Agency, Doyle Dane Bernbach.

Testimonial ad for El Al which breaks with tradition. Beautiful example of visual crystallization. Art Director, Bill Taubin. Agency, Doyle Dane Bernbach.

TWICE THE JETS TO TEXAS!

Only American offers you morning and afternoon 707 jets nonstop to Dallas-Ft. Worth. First with jets to Texas, American has twice the experience and twice as many flights to Dallas-Ft. Worth . . . which makes it twice as convenient for you. ¶ The morning jet leaves at 9:00 a.m., arrives 11:30 a.m. An afternoon 707 jet flight leaves at 4:15 p.m. daily, arrives 6:45 p.m. There are morning and afternoon jets returning to New York, too. ¶ Going or coming, you'll find American's Jet Flagship as comfortable as your own living room. Meals are marvelous, service impeccable, a special Baggage Expediter System has your baggage waiting when you land. ¶ Choose de luxe Mercury or economical Royal Coachman service. Just see your Travel Agent or call American Airlines —first choice of experienced travelers. In New York, call LOngacre 4-2000. In Newark, call Mitchell 2-8570.

AMERICAN AIRLINES The Jet Airline

The virtue of this newspaper ad lies in the simplicity and directness in which it gets the message across. Art Director, Kevin McNally. Agency, Young and Rubicam.

EL AL Israel Airlines is now flying Preminger and company to Israel for the filming of "Exodus." Paul Newman, Eva Marie Saint, Peter Lawford, Hugh Griffith, John Derek, Lee J. Cobb, Sal Mineo, David Opatashu, Michael Wager and Sir Ralph Richardson. Cast, crew, cameras—the whole shooting works—are being airlifted 5,000 miles on the split-second timetable for which Hollywood is known, and EL AL too.

distinction means sales . . .

The most meaningful medals for advertising management, copywriting, or art direction, are won daily by some retail advertisers. You run on Thursday. And Thursday morning at 9 — you don't have to wait till the doors close at night — you know how good you are.

It is no coincidence that two of the country's most successful retail stores win art direction medals every year. Neiman-Marcus' Art Shipman and Cox's Arnold Varga believe that distinction means sales, that sophistication builds volume and profits.

It seems like the dark ages, although it was only yesterday, when contemporary visual treatment was thought harmful to an ad. And today, while many agree good advertising can have contemporary design, only few feel it must. It is significant that among the few are leading retailers who can measure their ads, not for seen-noted, but for sales, every day.

retail advertising . . . *a trend is needed, away from look-alike, hodge-podge, sales minimizing ads*

by ARNOLD VARGA

There's a tired formula for most of today's retail advertising. Its main ingredient is an imitation flavor. If you were to cover up the signatures of all retail advertisements in a Sunday edition of the New York Times, you would have a hard time telling the advertisers apart . . . with a few exceptions. This look-alike quality can only be attributed to imitation. Ironically, the need to compete has caused these stores to do that which is least competitive: imitate. Small wonder that those stores which imitate most are having so much trouble building sales. Imitative advertising fails to reflect the true personality of a store, prevents it being a sales leader.

People tend to personalize stores. They like to deal with places that are pleasant to shop and that "feel right" for them. A store has two ways to project this "right" image: through its operations and through its advertising. If the advertising fails, many people will not bother to explore a store's operations.

distinctive store personality a must

Before management can expect its establishment to grow and increase its profits, it must first build a distinct personality that appeals to the shopper and then reflect that character in its advertising so strongly that it is felt instantly by the reader. Otherwise, there's bound to be trouble in the cash register. As an example, there were two department stores in a large metropolitan area that had never made the effort to establish individual personalities. Very much aware of the success of their competition, they both adapted bits of everybody else's advertising in an effort to become as successful. Their cluttered and sometimes vulgar appearing ads looked like, and were the work of a confused committee. Eventually both stores were forced to liquidate, and the more genuine stores which they imitated absorbed their trade.

Committee work is indeed largely to blame for a store's lack of personality and its dull, unimaginative advertising. Managing directors who organize committees from buyers, merchandise managers, fashion coordinators and the like should be shot from a cannon. They are only putting a damper on creative inventiveness. Retail advertising will not improve until the committee is erased and this responsibility belongs to the artist and his creative cohort, the advertising writer whose thinking can contribute to his best efforts. Management will open its eyes and ears to ideas that will build a better business. Good ideas which answer the store's needs are seldom turned away. And when they

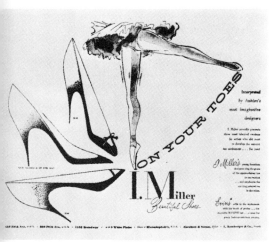

1. I. Miller's 1953 advertisement didn't reflect the integrity of the store as a style center for footwear.

2. I. Miller's half-page 1960 advertisement displays a refreshing approach to retail shoe advertising. Inventive photography is underscored by well composed typography. The overall design has clarity and an organized look that dominates the page. And it gives the store a look of fashion conviction that was lacking in some of the earlier ads.

are enthusiastically received, a wonderful world of "type", "pictures" and "design" can be accomplished.

hodge-podge layouts illegible typography

Currently, the most neglected yet largest facet of retail advertising is in the presentation of goods. The jumbled hodge-podge arrangements of merchandise drawings and illegible typography must be reorganized into freshly composed messages that will attract and be understood by everyone.

the trend that isn't

If there is to be a trend in retail advertising, it should be one directed toward exploring all the untouched areas and to destroy the damage already done through the trend of imitation. This will require a lot of power on the part of artists and writers to create new means of communication, lift the face of newspaper advertising and contribute to more successful retail merchandising. Some stores have already done this. They have invented new ways to say "sale"—far more energetic and profitable; illustrations for fashions, home furnishings, cosmetics, etc. have been given a fresh twist; type has been treated more usefully and legibly.

Among the thousands of retailers only a handful create vital, distinctive, sales dynamic ads. Some of these are shown in the accompanying examples. Most of these are products of stores where there has been a direct relationship between top management and creator. Sound, organized thinking has clearly stated the distinct personality of each. These stores have dared to do it "differently" without losing sight of their one big purpose, and in every case their advertising has proven highly beneficial.

Dashing Amelia And The 2-Pants-Suit

Dashing Amelia, look what you started! You put women in bloomers, you helped get them the vote—now they're running for Congress and wearing the 2-pants-suit. Amelia Jenks Bloomer would smile with pride and rest in peace if she could see the final effects of her famous cause. She got the first daring soul to step into bloomers just 100 years ago and that was the beginning of the trend you're seeing here : the very first of the fandabulous 2-pants-suits and man's last bold on a wardrobe of his own. One pair of our 2 suit-pants is cut like culottes (for climbing in and out of itty-bitty cabs) and the other is tweedy trousers for country brambles. Both are tailored by Robert Sloan with enough finesse to delight a fuss-budget Englishman. Wool tweed pants, 12.98 each. Orlon* acrylic fleece jacket in taxi-cab yellow, 39.98. Wool jersey top, 14.98, 10 to 16 sizes. Sportswear Shop.

Franklin Simon

3. This Franklin Simon advertisement marks the store as a conscientious authority on fashion. A well-conceived drawing, complemented by a simple handling of type, creates a favorable store personality. Copy and art are beautifully blended into an effective message both entertaining and informative. The deletion of the circular signature used in the past helps to contribute to a warmer and more personal image that is built in.

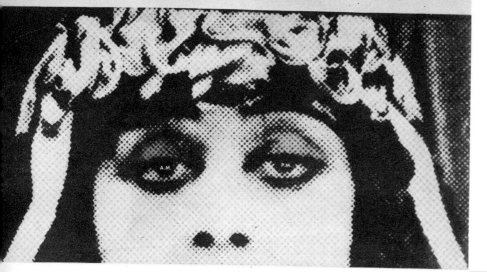

4. Neiman-Marcus is a pioneer of the most unique form of merchandise advertising. The store's flexible advertising philosophy is exemplified in this advertisement, almost witty in feeling. It sells eye shadow — one wears purple — the other yellow. Also a good example of N.M.'s ingenious use of R.O.P. color.

5. Ten years ago, Cox's crammed its pages with disorderly arrangements of everything except the locations of the rest rooms. This ad was apparently the work of a committee and it looked like all the other ads in the newspaper. No matter how large the signature cut appeared, Cox's looked like any other store in its area. Little if any effort was devoted to reflecting the store's real personality. It was downstairs advertising for an upstairs store.

6. This advertisement appeared 10 years later and ran on exactly the same subject—"July Clearance." Type was integrated with art to add to the impact of the page. An idea replaced the garbage collection of the past and a strong image that reflected the store's personality didn't require a signature. The signature is inherent here. Today, Cox's leads in sales.

2 Art Director, Designer ● Robert Fabian
Artist ● Evelyn Hofer
Date Run ● May, 1960
Publication ● New York Times

3 Art Director ● Hal Dows
Artist ● Mia Carpenter
Designer agency ● Jane Trahey Associates

4 Art Director ● Art Shipman
Designer ● David Renning

6 Art Director, Designer, Artist ● Arnold Varga

if products and services, manufacturers and retailers find their customers more sophisticated, media find their audiences likewise. And that's hardly strange, since they are one and the same. Here William Duffy explains why today's audience is sophisticated, why tomorrow's will be more so, and what TV is doing to keep pace with its audience.

TV today and tomorrow...

by WILLIAM R. DUFFY

Television is no longer a baby. The last dozen years have seen it grow rapidly from infant . . . to toddler . . . to preteen . . . to its present rather troubled adolesence. Now, ready or not, it must enter adulthood. In considering the past, present and future of Television, attention should be given to the audience, the sponsor, and the communicator. They are responsible for what Television was, is, and will be.

yesterday's audience was comparatively small. Imbued with a pioneer spirit and a great sense of kinship . . . of curiosity, they enjoyed its conversation piece value. Wrestling, roller derbys . . . and even the errors . . . they enjoyed the novelty of just turning a dial and seeing a picture.

yesterday's sponsor was also a pioneer. One who played and encouraged experimentation in this new communications form. He was intrigued by unquestioning acceptance. He would sponsor almost anything.

yesterday's communicator was a creative explorer. One who was stimulated by the excitement and challenge of this new medium of expression. With no precedents to fall back upon, he exercised ingenuity and inventiveness.

today's audience has grown increasingly larger and selective. The pioneer spirit has dimmed. Viewers expect, and rightly so, a more professional commercial and program.

today's sponsor . . . that same sponsor perhaps . . . expects and demands better representation and results . . . especially in view of the ever rising cost of the medium. Less tolerant of errors, he no longer considers his expenditures experimental.

today's communicator grows more numerous by the day. And, intermixed with those who have made great creative advances, there are far too many who are willing to fall back on the "usual" . . . the "safe" . . . "the "pedestrian." Television, with its voracious appetite for people and material, isn't as discriminating as it should be.

tomorrow's audience, influenced by advances made in allied mediums, will be even more selective and demanding. They will expect new concepts, new directions and more significant productions of both commercials and shows. Raised on Golden Books, exposed to the influences of the Ivy League and the improved taste and design of their clothes, their homes and most of the things which surround them, they will be better oriented, more sophisticated.

tomorrow's sponsor will be an educated sponsor . . . one who is more fully aware of Television's value and potentials. Ideally, he may even sponsor a show or commercial approach that subjectively he may dislike, if it is proven most effective for his product and corporate image by research (by forms of research yet to be developed). The competitiveness of the medium may be Television's salvation . . . and his.

tomorrow's communicator . . . thoughtful consideration of the past, present and future of the medium should enable a truly creative person to decide what tomorrow's successful Television communicator will be. During the past twelve years, many creative breakthroughs have been made by people who have striven to understand the medium and who have been equipped to accept its challenge. Those responsible for the following examples are representative of Television's future.

132

A. Design has been second only to ideas in the advancement of the medium. The creative mind, stimulated by the challenges of television, has greatly broadened TV's scope with the use of new concepts and new techniques.

B. Television commercials have given impetus to the development of more dramatic . . . and consequently more interest gaining and interest holding . . . staging methods.

The concept and use of settings and locations show more uniqueness and inventiveness than the film industry has exhibited in the foregoing half century.

C. In varied forms, depending upon the need . . . drama, believability, softness, warmth or starkness of situation . . . tastefulness has come into its own . . . and in its own way.

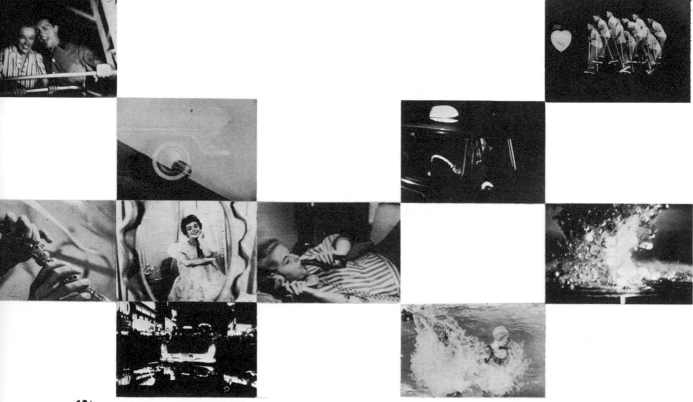

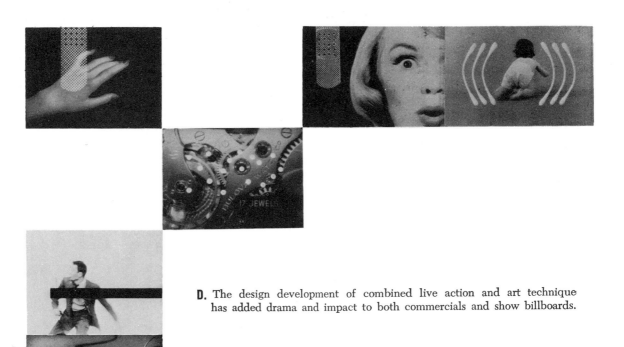

D. The design development of combined live action and art technique has added drama and impact to both commercials and show billboards.

E. Of recent vintage, the inventive use of still photography in a "squeeze motion" technique is another example of the medium's ingenuity.

F. . . .And then there are panels and shapes that make the picture smaller . . . but the interest larger.

G. Humor in a variety of forms and techniques and with a greater degree of sophistication, is one of television's most fruitful approaches.

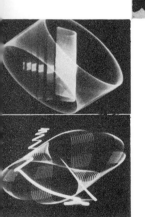

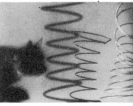

H. The creative application of many advanced and unusual techniques, such as: stop motion; strobe; over lap photography; elastic lens; high speed and microphotography is being used to great effect.

As in all good television commercials, evidence of co-creativity can be seen in the writing, design, casting, styling, sound, music, audio and video effects, performance, staging and direction.

For the examples shown here, the following are primarily responsible for the advancement of the visual aspects.

Clark Agnew
Saul Bass
Lawrence Berger • BBDO
Frank Broadhurst • McCann-Erickson
Herbert Bull • J. Walter Thompson
Mary Ellen Butte • Nemeth Studios
Gene Deitch • Deitch Productions
William Duffy • McCann-Erickson
Stephan Frankfurt • Young & Rubicam
Robert Gage • Doyle Dane Bernbach
Jack Goodford • Elektra Productions
Ed Graham Jr. • Goulding-Elliott-Graham Productions
Chad Grothkopft • Chad Inc.
Rollins Guild • McCann-Erickson
John Hubley • Storyboards Inc.
Chris Ishii
Paul Kim • Gifford-Kim Productions
Abe Liss • Elektra Productions
Raymond Lind • Benton & Bowles
Martin Nodell • Cunningham & Walsh
Irving Penn
Wingate Paine
Ray Richards • McCann-Erickson
Lee Savage • J. Walter Thompson
Jack Sidebotham • Young & Rubicam
Norman Tate • N. W. Ayer
Robert Wickersham • Chad Inc.
Jack Wohl • J. Walter Thompson
Howard Zieff

the super-additive . . .

"The super-additive is convenience and the American consumer has come to expect it." That's what J. Walter Thompson's Ward F. Parker told Australian ad men in 1960.

And the two great areas of consumer convenience are the product and the package. The multi-purpose package, the package that makes it easier to use the product, is the big packaging direction. There may be more sophistication in surface design, but increased functionalism in the package has pushed surface sophistication into second place as a packaging direction.

packaging design trends...

more products . . . more self-selling . . . more consumer conveniences create new directions in surface design and construction

by DONALD R. RUTHER

Even without a working crystal ball, it is evident that certain current facts will influence future packaging trends. Not only surface design, but package construction, convenience features, new machinery, merchandising innovations and the development and use of new materials will have great impact on the packages of the future. Designers must be aware of these changes and their significance.

Packaging, which dates its recognition from the '20s, is entering its fifth decade, which, from all indications, will outstrip any that have gone before in the increased use of packaged goods.

What makes the 10-year outlook particularly bright is the unrelenting surge of a marketing trend established during the past few years: the demand by dealers for self-selling, self-service packaging and by consumers for convenience packaging of a growing number of different products moving through an increasingly greater variety of retail outlets.

The significance of this revolution in retailing is that marketing or merchandising strategy is becoming more than ever packaging strategy. The product's package—its characteristics, its protective properties and construction, and its surface design—more and more will set the sales pace. Surface design is following the almost universal objective of design upgrading to cater to the more sophisticated tastes of today's consumers—a trend apparent also outside the field of packaging. In packaging itself, a concerted effort is being made to create graphic design that gives more pleasing shelf impressions without resort to garish devices of screaming bull's eyes, cluttered arrangements and harsh colors once regarded as necessary for standouts.

More and more sophisticated design principles will be used for popular-priced items as well as for expensive items, where the trend began. Emphasized will be more tasteful arrangements, greater legibility of informational copy, more careful selection of type faces and the judicious use of color.

More significant new packages reached store shelves last year than in any previous year. These are making retailing more dynamic, and shopping much more interesting for the customer.

The concept of the supermarket—in less than 30 years—has turned traditional merchandising topsy-turvy. The package is the strongest single factor in the successful development of self-service selling. Its growth has changed many ideas of package design.

Economic, technological and social forces are challenging the imagination of marketers of packaged goods. Working wives, for instance, will increase from 18 million to about 24 million in the next 10 years. This means a greater demand for packaged products, particularly those that save time and effort.

1. The aerosol
This was originally a heavyweight, military insecticide bomb. Today it is used for dispensing products all the way from whipped cream to cosmetics.

2. The flip-top box
It made a smash success for Marlboro's and was intended for cigarettes only. Today, different versions of it market lozenges, crayons, plant fertilizers, tacks, and paper cups.

3. The pump-type fiber can
that started out as an insecticide duster inspired the idea for the bellows package to inflate toy balloons and now becomes a handy dispenser for a grit sprayer that provides instant traction for cars stalled on icy roads or to do away with slippery steps and sidewalks.

Successful packages with convenience dispensing features

4. The polyethylene squeeze bottle
Developed as an atomizing package for underarm deodorant, within six years no less than 2,000 other products in 30 different industries were using it.

5. The roll-on applicator
Originated by Bristol-Meyers for "Ban" deodorant, the principle has since been adapted to products ranging from mucilage to garlic seasoning.

Solutions to the problem of providing conveniences are not simple, but there is almost an insatiable demand for packages that reduce menu planning, food preparation and clean-up—termed "built-in maid service." This is why so many companies are now engaged in programs—both immediate and long-range—to develop such packages which still could compete with current packages.

Meanwhile, packaging people are becoming more expert in their specialties. Evidence of this can be seen in the appointment of packaging coordinators at staff level for many of the country's large concerns.

Another event of importance, in the immediate future, will be the impact of the new Food Additives Amendment and the new Textile Labeling Act. Manufacturers faced with a little packaging revision to comply with the law will find it practical and rewarding to go all the way. Package change and revision will be a fact of life to an extent not previously experienced.

Just as the aerosol, the pump-type fibre can, the flip-top box, the polyethylene squeeze bottle and the roll-on applicator have been successful so will others be developed through the invention of new machinery, ingenious use of new materials and creation of new packaging ideas.

Today, aluminum challenges tinplate for cans. Plastics challenge established materials right across the board—from paperboard on up. But where they can't like the new materials, many old ones combine with them and they advance together.

The designer's role will be bigger than it ever was and his understanding of the part that packaging will play in the overall picture of America's growth will help him to create even more functionally designed packages.

All illustrations for this story were supplied by Modern Packaging magazine.

Surface design indicates a trend toward sophistication for even the lowest-priced items. The examples shown here are from the 1960 AIGA Packaging Show. Marketing and design development data supplied with the entries are briefed here.

6. Supermarket sponge line is given a new, coordinated graphic treatment. Emphasis is on brand image (large B prominently displayed). Polyethylene is printed in two colors of transparent inks plus opaque white for a calico 'feminine' appeal.

8. Required was a physician's sample for children's drops, printed in two colors. Design indicates content (plastic bottle) and appropriate symbol for children's product. Cover of the leaflet which is attached to the box carries same symbol.

10. High styling for a low-end product was client's aim. White sticks suggest white chalk; colored sticks, colored chalks. Format helps establish identity with a motif that illustrates product.

7. Two boxes embody the "gourmet look" to promote new decorated tool handles. Photographic cover increases the promotional value of the box, makes it an attractive gift package.

9. Set-up boxes to provide inexpensive gift package for cutlery sets. Boxes were designed for stacking to make point-of-sale displays—one of purposes of bold design treatment and three different-colored boxes.

11. In a product area hitherto lacking in color and in product appeal, this stock carton was designed to achieve a high level of product appeal, impulse and quality.

12. 1st package in redesign program. Existing symbol was used, but with a new look for an inexpensive product by the use of red, gold and white on black, with illustrations of product in both assembled and knocked-down kit form.

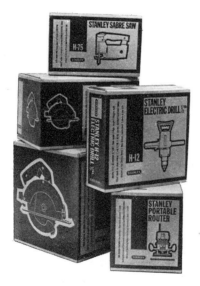

13. Selected cartons from a group of 40 different redesigned display packages and shipping containers. Problem was to develop a strong yet flexible family resemblance to overcome confusion among different sizes, shapes and uses.

14. Marketing objective was to create an auxiliary Hap package to compete in lower-price range. Design was limited to two colors. Photographic illustration ties in with family design and Hap shield maintains identity with other Hap pet foods. Rubber stamp informs of special value.

Some recent packaging developments of growing significance for the 1960's

15. High-density polyethylene bottles
Plastic bottles are now a major challenge on the basis of light weight, attractiveness and economy. Use of other plastics will enhance this competition with established materials.

16. Light-weight glass
Containers like the new one-way "shorty" beer bottle make glass increasingly more convenient and economical. New coatings are improving glass strength. New colorings methods are available.

17. Aluminum cans
Major advantage at present is wide choice of styles, sizes and attractive forms—especially advantageous for aerosols. Foothold in beer, foods and oil is likely to spread gradually.

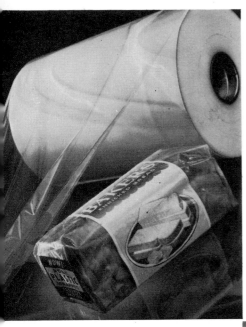

18. Polyethylene bread wraps
Successful handling of polyethylene and other plastic films for bread, tobacco and similar products is here or near and will have far-reaching effect.

19. Foil pans
Anticipated trends to cook-and-serve packaging will rely on these excellent and improving containers. Continuing additions in types, decoration, filling equipment are setting a fast pace.

20. Tetrahedral cartons
Continuing progress in packaging of milk and other liquid products will undoubtedly stem from the use of tetrahedron types.

21. New thermoforms

Blister, skin and all-plastic packs will continue to make large share of packaging news based on new materials, techniques and equipment. Advantages and successful applications will grow steadily.

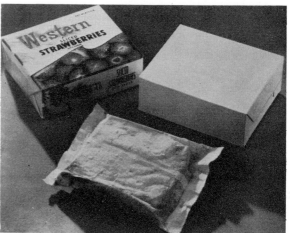

22. Pouches in cartons

Packaging systems based on a combination of carton and pouch are increasingly important for their function and performance for semi-liquids and especially for new convenience products.

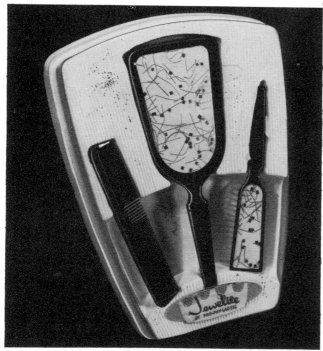

23. Molded foams

Many new properties and applications of plastic foams are possible. Molded polystyrene packages give solid support, reduce loading and handling costs.

6   Designer • Hal Hester
Client • Burgess Cellulose Co.

7   Designer/AD • Don Smith
Client • Ekco Products Co.

8   Designer • Rolf Harder
AD • H. P. Decker
Client • Hoffman-La Roche

9   Designer • Richard Schiffler
AD • Michael Lax
Client • Ontario Knife Co.

10   Designer • Ben Rosen & Irv Koons
Client • Art Crayon Co.

11   Designer/AD • Roy H. Johnson
Client • KVP Sutherland Paper Co.

12   Designer • Richard Schiffer & George Nelson Co.
AD • Ronald Beckman
Client • Rek-O-Kut Co.

13   Designer • Lester Beall & Richard Rogers
Client • Stanley Electric Tools

14   Designer • Vance Jonson
Photographer • Joe Maddocks
Client • Hap Pet Foods Co.

in direct mail it's showmaship . . .
If the stress is on functionalism in packaging design, in direct mail it is on showmanship. And the showmanship goes beyond surface design and fresh formats to a search for new ways to use paper colors and textures. As with other forms of advertising, costs have gone up, competition for reader's time is intensifying. To justify costs, the direct mailer is seeking more returns per mailing. To get more returns, he's turning to creative design.

trends in direct mail . . .

disregard the standard layout, reach for new format directions and new ways of using paper colors and textures

by ART SCHLOSSER

Trends in direct mail? Certainly, there are many. There always have been . . . from the day the first Pony Express rider took off from St. Joseph, Missouri, a hundred years ago, to today's $2½ billion medium selling every conceivable kind of product and service. From 1860 to 1960, business communication by mail has literally grown up with new trends, new ideas, new creative approaches and new production methods into the most flexible of all promotion vehicles.

Probably the most significant of all trends in direct mail today are:

1. Increasing costs of higher postage rates and per-thousand production expense.

2. Increasing competition for prospects' time, attention, readership and response.

3. Increasing need to meet both of these problems *creatively,* to make any direct mail budget do a more impressive and effective selling job.

Significant, too, is the fact that all too many direct mail advertisers caught in this "trend triangle" are stopped short by nothing more than semantics . . . direct mail lexicon that in itself has been an inhibiting "trend" in this medium for decades. They realize that costs have certainly gone up. They know the value of greater selectivity in prospect lists. They are infatuated by continuous microscopic testing, testing, testing. And they are quick to utilize the latest time and cost saving production automation. But when it comes to creatively breaking through the competitive barrier of voluminous messages compounded by *all* growing mediums, they shun the sound showmanship advice offered so well in the hit musical, *Gypsy:*

"You gotta have a gimmick."

Those who shudder at such a suggestion do so only because years of stodgy direct mail semantics have led them to believe "gimmicks" per se may be all right for burlesque, but they have no "dignified" place in the mail bag. Today's trend setters, however, realize there is a vast difference between "gimmicks" and "gadgets." Unlike the sparkling "gadget" employed by the buxom burly queen in *Gypsy,* the "gimmick" we're talking about is of the highest quality, finest taste. It builds prestige with dignity.

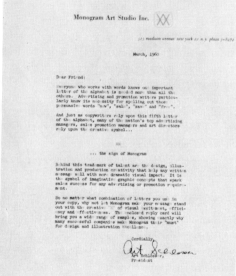

Increasing use of illustrated letterheads is evidenced by **Saturday Evening Post** subscription appeal in full color. Monogram promotion letter with every letter "e" in red shows how even copy is being created for design effect.

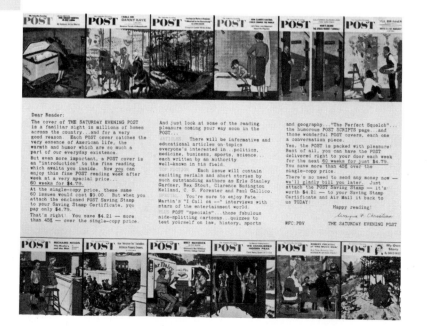

It is simply the dramatic, unrestricted art direction that most creatively allows a mailing to take new and different format directions.

There is an important growing trend toward these new format directions, new dimensions of layout, color and paper stock application. The reasons behind this trend toward more high-impact "gimmickery" are economic as much as they are creative. The most outstanding mail advertisers—those whose office walls are lined with direct mail awards, while their sales departments are lined up with continuing orders—are ones who apply this principle to their direct mail costs:

The best defense is a good offense. The best economy in direct mail is a mailing that is too visually dramatic not to get through . . . so impressive and interesting that it compels greater readership . . . and so influential in both design and copy presentation that it creates a larger response from a bigger segment of the list.

Followers of this proven reality are mailers who also realize that to accomplish this in any busy market today, "you gotta have a gimmick." The highly successful advertisers showcased on the next few pages did. They are among the dynamic direct mailers whose bold decision to be dramatically, dimensionally different is setting the trend toward the most effective way to meet higher costs and competition.

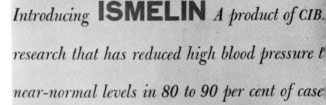

Window envelopes are gaining more popularity for both economy and visual impact. Double window was used effectively by **Life** for subscription appeal using miniature magazines inside. Ciba created ultimate in attention-getting "show-through" with complete cellophane envelope using address label.

Introducing **ISMELIN** *A product of CIBA research that has reduced high blood pressure to near-normal levels in 80 to 90 per cent of cases*

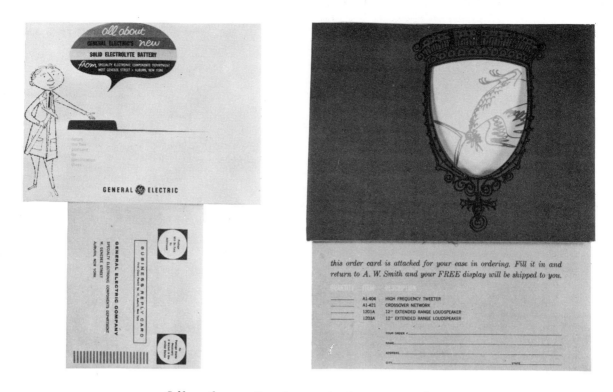

Self mailer creation is experiencing new trends in increased impact and reduction of prospect's required effort to reply. General Electric self mailer series with pre-addressed gimmick reply card, window teaser, bold type design, etc. sparked a 34% response.

Die-cut pop-ups, long a direct mail attention-getter, are taking new dramatic dimensions. Pop-up aluminum outhouse miniature created for Alcoa by Jannes Associates, and Modess series are examples of trend toward more action and realism.

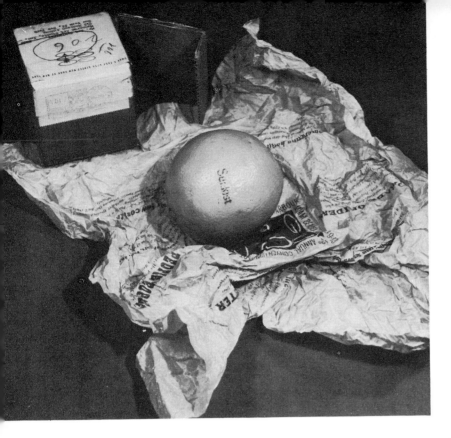

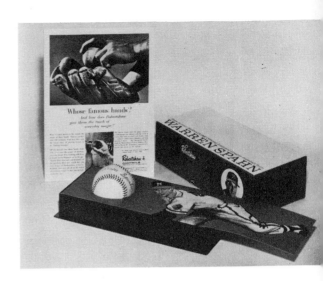

Useful "gimmicks" are increasing mailing's visual impact, actual value and longevity. Campaign created for Robertshaw-Fulton Controls by Cargill, Wilson & Acree agency gave financial leaders a deck of playing cards, classical phonograph record, baseball and golfball. Prospects for Direct Mail Advertising 1960 Florida Convention received an orange promotion mailed from Miami.

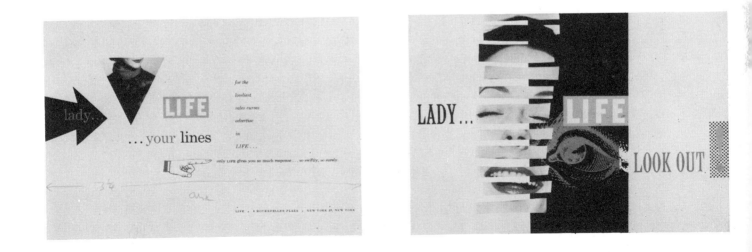

Combination of photography and illustration is creating new striking design effects for dramatic impact, as in these merchandising mailers designed for **Life.**

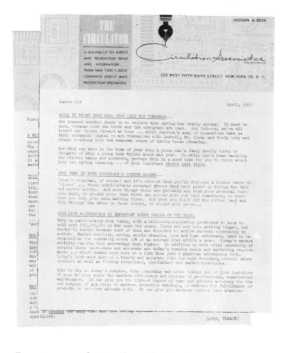

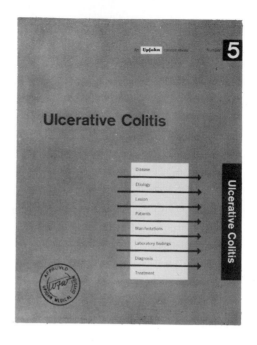

Booming popularity of newsletters is another noticeable trend in direct mail. Their "gimmick" is an illustrated masthead for continuity, identity, and light breezy editorial style copy with more information than sell. Circulation Associates' **Circulator** gives direct mail users ideas and information on new trends in direct mail production.

More interesting presentation of highly technical information is being noted, particularly in the pharmaceutical field. Upjohn's technical series on Medrol gave doctors vivid demonstrations with X-ray photo inserts.

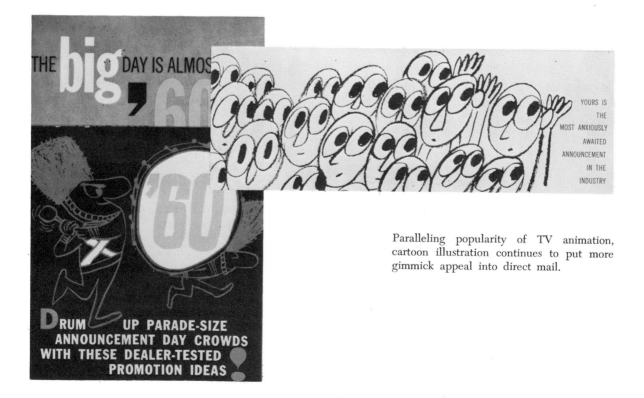

Paralleling popularity of TV animation, cartoon illustration continues to put more gimmick appeal into direct mail.

IMPERIAL

FOR NINETEEN FIFTY-NINE

IDEAS LIBRARY SAMPLES
Please Return to
5 East 57th Street, NYC 22

Blind embossing for richness and elegance is choice of more and more direct mail art directors. Imperial eagle and Monogram studio trademark are typical of regal look created for booklets and letterheads.

Paper sculpture and other illustration forms are getting more attention as direct mail "gimmicks." Eli Lilly series for Sandril c̄ Pyronil nasal congestion relief featured paper sculpture by Jerry Kuhlé. Eaton Laboratories utilized unique dolls created by Abe Seltzer.

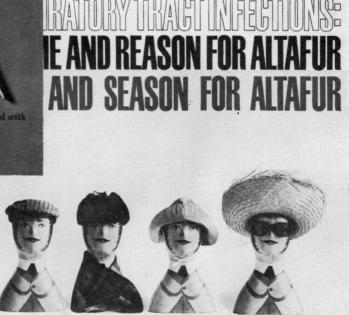

the most common side-effect of reserpine may be avoided with
SANDRIL c̄ PYRONIL

Fine art influence is being felt in more direct mail where quality is main appeal. West Virginia Pulp & Paper Company's fine paper sample series is one example, along with their well-known house magazine, **Westvaco Inspirations** designed by Bradbury Thompson.

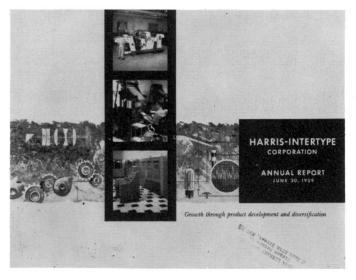

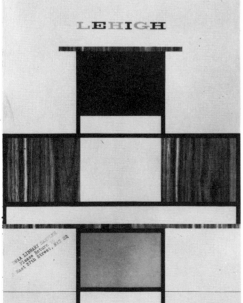

European Mondrian influence of heavy black border effects is being noticed more frequently, particularly in catalogs, annual reports and other publications. Lehigh Furniture Corporation catalog and Harris-Intertype Corporation annual report are two good examples.

. . . Direct mail is a pacesetter in graphic creativity, in expressive use of type, paper and contemporary design. Outdoor advertising may well be the most visually static of our media. Here Orville Sheldon explains why outdoor creativity has tapered off from the golden 20's and early 30's, notes five current changes in attitude toward poster design that hold hope for a visual breakthrough. . . .

trends in outdoor posters...

by ORVILLE SHELDON

Increased sophistication, photography, humor, and creative freedom making trend breakthroughs possible

In a business that spent $193,200,000 in 1959, employs some 11,000 people, and on any given working day posts some 10,000 posters in the United States, it would seem logical that some indication of a trend in the poster would be apparent. If there is, it is so well hidden, so subtle, there seems to be little or none at all.

Webster says that a "trend is to have or take a general direction or course." Let us look for this general direction.

We think forward and remember backward. Since the past influences our present (and this is particularly true of the poster, since the ground rules laid out years ago are still adhered to) no one dares break them. Since the present should effect our future, I should like to remember backward to the times and the people who created "trends." Retrospection may only point out the necessity of reviewing the ground rules—of taking another look at poster fundamentals. Then, with reason and good taste, we may dare to break some of these rules, to be original, to start a trend!

A poster is conceived of as a direct *simple* unit. One of the greatest posters ever designed is the national flag of Japan—the sun spot. It is the perfect poster—the perfect symbol.

But look at many posters today. They resemble magazine advertising, *outdoors!* The poster needs strong colors, stronger silhouettes, done with taste, done *simply, simply, simply.* I hope all of you may judge an outdoor poster show so that you can compare the power of the simple poster with the "outdoor magazine ad."

The poster, which came down to us more or less from the Japanese print, and was utilized exquisitely by such men as Toulouse-Lautrec in the late 1800's and early 1900's, was the forerunner of modern poster design.

This was a period of trends.

The poster as we know it today had its golden period in the mid-twenties and early thirties. Never before or since has there been such an area of creativity, of poster trends. The reason, perhaps, was because of the long years of peace following the first world war. It was a time for reflection and contemplation. Things were created with a sense of happiness. There wasn't the tension that exists today.

The trend-setters were many. Ludwig Hohlwein influenced the art of the poster, perhaps more than anyone. He was followed closely by A. M. Cassandre, Joseph Binder, and America's McKnight Kauffer who lived in England. Such men as J. C. Leyendecker and his Arrow Collar period, Edward Penfield, Cole Phillips and Ervine Metzl continued to set trends in poster design. They worked in bold, flat colors, in daring arrangements.

The outstanding trend was a spirit of gaiety. These men developed a gentle simplicity that took the reader into their confidence quickly and comfortably. Even today their work has a spark of freshness—and a wonderful ingredient—*remembrance!* Did you see any trend-setting posters on your way to work today?

Why could these men develop poster trends? Because they *specialized* in posters. They were bought as poster artists—they loved and understood the medium—they loved its challenge. They were *given a freer hand.*

1924—J. C. Leyendecker

1924—H. de Toulouse-Lautrec

The Art Director of that period (and I'm not suggesting he is non-existent today) was an art director in the truest sense. He had imagination. With advertising budgets unlike those today, he had little money to operate with. He had smaller areas to work from. Seldom could he go to New York if he lived in Chicago, or go to Chicago if he lived in New York, to pick a special artist. He had to find, develop and work with the talent where he worked. A man gleaned his reputation as a *poster* artist, was purchased as a *poster* artist.

Today, a poster is usually designed by an art director. An artist does the pictorial, a letterer the copy. Too often, the result of this working procedure creates a disjointed, many-sided picture. In many cases the lettering is far better than the pictorial, or vice-versa. There is a conflict in shapes and patterns.

1924—Ervine Metzl

Many art directors take the poster assignment as a step-child to the magazine page. They don't devote the time and the energies needed to set the trend to create a fresh idea. Compare them with the consistent quality in the Ford posters, the freshness and the inventiveness of the Morton Salt designs.

Despite this, there are some noticeable things happening. Among the trends or trend influences::
1. Art director's or designer's awareness of the higher level of sophistication in his viewing audience.
2. Increasing use of photography, and the photographer's simplicity necessary to the good poster.
3. Increase of humor—designs excellent for effectiveness, and for sheer pleasure.
4. Awareness by art directors of the necessity for *selling* good poster design.
5. Awareness (though slight) by advertising managers to allow a freer hand both to the art director and the poster artist.

The future holds unlimited possibilities. Although American leadership is unquestioned in many fields of advertising, the colorfulness, the gaiety, and the audacity of the European poster makes us a poor second in this field. Perhaps tomorrow's poster designer will break a few rules, set some new marks, and bring the poster up to the quality of our magazine advertising today.

1924—Ludwig Hohlwein

1926

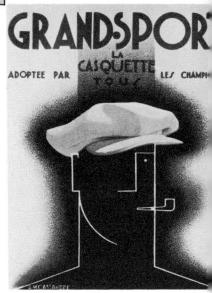

1927—A. M. Cassandre

1927—Joseph Binder

1937

1945

1949—The first teaser poster. It ran without copy
for days. None since has equalled its impact.

1951

1953

1954

1954—Savignac

1955

1956—Savignac

1958—Renfro

1960

1960

1960

at once more practical, more eye-appealing . . .
Like retail advertising, point-of-sale material is more easily measured to its effectiveness than are most media. And like packaging, function is often more important than form. But even in this traditionally hard-sell field, the beginning of a move toward sophistication is noted. David Flasterstein sees as a new function of the display the combatting of consumer boredom. Some of the trends noted: more whimsy, displays easier to ship and erect, increasing variety of materials and techniques, fewer window displays, more product dispensers, and, as has been noted of direct mail, more showmanship.

in point-of-purchase, design sells or else...

to move more merchandise, designers are using more whimsy

by DAVID FLASTERSTEIN

In no other advertising media does design play as important a role as in point-of-purchase advertising. Display space in a store is the one medium which cannot be bought and paid for on a dollar and cents basis. Here creativity is almost completely responsible for success or failure. As more products and companies compete for space, the design, and the esthetic appeal of the display to the retailer and consumer have become the all important factor. Point-of-purchase advertising in the United States has grown enormously because of self-service selling, and as the final link between pre-selling and actual in-store purchasing decision.

As more and more stores are designed along uniform lines, bare and antiseptic, with no marked distinction between them, point-of-purchase advertising adds color and excitement to the store. Displays create appetite appeal in a store full of similarly packaged products. New displays coming into a store tend to alleviate consumer boredom. Of growing importance are fixtures which coordinate products by style, color, size, price; they can make a sale on their own.

Design in this field is in almost constant flux. Designs, materials, types of displays become popular for a while and then fall off as the retailer becomes surfeited with the imitators. Retailers have an enormous display appetite—they are always looking for something new, unique, different. Displays transferred from four-color magazine advertising almost always fail because of the special communication problem in the store.

current design trends

The displays on these pages illustrate some current design trends. There is a growing use of humor and whimsy—humor being one commodity that is in short supply in most of today's stores. More attention is being paid to a display's structural design as designers learn that shape can communicate to the consumer. Designers are constantly simplifying construction to solve shipping problems, and display installation.

The point-of-purchase designer must solve merchandising problems in every size and type of outlet in all parts of the country. His designs must satisfy the advertiser, the salesmen who put up the display, the retailer, and the consumer. He works in three dimension with practically every basic material. He uses die-cutting, motion, and lights.

window displays off

The most dramatic trend in recent years has been the fall off in use of the window display. While still popular in some outlets, the window display has practically disappeared in drug stores and supermarkets as these turned to open windows.

Advertisers use more and more display merchandisers which actually dispense the product in the store. Merchandisers are being built of semi-permanent and permanent materials to stay in the store anywhere from three weeks to years. Color and structural design in corrugated displays have improved enormously; corrugated is also being combined with wire, plastic and other materials for more durability.

more sophistication

Design standards in motion displays grow more sophisticated each year. Motion was once used simply as an eye-catcher, most animation consisting of moving arrows, winking eyes, waving hands. Today it is more functional. It must perform a direct merchandising service for the product. A good motion display brings an element of showmanship to the retail store.

The display spectacular is still popular in supermarkets but is also being used more in other types of stores. Spectaculars now rise 12 to 15 feet high—more often than before they have mass displays of merchandise around them for self-service sales.

A display can only succeed by stimulating the imagination, enchanting the eye. Look at the samples here to see how some of the top displays of the past year were both customer stoppers and merchandise movers.

1. Wire window display used by Du Pont Fabrics to merchandise convenience and wearability of slacks made from Du Pont fibers in any climate. Wire is twisted into attention getting litter-bearers; mat motif suggests tropical atmosphere. (Designer, Arrow Display Associates; Advertiser, E. I. du Pont de Nemours and Co.)

2. Wire merchandiser forms an "Animal Tree" for Ideal toys for counter display in department stores. Made of white wire, the display has leaf-like branches which hold full line of stuffed animals. Open-work design does not detract from appeal of animals. (Designer, Product Presentation, Inc.; Advertiser, Ideal Toy Corporation)

3. Window display for Bulova transistor radios has brass plated wires converging at small Bulova trademark. Deep red velvet background adds touch of richness to radios. (Designer, Joseph E. Mason; Advertiser, Bulova Company)

4. Cardboard window display kit for Sucrets features a die-cut tubular construction for easy shipping and construction. Interiors of displays are printed in red Day-Glo inks to represent a raw sore throat. Figures take advantage of ceiling lights to emphasize color of throat. (Designer, Great Lakes Press Corp.; Advertiser, Merck Sharp & Dohme)

5. Cardboard display used to promote Ferris bacon shows cartoon figure and ad slogan carried through from media advertising. Complete integration of copy and design brings humor to the supermarket meat counter. (Designer, Thomson-Leeds Co., Inc.; Advertiser, Stahl-Meyer, Inc.)

6. Cardboard spectacular stands 10 feet high in supermarkets, was used by the Pet Milk Co. to promote new Personality Package for Instant Dry Milk. Girl jumping up and down, through an electric motor, creates an atmosphere of youthfulness and vitality. (Designer, Chicago Show Printing Co.; Advertiser, The Pet Milk Co.)

7. Counter display made of brass and walnut is used in department stores by Kayser hosiery. Petite brass wire ballerina holds a single stocking around her shoulders as a stole. Display adds a touch of whimsy to hosiery departments. (Designer, Dwaine Meek; Advertiser, Julius Kayser & Co.)

8. Corrugated floor spectacular to sell a complete line of National Distillers' brands. Display is printed in gold on a white background. Carousel rotates on a turntable with featured item highlighted by flashing lights. (Designer, Gibralter Display Division of Mead Containers; Advertiser, National Distillers Products Corp.)

9. Corrugated floor spectacular in the form of an old-time car was used for self-service selling in liquor stores by Early Age Bourbon. Display tied in with media advertising, stands five feet high and holds a case and a half of whiskey. (Designer, Container Corporation of America; Advertiser, Early Times Bourbon)

10. Motion display used by Enna Jettick shoes shows furry cat bending shoe with his paw to demonstrate softness and flexibility. Design and motion are integrated to put across the message at a glance. (Designers, Sculptural Promotions, Inc.; Advertiser, Enna Jettick)

11. Corrugated floor stand used by Nescafe to tie in with "43 beans in every cup" promotion. The burlap bag, stapled to the corrugated backing, brought realism to the supermarket, established a mood of "real" coffee for the instant product. Display was a one piece oval that sets up in three minutes. (Designer, Interstate-Boochever Corporation; Advertiser, Nestle Company)

12. Cardboard is combined with plastic in Revlon's deodorant display. Unique construction allows it to be shipped flat, automatically positioned into hexagon when opened. Package is designed to fit tightly into display for pilferage protection. (Designer, Graficon, Inc.; Advertiser, Revlon, Inc.)

14. Motion display used by the Sherwin-Williams Company featured a series of house silhouettes rising from the open paint can to spell out various features of the paint being promoted. Solved problem of presenting continuous series of messages. (Designer, W. L. Stensgaard and Associates; Advertiser, The Sherwin-Williams Company)

13. Motion display used by General Electric to introduce a new spray steam and dry iron created the illusion of steam spray through use of vibrating springs. Designed to show unique feature. (Designer, Dechar Corporation; Advertiser, General Electric Company)

15. Plastic outdoor sign used by DX Sunray Oil Co. stresses crisp clean design in trademark to give gasoline stations a modern brand image. Signs are red, white and blue; can be seen from a long distance when illuminated. (Designer, Lippincott & Margulies; Advertiser, DX Sunray Oil Co.)

Corrugated floor ad used by Longines-Wittnauer to merchandise Cine-Twin camera and projector. Column construction holds a full color stage which dramatically puts across the story of the product as complete home movie studio. (Designer, Liberty Corrugated Container Corp.; Advertiser, Longines-Wittnauer Company)

17. Plastic wall display used by Schmidt's beer in bars shows a series of changing colors being transmitted through the clear plastic fins. (Designer, Thomas A. Schutz Co. Inc.; Advertiser, Schmidt's Of Philadelphia)

18. A black and yellow honey bee dramatically focuses attention on Hiram Walker recipe for "Stinger" cocktail featuring Creme de Menthe and Brandy. Outsize cocktail glass, purple grapes and green mint leaves are made of styrofoam; appear realistic. (Designer, Craft House Plastics Corp.; Advertiser, Hiram Walker & Sons, Inc.)

19. Motion spectacular to merchandise King Size bottle of Coke is ten and a half feet high, stands in center of mass display of cartons. Lion instantly puts over theme of promotion; light touch is added when lion turns his head from side to side, rolls eyes in corresponding direction. (Designer, Snyder & Black & Schlegel; Advertiser, The Coca-Cola Company)

20. Plastic display demonstrates full line of Jantzen bras in full color; also shows actual sample of product. Unit takes up small area of counter, is designed for permanent use. (Designer, Kirby-Cogeshall-Steinau Co., Inc.; Advertiser, Jantzen, Inc.)

The more practical approach of both record albums and pharmaceutical design seems to point to a special trend. Here are two of the three pioneer areas (network advertising and promotion was the third) of sophisticated copy and design.

What's up?

In the first place, neither is abandoning top-flight, contemporary graphics. But, as in every field, you've got to keep changing to keep them interested. Because they lead the field in visual sophistication, these media had the choice, in order to change, of reverting to old-fashioned approaches or of coupling a practical copy approach with powerful, contemporary graphics. They chose the latter.

And just as these media led in the adoption of good graphics, they may again be showing the pace to other media, products and services.

Good graphics, as essential as they are, are no substitute for good copy. The scales may be swinging back to an attitude that says, "We want the best art with the best copy" rather than assuming one or the other can do the whole job. Thus, with ever increasing emphasis on the visual, there may be coupled a renewed concern with good words. . . .

record album directions . . .

photography still dominates, but trends are toward hard-sell copy, graphics, interpretation of contents

by ROBERT M. JONES

Color photography continues to dominate, by a large percentage, the 7,500 to 8,000 pieces of art prepared for record covers produced annually in the United States. Virtually every known art form available for reproduction is being employed for packaging by the some 300 different phonograph record labels in this country. The art media include, beside color photography, paintings both contemporary and the old masters, mosaics, collages, typographic, illustrations in all mediums, drawings, wood-cuts, graphic design and so on through the entire catalog of visual expression.

The most evident change is the recent emphasis on "hard sell." Sell tabs and quotes are being integrated into this basically point-of-purchase packaging. Listing titles of the repertoire on covers occurs with greater frequency. Graphics in conjunction with color photos appear to be increasing with each company's record releases. The challenge to the designer for additional copy is creating a more thoughtful attitude toward typography and letter forms. Fortunately for all concerned, the record buyer seems to be demanding a more sophisticated art form. There has been a considerable decrease in the use of semi-nude girlie pictures with absolutely no bearing on the contents of the package. It has become increasingly important that the cover, whatever its medium, must explain or interpret the musical content of the album.

The three major obligations of art to album covers remain unchanged. The first responsibility is to interest, secondly to inform and finally to influence.

Jo Low's admirable personal expression airily accommodates a striking illustration and considerable copy. A refreshing relief from four color photography. AD Jules Halfant; Artist/Designer, Joseph Low; Advertiser, Vanguard Records.

Jim Flora's wonderfully wild two-color illustration points up what the inventive designer can do when challenged with the restriction of limited color. AD, Robert M. Jones; Artist, James Flora; Advertiser, RCA Victor Records.

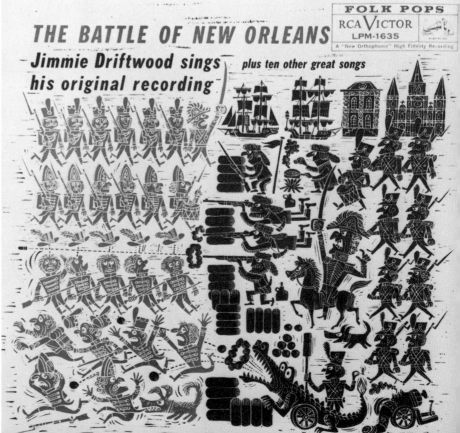

Another highly personal expression by one of America's most talented graphic artists results in a bold and vigorous sales tool. AD, Jules Halfant; Artist/Designer, Antonio Frasconi; Advertiser, Vanguard Records.

A dynamically simple poster enhanced by a minimum of copy. The single figure conveys the vitality, charm and gayety of the ballet. AD, Robert M. Jones; Photographer, David B. Hecht; Advertiser, RCA Victor Records.

Unabashed whimsy of art and title makes for a delightful point-of-purchase poster. AD, Nesuhi Ertegun; Artist, Reynold Ruffins; Advertiser, Atlantic Records.

Federico Castellon's unusual "fine arts" technique and isolated typography results in a compelling, story-telling, packaging job. AD, Robert M. Jones; Artist, Federico Castellon; Advertiser, RCA Victor Records.

Colorful letter forms forcefully integrated with powerful illustration results in a most vital and colorful resolution to the problem of excessive copy. AD, John Murello; Artist, Jerry Martin; Advertiser, RCA Camden Records.

A delightful typographic tour-de-force that explains in detail the contents of the package. The decorative typographic symbolism used as illustration is most effective. AD, Robert Cato; Designer, Noel Martin; Advertiser, Columbia Records.

Tasteful simplicity and a thoughtful use of white space combined with descriptive copy results in a bold and dignified design. AD, Designer, Irving Werbin; Artist, Old Print; Advertiser, Kapp Records.

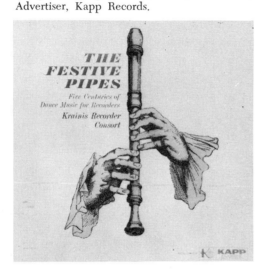

Clever use of paper sculpture takes advantage of four color process reproduction to achieve a mannered and unique album cover. AD, Acy R. Lehman; Artist, Blake Hampton; Agency, Donahue and Coe.; Advertiser, MGM Records.

An expressive, dramatic photograph, derivative typography, and a lively, contemporary sense of graphics produces this superb poster-cover for unusual repertoire. AD, Paul Bacon; Photographer, Melvin Sokolsky; Advertiser, Riverside Records.

Direct and straightforward approach to a complex listing problem. The handsome collage serves well as a colorful attention getter. AD, Arnold Meyers; Designer, Brownjohn, Chermayeff, & Geismar; Advertiser, Roulette Records.

an updating

Trends in advertising of food, cigarettes, liquor, autos and fashion were covered in depth in the first edition of Advertising Directions. Here leading art directors in each field have been asked to update the previous report.

Some of the trends in these areas:

• food advertising, the house of realism, is moving slightly away from straight realism, putting more emphasis on impact and individuality. Could this be a result of McCall's food pages?

• cigarettes, like beer, are turning to art/design distinction to create personality differences among too many brands with too few product differences.

• liquor advertising's new look comes from frank art and copy. No defenses, no apologies. No coyness nor cuteness. Liquor is now part of the normal, American scene.

• the ads, if not the cars, in the small, foreign area are the best. If so, it could be, as George Lois suggests, because they bypass committees. The sales success of these cars is largely due to changes in market demand. The emphasis is on economy in original price, operation and maintenance. The foreign cars were the first to meet this demand. Now that American manufacturers are in this market, mostly with less creative advertising but with more space and bigger distribution facilities, it will be interesting to see which foreign cars best hold to their former sales pace.

fashion goes

middle volume...

by GENE FEDERICO

Fashion knows . . .
- it cannot be sold like Ford or Fab.
- its strength lies in the power to make its advertising dollar do the work of five.
- "volume follows class introduction and identification" (See Editor's note).
- its art director is the key man in this area of motivation.

Of the various techniques evident in this year's work nothing of earth-shattering newness has been advanced. Facility, good taste, and the imaginative use of the relevant continue to be the stock in trade of the fashion art director.

However, the random examples of this year's work show that fashion advertising hasn't stood still either.

Although straight reportage photography has not found a place in fashion advertising (and so long as fashion represents an escape from reality for women, it probably never will) a sort of near-reportage is effectively used in the "Daphne knows" series. The fantasy of a little girl's world is enchantingly explored in the Girltown series. As modern girls go, Stacy Ames is ingenuous but that Springmaid is stripped for action. The out-of-scale small prop of L'Aiglon; the inscale gigantic prop of Borgana; the raw lean meat, no fat approach of Evan-Picone; the "corporate image" of Sidney Blumenthal; etc. etc. All these make clear, memorable associations of the manufacturer with his product.

Grandoe Gloves must show 3 gloves in their ads to push a color promotion. This was turned into a considerable advantage and the triple-armed Grandoe girl was born. Photo, M e l v i n Sokolsky; AD, Ken Duskin; Agency, Mervin & Jesse Levine.

This tweedy character is saying rather confidentially that "E v e wears this." Undoubtedly his name is Adam. Photo, Wingate Paine; AD, Lee Batlin; Agency, Altman-Stoller.

Why little girls leave home? Because Joe Nissen has founded a town for them to go to. He's put Girltown on the map. Photo, C a r m e n Schiavone; AD, Joseph Nissen; Agency, Altman-Stoller.

Product superiority of this man-made fabric is proven by Darwin. Photo, John Shannon, AD, Peter H i r s c h; Agency, Douglas D. Simon.

This is as close to reportage photography as fashion will ever get, though the girl is as idealized as a fashion model should never cease being. The naivete of the type treatment has great strength. Photo, Karen Radkai; AD, Alvin Chereskin; Agency, Hockaday Associates.

Editors' note:

Fashions used to be introduced in Paris September 1 and in the United States by mid-October. Today Macy's, Orbach's etc. have knocked them off by September 10. Result: according to Harper's Bazaar publisher William Fine, "Volume follows class introduction and identification." It reaches middle volume class much more quickly than it used to.

What does this mean to the advertising program? "Uniqueness, untogetherness, apartness" and selective marketing are essential. Sales records show that high fashion appeal wins out over diffuseness aimed at volume markets for many items. High fashion also implies an appeal to personal and social meaning in addition to function.

One of the chief approaches of art directors trying to build sales volume while creating and maintaining a unique identity is an aura of fantasy. Here Gene Federico shows, via a few of the year's top fashion ads, how different ADs meet this challenge.

This approach reflects the modern girl down to earth and off the pedestal. Photo, Ray Kellman; AD, Richard Gertner, Agency, Irving Serwer.

Mammoth eyeglasses? Or Lilliputian lady? The effect is arresting. Photo, Wingate Paine; AD, Peter Hirsch; Agency Douglas D. Simon Advertising.

Cropping accentuates the tension in this photo giving the figures importance beyond their size. Even the stuttering typography of the trademark is not unclear. Photo, Jerrold Schatzberg; AD, Gene Garlanda; Agency, Gilbert Advertising.

The grainy photography of Charles of the Ritz has become their trademark. Great elegance and good taste. Photo, Don Briggs; AD, Ched Vuckovic; Agency, The Rockmore Company.

Tension between used and unused space concentrates attention on Lois Gunnis in her 100 per cent wool sweater. Photo, Jerrold Schatzberg; AD Gene Garlanda; Agency, Gilbert Advertising.

The Springmaid tradition of provocative suggestion has not been lost. Neither has the emphasis on merchandise. Photo, Norman Nishimura; AD, Lee Batlin; Agency, Altman-Stoller.

A visual pun plays up the fun of dressing in Aileen clothes. The format makes the most of vacation-time snapshots. Photo, Jerrold Schatzberg; AD, Gene Garlanda; Agency, Gilbert Advertising.

food advertising: fewer recipes, more brand distinction...

by ROBERT W. WHEELER

In many an endeavor there are the vintage years, and the years in-between. Based on the comments of a small but select group of food advertising experts reporting here, 1960 appears to be one of those in-between years for food advertising.

This group of people from the editorial and advertising fields were asked to clip a food ad of late 1959 or 1960 which they considered to represent a trend or to have some characteristic that could promote a trend. Each was asked to comment on his selection.

Looking for trends in graphic presentation is an interesting past-time, but following a trend (from an advertising point of view) may be a very questionable pursuit.

The respondents were: 2 food editors of national magazines; 1 national magazine art director; 2 advertising agency art directors; 2 advertising agency copy directors, and 3 advertising agency creative department heads.

It is not surprising that all the ads submitted used photography for the illustration. Among the things that become apparent in looking at the ads selected is the lack of bounce light, high key photography so popular with photographers in recent years. Now, what looks like candle light seems to be the fashion. There is much more saturation of color. The photographers have become painters with 4-color process ink as the medium.

Simple typography against white paper is a rarity in 1960 food advertising. Type, both positive and negative, over pictures, panels, tints and shades seems to be the rage. McCall's rightfully gets the credit for leading this parade. It will be interesting to add up the researchers' findings when available.

The comments on the following pages show how 1960 food advertising fared among this group of experts . . .

fewer words for greater impact . . .

"We write copy only necessary to say what the picture can't or doesn't say. This may not be a 'general trend' but it could be. However, it is the direction we are taking to give our clients page impact and quick reading."

—Fred Ludekens, FC&B

representative . . . with distinction

"I will be pleased to select a recent food ad which I consider representative of a trend . . . the Hunt series which has brought so much distinction to food advertising for the past few years."

—Paul Smith, Grant Ad.

clean, postery, copyless . . .

". . . hits an entirely new note in appetite illustrations of food. I think it will accentuate the already-prevailing trend toward clean, postery ads which rely almost entirely on the appetite appeal of the picture. With today's advertisement —heavy publications such a trend is almost inevitable. I doubt that this will be copied as much as McCall's editorial experiments with food, but I think it will contribute to a move which will make the copywriter almost obsolete."

Draper Daniels, Leo Burnett

the picture is the copy . . .

"This Hunt's advertisement tells a complete story in one picture. It shows the trademark, the container, the product itself and its enjoyment in one good graphic idea. One look quickly shows that it needs no preparation and is good to eat just the way it comes out of the can. The child's expression of enjoyment tells me it is fun to eat like ice cream or dessert and creates a real desire for peaches. I think a good communicative idea like this plus its excellent presentation will influence other food advertising."

—Otto Storch, McCall's

editorial style . . .

"These two advertisements represent a trend. One is an ice cream ad from the American Dairy Association which is editorial in concept. This is relatively easy for an association to accomplish but I feel General Foods has done very much the same thing with the hors d'oeuvre."

—Mercedes Bates, McCall's

less recipe . . . more brand differentiation

"There is a trend away from sheer appetite appeal, recipe, and extravagant copy in food advertising, and toward some reason-why and an attempt to differentiate a brand from all others in its category. Pream is an example of this trend."

—Wm. Tyler, B&B

darker backgrounds . . .

"Generally speaking . . . foods are being treated in a less literal or less realistic way than in months past. There is more staging in setting up food photographs. Backgrounds are increasingly important. Dark backgrounds which give you a look of elegance are in vogue. Backgrounds often spotlight the romance of the product. Of course, the product is displayed in the bold manner, 'the big-image look,' so in fashion at the moment."

—Myrna Johnston, BH&G

overprinting, despite research . . .

". . . the bleed page with a complete over-printing of headline, body copy and recipe right on the picture. I think Wesson Pepper Steak ad is typical of this technique . . . Gallup-Robinson has long said don't overprint the message on tone. However, in this case, as in the case of the brilliant and apparently successful disregard of McCall's for this dictum, this is not overprinting the 'tone' but really more exactly overprinting a 'picture.' I must say that I don't think any particular food advertiser has done as much to create a big trend as have the McCall's food pages."

Rector Wooten, Fitzgerald

cigarette advertising:
copy similarity forces
design distinction...

by ROBERT WEST

With 36 or more brands fiercely competing for the approximately 450 billion cigarette market, it is necessary to create a distinctive impression for a brand and to make it exclusive, if possible.

Cigarette advertising today tries to create the mood, or look that registers with consumers.

Marlboro has allowed the tattooed man to relax and be seated. Viceroy keeps plugging the thinking man. Philip Morris is showing giant packages. Newport models only smoke in the water. Alpine has taken to the mountains. We have porus paper, double filters, white tips, cork tips, soft packs, hard packs, each one hoping for the consumers eye and ear.

It must be understood that all of these brands fall into four broad cigarette classification: Regular, King Size, Filters and Menthol Filters

Since Filters now account for over 50% of cigarette sales, it is not surprising to find the non-filter brands leveling their guns at the filter market. The filters aim at the non-filters for their sales increases while proclaiming they taste like non-filter cigarettes.

In copy all brands hover around the hive of flavor, taste, satisfaction, and mildness in "follow the leader fashion."

To rise above the sameness in copy claims, it is up to Art Directors to create a distinctive look, or impression, to a campaign that sets it apart from the rest, is memorable, and above all, sells.

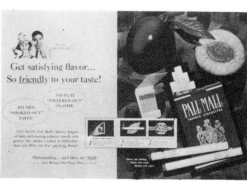

Pall Mall—the leading King size cigarette—continues to feature this package. Formerly this was created in artwork and this year it is in photography that combines pack, cigarettes and fruit on an art work background. Photography by Alan Fontaine, for Sullivan, Stauffer, Colwell & Bayles, conveys the story of flavor and taste. The black outline around the package has become a Pall Mall trademark.

Chesterfield — the number two King size cigarette—uses boy-girl smoking pictures. Since the product uses porous paper the copy features air-softened, just as Salem is doing. AD, John Iapalucci, McCann Erickson; photo, Ben Rose.

Lucky Strike—the number two cigarette in the sales of regulars—uses real people instead of professional models. They could be your neighbors or friends, and look convincingly happy smoking their Luckies. Photo by Jon Abbot. Layout by Vic Capellupo of Batten, Barton, Durstine & Osborn.

Camel—the number one in regular size cigarettes—creates a definite masculine impression. In this ad, we have the testimonial of Orin Murry—field survey engineer—relaxing with his Camels. Testimonial plus fine photography by Ray Manley registers a strong he-man look. Layout by Eugene Hooker of Wm. Esty Company.

Salem—the top selling menthol filter—creates the impression of freshness by using the outdoor shots of Arik Nepo. The photos are full size bleed with copy superimposed on the foliage. Winter and summer, these ads look like springtime. Since Salem is using porous paper they feature "air-softens" in the headline. Layout by Andrew Maddalone of Wm. Esty Company.

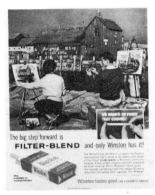

Winston—the leading filter cigarette—uses boy-girl situations. In this photograph by Arnold A. Freedman, the boy is demonstrating "It's what's up front that counts." Winston's impression is of people enjoying themselves. Layout by John Hill of the Wm. Esty Company.

Bowling Night

How smoothly Seagram's 7 Crown completes the evening's pleasure

Say Seagram's and be Sure

Seagram's 7 is the leading selling whiskey in the United States and no wonder. These smart, wholesome ads show the product in **today**'s setting. They say whiskey has a regular place with healthy, normal young American couples. The art direction, the photography, the overall sense of taste is impeccable. Photographer, William Helburn; AD, Leslie Silvas and Sidney Rothberg; Agency, Warwick & Legler.

THE DAY
OLD CROW
WAS BORN ~ *125 years ago*

Old Crow is the nation's #1 bourbon. No other bourbon is even close in sales. The theme of the great men in American history drinking Old Crow has been sheer magic. It has given every buyer a sense of reassurance, trust, confidence in the product. The art work by Carroll Jones is fine arts. Artist, Carroll Jones; AD, Fred Widlicka; Agency, Lawrence Fertig & Co.

liquor advertising's

new look...

by FRED WIDLICKA

Liquor is probably the most difficult product to sell. It is legally restricted, ambivalent, sinful—and inspiring. It makes you feel happy—and it is a depressant. It is a tonic—and a poison. Visually, the juxtaposition of a bottle of liquor against the ordinary illustrations used in other advertising produces bizarre associations.

Despite these difficulties liquor advertising has been successful and most of it well done. Great brand names have been built. Consumers feel enormous loyalty to these brands. Liquor is accepted as a normal and intelligent part of American living and entertainment.

The advertising agencies and creative people involved must therefore have a special know-how and a feeling for this product. It is a sort of trained intuition. Ordinary "hucksterism" is death to a liquor brand. The essential creative quality required for liquor advertising is an honesty that places liquor in its advertising setting without apology or defensiveness.

There is a great new trend apparent in liquor advertising today. It is a new look that comes from an "Honest John" approach in both copy and art. A subtle up-grading educational campaign is going on that gives liquor a definite place in the normal, healthy American scene. This is being done without coyness or cuteness. The other part of the new look is in copy. For many years it was thought that people would not read about liquor. Today we know better. People do read intelligent, sensible copy about their brands and the sales show great response.

Long strides have been made from the old picture of a bottle in a wealthy setting and a reminder of the brand name. Today liquor advertising has become adult. This honesty of liquor advertising requires a conviction on the part of its creators. The fashionable, shock-the-people, imitative techniques do not work.

184

Dignity in art, superbly painted, has made V.O. Isn't it amazing how an advertising approach can make a product not just appear to be, but actually become one of the finer things of life? Artist, Bernie Fuchs; AD, Sidney Rothberg and Bill Simms; Agency, Warwick & Legler.

Nothing as obvious as a drink here. This campaign has changed a respectable (but just another) blend into a smart buy. You wouldn't be ashamed to have a bottle of Imperial on your table. How did they do it? Creativity! Photographer, John Bryson; AD, Martin M. Krein; Agency, Foote, Cone & Belding, Chicago.

This provocative series represents one of the best **new** looks in liquor advertising. The problem was to sell Old Crow bourbon in an area where bourbon is not the big drink. Copy carries the ad but the whole look and logic are aimed to appeal to and inform the sophisticated market that sets trends. Artist, Otto Muhfield; AD, Fred Widlicka; Agency, Lawrence Fertig

Newspaper reproduction is often a nightmare. But this West Coast campaign with woodcut art by Bernard Brussel-Smith was foolproof. Its theme, its art simplicity make the product desirable. Fields of golden grain, skill, time—all make this "Nature's Finest Bourbon." 4-color woodcuts were also done with stunning effect. Agency, Lawrence Fertig

This consistently brilliant campaign not only made vodka but made Smirnoff the name for vodka. This example almost makes still life move. Four individual photos create the impression of one and seem to move from the distance to a close-up. Advertising quality that leaves you breathless. Photographer, Bert Stern; AD, Hershel Bramson; Agency, Lawrence C. Gumbinner.

It took fine and subtle art direction to make this direct ad this simple. It is clear, clean, honest and DE LUXE as its product. And the big thing is it **worked.** Sales of PM have increased since this campaign started. Artist and AD, Ned Wheaton; Agency, Lawrence Fertig & Co.

The idea of keeping up with the Jones' is an American social concept which is propagated by Detroit to get Americans to buy new models every year. This Volkswagen ad challenges that concept. Photographer, Frank Cowan; AD Helmut Krone; Agency, Doyle Dane Bernbach.

car advertising: compact agencies for big creativity

by GEORGE LOIS

There are good admakers and there are bad admakers. The good admakers will make good ads for whatever product they work on, automobiles or bubble gum, regardless of what's been done before.

The best campaign of the year was an automobile campaign. It was for Volkswagen. There will be many copies of these ads attempted for other cars. The "gimmick" is to dramatize a special feature of any car. But the copiers will make bad ads while the originators go on to new exciting ideas.

Who are these originators? They work in the smaller agencies where the atmosphere is conducive to creativity. It's no mystery why the best campaigns are done for foreign cars. The American manufacturers go to the biggest agencies, where, if there are any creative ideas around, they are drowned in a sea of committee before they ever reach the client.

On these pages I show what I believe to be the best recent car ads.

Pages back to back emphasize the capacity of the Volkswagon station wagon. Photographer, Carl Fisher; AD, George Low.

JAGUAR

ROVER 3-LITRE

Think small.

Once in a lifetime comes an ad with such a powerful idea that it challenges the whole American concept of "bigness" as a necessity in a car. Photographer, Wingate Paine; AD, Helmut Krone.

Diagrammatical way of showing that the Volkswagen stationwagon is just a little bit longer than the Volkswagon sedan and 4 feet shorter than American station wagons.

One of the very few fresh American ads. AD, Guido & Ed Thomas; Agency, Campbell-Ewald Co,, Inc.

A message to owners of cars that can overheat.

RENAULT RUNS RINGS INSIDE OTHER CARS

Dramatically emphasizes the selling point of the small turning radius of the Renault as compared to other cars. Photographer, Carl Fisher; AD, George Lois; Agency, Popert, Koenig, Lois, Inc.

This ad uses women to illustrate the easy maneuverability of the Renault.

This graphically expresses the expectation of great things to come. Photographer, Charles Kerlee; AD, Stephen Baker; Agency, Cunningham & Walsh.

A guide to Rolls-Royce comforts and graces

Rolls Royce . . . comforts and graces. Photographer, Charles Kerlee; AD, Rollin C. Smith, Jr., Agency, Ogilvy, Benson & Mather, Inc.

This simple reprint of a road test is authentic and believable. Photographer, Carl Fischer; AD, Herb Lubalin and Rene Bittel; Agency, Sudler & Hennessey

is anyone listening?

If the big idea is the one that can be successfully applied, ideas must be communicated effectively. Are they? Elwood Whitney says no. In the office, in advertising, in international politics, almost everywhere, the trend is toward confusion.

For all the emphasis on images and creativity, on believability and sophistication, too often we are not even being heard.

The trend is away from understanding. We are saying more. We are reading and hearing more. But we are understanding less. This paradox, says Mr. Whitney, is due to the clash between the numerical increase and technical improvements in vehicles of communication and archaic language. Mr. Whitney considers communications confusion a major contribution to many of the world's ills. Here he defines and illustrates the problem, suggests a way out.

in communications, the trend is toward confusion

by ELWOOD WHITNEY

This is a book about trends, trends in the media and techniques of communication. Unfortunately, the only traceable trend in communications itself is toward confusion.

Let's concentrate on several important but diverse areas wherein communications bog down—in the hope that more voices will protest the antiquated practices and procedures in common, every-day use—and that more rigid disciplinary controls be self-applied.

Some, because they are fairly traditional, are often overlooked; others, because they occur in such high places, seem to be above criticism. But examine each and every one we must, for our freedom, our economy and our way of life may depend on it.

Let's begin with the more pedestrian problems of communication in the advertising business.

basic communications problems in advertising

There are two basic communication problems in advertising: one is common to any kind of business—and that's the communication of *transacting* business; the other is the technical, yet highly imaginative, job of the communication of advertising *itself*.

Advertising is the process of communicating sales-producing ideas, desires and feelings to people. There is no pat formula for this. For each product it must be decided what rational and emotional messages to communicate, how many and what channels of communication to use, and whether to address the mass or a selected group of prospects.

Since advertising is essentially a *service* business, problems of communication may be more complex. There is no *product* manufactured in an advertising agency. *Creativity* is supplied by the brains and spirit of the agency *staff*. The inventory rides home every night. But the advertising *services* an agency furnishes its clients—in copy, art, research, marketing, media, merchandising, promotion and production—and, in many instances, public relations—add up to an interwoven, complex problem in communications. Couple this to an agency in the "top ten" classification, with offices in the United States and abroad, serving both national and international clients, with a staff of twelve hundred or more people, and you have a pretty sticky business of inter-departmental and inter-office communications.

the communications of transacting business

The simplest possible communications system is one which reports every meeting, every conference immediately after it takes place, and furnishes everyone concerned with a copy of the report. Each account executive should keep a diary of day-to-day activities and decisions, regardless of how small these may be—including the gist of all telephone conversations.

If followed religiously, this system is almost foolproof. Human frailty, of course, sometimes can cause a breakdown. For many of the larger clients the possibility of error is multiplied, particularly among those who have multi-product, multi-office and *multi-agency* relationships.

This is just *one* form of communication. It is horrifying to observe how lax we *all* are in this simple area. The fault, when one occurs, is largely one of omission, which, though frequently embarrassing, is easiest to correct.

All of us should develop a greater consciousness of the results of omission in such communications, because if it could be overcome, there would be a tremendous increase in our over-all operating efficiency.

communicating advertising

Advertising is another thing entirely—projecting ideas and feelings to people. This involves all the accepted vehicles of communication: 1) national consumer media—magazines, newspapers, radio and television; 2) trade media, such as the building industry, architecture, grocery, jewelry, automobile trades and accessories and hundreds of others; 3) and the specialized technical media—scientific, medical, engineering, scholastic and other such publications.

For national consumer media quite separate and ingenious techniques in communications must be devised if the message is to be memorable and identifiable with the product, commodity or service being publicized.

The techniques employed would encompass all *forms* of communication—verbal and non-verbal; symbology; illustration, cartoon, caricature and word-picture imagery.

In radio and television, still another dimension of communication is used—the imagery of sound. Before considering the still wider field of communication, remember that communication devices in advertising wear out quickly, putting a *heavy* premium on all facets of creativity. This is particularly true of television.

In international *advertising* and international *commerce,* communication is additionally complex because of language barriers, ideological hurdles and differences in the interpretation of visual symbols and imagery.

two important conferences

An appreciation of the confusion surrounding one area of *visual* communication—symbology—led to a two-day conference on the subject in New York City two years ago. Its objective was to point up the need for a codified and reciprocal nomenclature of symbology.

Since I was the Program Director of that seminar, I was especially pleased to discover that the Ford Foundation was conducting an exploratory study to determine the world-wide need for a *science* of symbology.

In July of this year, Colorado State University held its *Third* Annual Institute in Technical and Industrial Communications—a week-long conference devoted to studying, analyzing, exposing and helping to resolve some of the more malignant problems of communication. From an attendance standpoint alone, these two meetings are tangible evidence of the widespread interest of manufacturers, exporters, businessmen from almost every category; marketing people, research people, educators, publishers and government representatives, as well as the advertising profession.

the important single problem Palmer Hoyt, the distinguished editor of THE DENVER POST, speaking at the opening of one such conference, observed:

"... It is my substantial and sustained belief that communication (and thus communications) is the most important single problem that we have to solve in this age of A and H bombs. Because we can take it as a fact, and I don't think we have to argue the point, that if people can communicate, they can understand; and if they can understand, they can agree on things that are of common interest."

Amen to that, Mr. Hoyt.

What is implied is the horrendous possibility that we may not be able to communicate *in time*.

We have had several recent international crises: Russia—over the U-2; the collapse of the Summit Conference; Japan; and our hirsute Caribbean neighbor, Castro; the Congo, *to name a few*. The simple equation is whether or not we hopefully reach the *understanding* Mr. Hoyt mentions *before* we reach the blow-off point.

Hence the meaning of my phrase, "in time."

Understanding is not always based on logic and the clarity of the communication. Apropos of this, I recommend a most fascinating article in the July 9th 1960 issue of the SATURDAY EVENING POST—one of its "Adventures of the Mind" series, entitled, "Words that Divide the World," by Stefan T. Possony, Professor of International Politics of the Graduate School of Georgetown University. The author explains a rather more subtle, complex and most insidious technique in communications—*semantic deception*.

illiteracy Speaking further to the point about understanding. . . . One of the best informed on the subject of communications is Dr. Frank C. Laubach. He is about 75 years old, and at least 50 of his years have been wholeheartedly devoted to a world-over crusade against illiteracy. He is credited with having taught 60 million illiterates to read, in 168 different languages and dialects in 48 different countries.

Dr. Laubach has a very simple philosophy. He allows no deviation from his charted course—except the time necessary to campaign for funds with which to carry out his work.

His philosophy is basic.

The hungry masses in the world are the illiterates . . . and the problem.

Fill their bellies first and then fill their minds.

Teach them—communicate with these people and they will understand and soon learn how to take care of themselves. When they learn to trust us they will become our friends and can then be taught many things; democracy, for instance —instead of communism.

His *system* of teaching is equally fundamental—associating a letter with a shape, a picture or recognizable symbol. Experience on every continent over the years indicates his method to be almost infallible.

Dr. Laubach is one of the foremost proponents for the adoption of a universal, common language. While agreeing with most linguists that English will eventually be the accepted, common language, he is equally vociferous in his *criticism* of English, primarily because of its "idiotic" spelling and lack of an understandable formula of pronunciation.

As an example, he demonstrates that our five vowels have an average of five sounds apiece; and that the most learned scholar, after a lifetime of study, doesn't know how to pronounce an unfamiliar English word simply because he gets no clue from the five *possible* vowel pronunciations.

Whether you agree or disagree, I doubt that *anyone* has had more practical, on-the-spot experience in communicating with people, *understanding* people—and getting *them* to understand!

There is presently being organized an "Association for a World Language." This has been gathering momentum over the years, and now its near-term goal is to hold a congress at some central place—such as Geneva—to which ministers of education from every country would be invited.

The "Association" does not advocate any one specific language. Its purpose would be to discuss the *need* for a universal language.

Many prominent men and women, essentially the same caliber of thinking people interested in all phases of communications, have been working long and hard toward this goal, and the interest stimulated *all over the world* has been astounding.

It is encouraging that there seems to be an increasing consciousness of our faults in communications, and that corrective measures, however piddling these may be at the moment, are being applied.

Further endorsement of this awareness is evidenced every day in the public press. During the past year, article after article has appeared, each of which, in some measure, bears on the problem.

A long article in the WALL STREET JOURNAL headed, "Government and Industry Rush Satellites to Aid World Communications," explained how a series of satellite communicators, for both military and civilian use, will be put into orbit. The forerunner of this space communications system, the 500 pound Courier satellite, orbited October 5, 1960.

Now that is in the area of a vastly improved—almost instantaneous, almost completely universal—*vehicle* of communications. But remember—however efficient the *medium,* we *still* have the basic problem of the *kind* of communications such carriers will transmit or reflect.

NATION'S BUSINESS had an article on, "Why You and Your Boss Disagree." Its subhead was, "These guidelines will help you master business's No. 1 communications problem." The article develops the point that faulty understanding between employer and employee today constitutes one of the most common and most costly business problems.

An article in BUSINESS WEEK contributed a piece on, "How to Tell Your Profit Story." This applied both internally to staff and employees and unions, and externally to stock holders and the public. Publicly owned corporations today are living in glass houses and subject to criticism from every angle, often unjustly. Nevertheless, if satisfactory answers *aren't* forthcoming, the hurt—both to management, the company *and* the stockholders—remains, and can become progressively cancerous.

It is very dangerous to assume that a reply to a stupid, irritating question from the floor at a stockholders meeting can justifiably be met by an equally thoughtless answer.

The NEW YORK TIMES and the NEW YORK WORLD TELEGRAM describe a research study on the much touted subject of "company image." The study was directed toward discovering the appropriate language to be used to project a favorable company image. Sixty-one commonly used terms, words and phrases in employee communications were examined. It was discovered that many such terms had an emotional impact management never intended. "Company," for instance, produced a more favorable reaction than the word "corporation." Adjectives such as "big," "selfish," "ruthless," were used to describe a corporation, while "good," "successful," and "necessary" were tied to a company. A large proportion of workers did not grasp the meaning of such words as, "capitalism," "dividends," "depletion," "productivity," "socialism" and "technology."

Where the communications objective is to create awareness and understanding for an issue in a *favorable* context, there is a premium in choosing words that convey clear and precise meaning. We must *always* try to be equally clear and concise.

ADVERTISING AGE points out the need for legal aid on the part of management negotiators, personnel directors and public relations people and goes on to state that "... The entrapments by such 'pros' as head this country's large unions are substantial." The PR man "... is invited to bear in mind that he'd better be on sound legal ground before taking off on loose statements involving company policy.... A pledge of performance on management's part, allowed to slip unwittingly into an employee handbook, can cost hundreds of thousands of dollars at the bargaining table."

make communications understandable

Speaking to the point of the relationship between the humanities and sciences, Mr. Melvin Brorby, Senior Vice President of Needham, Louis and Brorby, said: "The present era of specialization, which has been intensifying as our knowledge horizons have been widening, has of course sent every scientist and every engineer down his own separate path. The sum total of knowledge and discovery and achievement has been as great and as exciting as it has been bewildering. These separate paths of analysis have had to merge finally into broad avenues of synthesis.

"That is our present need.

"But to make the separate pieces of knowledge understandable and useful, and to accomplish the needed synthesis and broader usefulness obviously requires the putting of that knowledge and that information into such simple, clear language that it can be understood by all those ordinary non-scientific people who share in the making of social, economic and political decisions, in and out of business."

This coterie of physicists, atomic scientists and advanced engineers of whom Mr. Brorby speaks, whose communications by means of mathematical hieroglyphics are necessarily accepted because of current limited understanding, may, perhaps, be excluded from the context of this accusation. However, what of all the other age-old professions which still attempt to communicate with the public in the highly technical idiom of their respective vocations?

Take legal terminology, for instance. Can anyone but another lawyer understand it? Can you understand a "simple," standard contract? There is no such animal.

Most leases and contracts are unnecessarily confusing, sometimes frightening and positively neolithic in terms of comprehension. They tend either to scare off most people or at the very least to make them highly distrustful.

Television and theatrical production and talent contracts are also beyond normal understanding. Often a contract for a national network television program is considered unacceptable long after the program has been on the air. Quite frequently, the TV season has ended; the cycle of 13, 26, 39 or even 52 weeks is over and done with before everyone gets around to satisfactorily completing the "official" contract.

A very fundamental question presents itself. . . . Why? Why, if all the people concerned have enough confidence in each other to proceed with the myriad of details and responsibilities in putting the program together, on purely verbal exchanges, why is such an inordinate amount of time required to complete the *written form* of an agreement covering a job which has, in the long interim, been completed? Here's another illustration of a product category—an industry which is a classic in terms of lack of communications and of understanding with the public.

Of all the products, commodities and services available for purchase in this enlightened democracy, none has as little public interest as insurance. Public interest in insurance is so low as to be almost apathetic. All research studies by independent insurance companies and by the Institute of Life Insurance itself reveal and attest to this fact. Yet this industry is a vital part of our economy and our financial security.

One of the most formidable barriers against such interest, communication and understanding exists in the product itself—the insurance policy. Its format is ancient, repelling and deadly; its phraseology oppressive, stifling, overwhelmingly legal and completely beyond the comprehension of anyone except a C.L.U.

And remember, the cover of an insurance policy is its package.

Can you think of any other product in the past ten years

of this kaleidoscopic America that hasn't changed its package in *some* manner?

There is no question but what improvements could be made both in the modernization of the policy format and simplification of phraseology. One big step in this direction would be a comprehensive condensation, a synopsis of what the individual policy purports to represent. This is one important but still minor move in the direction of building better communications and understanding. There are many others.

what of the future? There is an encouraging stirring and rumbling in this giant which is the life insurance industry, and we find it evidenced in many sources, one confirmation of which is from a speech delivered in December, 1959, at a meeting of the Life Insurance Association of America by Mr. Devereux C. Josephs, former Chairman of the Board of the New York Life Insurance Company. Mr. Josephs was pointing out that during the past eleven years he had witnessed many innovations in the life insurance industry which, by its nature, had not been under critical economic compulsion to change.

". . . Yet the industry led the parade in the use of new office equipment, simplified procedures, developed new products, met the advancing claims of government with intelligent modifications, adjusted its investments to new opportunities and persuaded some of the states to relax various restrictions that had long outlived their usefulness.

"But what of the future?

"In group pension business, have we let ourselves be hobbled by traditional definitions, distinctions and assumptions?

"Have we cooperated in persuading the legislatures to change the restrictions in procedures and investments required by changing times?

"Have we continued to impose our specialized vocabulary upon a public which has so often misunderstood our meaning?

"Have we made our dealings with the public as simple and as convenient as possible?"

Mr. Josephs' comments and questions posed are encouraging indications of awareness of those specific faults relating to communications in the insurance business, and that sound consideration *is* being given to remedying the situation.

Let's hope it will be soon.

There seems little sense in having sociologists, economists and other specialists study the needs and desires of people in order to develop and perfect new, more desirable products, created to fit the needs of the people's changing way of life, if such new products continue to be described in an archaic nomenclature or the stiflingly technical vocabulary of the profession, business, trade or science.

The high purpose of inspirational action on the one hand is *defeated* by the traditional reaction on the other.

And yet this same fault is repeated every day in business, in politics—even in affairs of State, for this seems to be a national trait.

no magic formula Americans, as a group, have another curious proclivity: We constantly struggle to find pat solutions for problems— formulas, panaceas—that can be pasted on like mustard plasters, then removed, with the hope that the inflammation has just "gone away."

If communications is indeed the vehicle for achieving understanding, comprehension and a higher degree of retention, then we must do more than hope, wear an amulet or "say our beads."

For there *is* no "magic solution."

What we can do, what we *must* do, individually, collectively and nationally, is to *THINK* more objectively toward achieving a better understanding.

We must think of *what* the problem is and of all possible approaches; its solution; and to the possible *reactions* of its resolution—*before* action is taken. Precipitate action is no substitute for sound thinking. Neither can investigation, research nor any amount of fact-finding automatically dictate the answer. All these, with analysis, help to *separate* fact from fiction; they help to light the way; but they do not of themselves constitute the solution—for there is no substitute for good judgment!

Mr. Donald K. David, Chairman of the Committee for Economic Development, made a statement at the opening of his address before the Investment Bankers Association of America which, I believe, aptly describes our peculiar penchant:

"As a nation, we tend to be quick solvers of the problem at hand. We pride ourselves on our ability to 'fly by the seat of our pants.' It is the immediate and the concrete that engage us more than the long-range and the theoretical. But now, more than at any time in our history, we need to combine our pragmatic problem-solving with long-range planning, with a philosophy and a sense of national purpose."

Perhaps the recent painful international issues will profit us in the future; perhaps we may begin to take to heart some of Mr. David's sage advice. Perhaps, too, we might give a good deal more thought as to how we can remove politics from *POLICY!*

This recitation could go on and on, because, unhappily, there are many more areas in which our communications are sadly at fault.

Why? We are not a blind, uninformed people. On the contrary, we have more *vehicles* of information than any other nation in the world. Quite frequently one hears complaints about this very point—about the plethora of communications media which threaten to inundate us on every front—trade and industry publications, newspapers, magazines, radio and television; and that these are so diffusing, confusing and suffusing as to make it impossible to *form* an opinion.

Or is it that careful, selective, retentive reading takes more energy, more brain power, more judgment—to separate the wheat from the chaff? Or are we again searching for that "magic formula," that prepared fact-sheet, that panacea—to supply the right answers?

Take a simple thing like reading. We've got to break with some of our constricted and constipated reading habits. We've got to extend ourselves beyond the narrow confines of our business, lest we tend "not to see the forest for the trees." We've got to stop *taking* pre-digested opinions and begin to *form* opinions of our very own.

living in a smaller world

We say, "*The world* is growing smaller." Fences and boundaries are being torn down faster than we can adjust to what this implies—both in business and the business of State. We endorse "free trade," but that's when it applies to *your* business—otherwise, we are protectionists.

It's a curious paradox. We should really say, "*The earth world* is growing smaller," because we are now thinking and planning in terms of *universe.*

Compared to our technology in vehicles of transmittal, our communications are still in the jungle-drum stage. The consequences of poor communications *and* contrasting, advanced technology in transmittal may result in an even lower degree of understanding and retention.

The implication of these advanced communicator devices could block penetration. In other words, people may be much more impressed (perhaps fearfully) by *how* we say something than by *what we said* ... which emphasizes the importance of strategy, planning and care in what we *mean* to say—to *actually* mean.

We must profit from past mistakes; certainly we must not repeat them. Our ineptness is *not* the result of a stumblebum policy, but rather, a kind of clubfooted progeny of a union between arrogance, strength, complacency and shortsightedness. It's difficult for us now, as a vastly expanding nation, to remember to politely "tip our hats" when for so long we had permitted ourselves the largesse of tossing a few coins in a tin cup.

"Kind friends" and "good neighbors" are not merely convenient terms. To be truly meaningful, they must be cultivated and nurtured by understanding and a continuing mutual exchange of thoughtfulness in deed and action. And unfortunately, discourtesy and rudeness have the same span of memory as have courtesy and patience. Omissions of the past are not so readily diffused by commissions of the present; even as a favorable "corporate" image in the world of commerce is a lot more things than a large investment in complimentary publicity.

Let us begin now to innoculate more thoughtfully the seeds we sow today in our international expansion, in our politics, as well as in our business and industry, against the reaping 25 years hence. Remember, too, that the degree of effectiveness in such chemical innoculation depends in large measure upon the quality of our communications. The pure essence of this distillation will be the understanding, the comprehension and the retention factor of what we say.

We have a lot to say, and we must say it to a lot of people. We'd better say it soon, and we'd better be sure we say it *right*, for the trend is away from understanding.

ideas are like D-rations . . .

Do you recall those rockhard chocolate bars used in combat areas during the war, to be eaten only in emergencies, to be taken in small bites, chewed carefully?

New ideas are something like D-rations, except they are better digested to prevent rather than to cope with emergencies.

The following pages are a compilation of ideas, new and old, talked about by advertising and ad/art leaders during the past year. Like the D-ration, ideas shouldn't be taken in big bites nor gulped down. Mental indigestion may result. Read in small bites and chew carefully.

ideas of the year

by

EDWARD GOTTSCHALL

"There are two worlds . . . the world of things and the world of ideas.

"Most people live in one or the other. But you have to live in both.

"All of us can laugh at the absent-minded professor who can comprehend the 4th dimension but stumbles over a chair.

"But what about the man who can walk around a chair and trip over an idea?

"Is that funny too?

"Not very. Because, maybe the success of mankind depends on keeping these two worlds stuck together . . . blended . . . communicating.

"And that's what you're here for.

"Not by accident. By design."

Chairman Bill Tara quoting Paul Keye at the 1960 International Design Conference

If 1959 was a year of many conferences, many speeches, and many answers, 1960 seemed a year of fewer conferences, more questions than answers.

Many of the year's questions were introspective, soul-searching, concerned with basic concepts. They were asked in hotel ballrooms, in Colorado tents, in Toronto and in Tokyo. They were asked by marketing and design executives, by students, by trade papers, by politicians, by researchers, psychologists, and author-sociologists.

The big questions were challenges, and counter challenges, and to date they have provoked still more questions, few answers. Some of 1960's big questions:

Can we, should we develop an international visual language?

How sales-effective is humor in advertising?

How can we communicate with Russia?

If visual drama can build magazine circulation and ad volume, how long can it surpass, or even keep its own pace? Does too much excitement lead to boredom?

How do we meet the challenge of sameness?

As communication speed increases, what happens to understanding?

Are the differences in people as important as their sameness?

If TV really gave the public what it wants, would we have a comic strip world?

How can we better use visual media to express ideas as well as facts?

What are designers in business for?

Should a professional design discipline be established, even at the expense of individual creativity?

What is the difference between creativity and innovation?

Is styled obsolescence immoral, or amoral? And if so, so what?

Was Malthus right, after all?

Should designers also be economists, sociologists, etc., etc.?

While we've preached "form follows function," have we practiced it? Should we? What happened to function? And to beauty?

Is "consumerism" as bad as Vance Packard cracks it up to be?

Is it necessary to force consumer waste to keep the economy growing? Is this ultimately good or bad?

Is "The Wastemakers" a pack of innuendoes, half-truths, exaggerated but basically true, a cynical creation of a best-seller regardless of consequences? How will the circulation of its ideas through a mass audience affect buying habits? How will it affect marketers, copywriters, art directors?

Are consumers becoming increasingly hostile to advertising? If so, why and what can be done about it?

What about "truth" and "taste" in advertising? Do they matter, morally? Economically? Where are they headed? What can we do about them?

Off-beat advertising...does it sell? Need on-beat be dead-beat?

Do consumers believe advertising in some media more than others?

Does the creative agency with a wall full of medals win and keep clients?

Does advertising really sell?

How do you really test an ad?

Is brand image building still considered vital or is it a fad?

Can aggressive marketing stop inflation? Even when coupled with a loose-money and a policy of hypoed economic growth?

What is disciplined creativeness?

Is sales promotion taking the play away from advertising?

The marketing, promotion and advertising man lives in a world where ideas must be spawned and communicated to move products and services. Here we shall see what, in 1960, he thinks about what he's doing and where he's going. Here we shall see some of the answers to the year's big questions.

advertising doesn't sell...

Robert M. Graham is field sales manager for Indian Head Mills, Inc. He has had 28 years of sales, sales management and sales promotion responsibilities. When he addressed the Sales Promotion Executive Association in the Spring of 1960 he spoke as one SPM to another. His opening salvo:

"We don't believe that advertising sells!

"We believe that if we took full page ads, properly created, in full color, in every magazine published in America; ran them simultaneously with the best TV show on the air and wrapped it up with car cards, outdoor spectaculars, cooperative newspaper ads in every newspaper and a direct mail piece in every mail box, we'd only show a slight increase in retail sales..."

What does Mr. Graham believe-

"...I do believe that sales promotion sells! And all of that advertising would give me a foundation for a wonderful, glorious Sales Promotion Program...advertising, market re-

search, product development, packaging, they all rank behind sales promotion in the selling program of our fabrics."

the coming man in management...

Theme of the SPEA conference was that the Sales Promotion Manager is the coming man in management. This viewpoint was keynoted by John D. Macomber of McKinsey & Co. Basis for the attitude is that sales promotion is close to the actual sale. He summed up: "I think we can see four major forces that are having a real effect upon the SPM's role in management...the dramatic shifts in world-wide population and spending power, the projected burst of new products...the growth of foreign competitions...the increasing pressure for earnings."

advertising sells...

While sales promotion men were listening to each other boost their role in marketing and management, ad men were taking much satisfaction from a series of heavily documented studies in Printers' Ink. The Van Diver reports, taking an industry at a time, were relating sales curves to advertising budgets, showing how companies with consistent ad programs fared better than those with sporadic programs, how companies continuing to advertise during recessions had smaller sales slumps, snapped back faster and further. The Van Diver studies were giving hard fact support for the first time to the theory that advertising sells.

off beat, on beat, plain beat

More concerned with finding advertising's most effective tone was Guild, Bascom & Bonfigli's Walter Guild. When on beat, he says, advertising sells like crazy. Mr. Guild was addressing Advertising Age's 3rd Annual Workshop on Creativity in Advertising. With much attention being given to a few agencies that have moved from the small to medium categories by using so-called off-beat approaches, Mr. Guild attempted to define off-beat, to question whether it is what it's cracked up to be.

"Off-beat is an expression which was once quite respectable, but it has since gotten into bad company.... It does not mean what it used to mean.... It used to mean exceptional, out-of-the-ordinary, different. The ex-

pression did not carry any connotation of esoteric, eccentric, beatnik or sick.... Nowadays off-beat suggests an image of guys with beards, bongo drums, and the advanced philosophies of maladjusted bums and wenches proudly living in sin in highly unsanitary surroundings."

Guild illustrated the specialized appeal of off-beat advertising by comparing it with such entertainers as Mort Sahl, Lenny Bruce, Dakota Staton and Thelonious Monk, and with advertising for Irish Mist. Woolite, Quaker State oil, Crane's stationery.

if it's so good, why so little of it?

"Off-beat advertising is not widely used because most of the products which might benefit by off-beat advertising do not have enough sales to afford any advertising...mass advertisers who can afford on-beat advertising, but who use off-beat advertising..., are wasting their money. I think they would reach more people more effectively if they used on-beat advertising, advertising that has universal appeal, that is a big hit, that has staying power."

To illustrate the universal appeal and distinctiveness of on-beat advertising, Guild compared it with entertainers Bob Hope and Dinah Shore, and with Volkswagen, Rolls-Royce, Skippy Peanut Butter and Ralston Cereal ads.

On-beat advertising must be original from start to finish. "It must be different from anything in its industry, from anything in all advertising. If it is less than that, it is not on-beat."

why not more on-beat?

"...too many cliches, too many sacred cows, the philosophy of playing it safe, the fear of losing the account, and very often dread of the dreadful drudgery involved in developing really first-class advertising."

clever, but does it sell?

Answering the payoff question, Guild cites the top and booming sales records of such on-beaters as Volkswagen, Skippy, and Ralston. "Volkswagen, through the first third of 1960 was 62% ahead of the same period in 1959.... Skippy Peanut Butter is leading the parade in all its established markets in the United States. ...Ralston's increase in share-of-market is more than five times that of the industry, is the highest of any

Pablo Casals is coming home
—to Puerto Rico

cereal in the cold cereal business, is increasing every month."

disciplined creativeness . . .

The need for marketing concepts based on "disciplined creativeness" of top management was emphasized to business leaders and agency executives at the Seminar for Management sponsored by the Container Corp. of America in Dallas. Summing up the conference, Edward C. Bursk, editor of The Harvard Business Review, said, "Disciplined creativeness for management means that all the efforts and elements of marketing must come together at the top where, after all the facts are gathered, management itself must think things through . . . you will never win at bridge if you don't bid to get the full potential of your hand . . . risk taking is the ultimate experience of management creativity."

does research inhibit creativity?

This is the "Which came first, the chicken or the egg?" controversy in advertising. The question is old, vital, answered repeatedly but unresolved. Speaking at the New York chapter of the American Marketing Association, David McCall, vice president of Ogilvy, Benson & Mather Inc., gave as his agency's answer an unqualified no. Considering the top creative rating of OBM, Mr. McCall's answer refocussed attention on this perpetual question.

"Research not only does not inhibit creativity, it is almost always a vital factor in the production of consistently good and exciting advertising.

"In other words, research is the search for facts. And facts are the straw with which great advertising is made.

"Research plays at least three major roles in an advertising agency like Ogilvy, Benson and Mather.

readership research . . .

"First, research conducted by men like Dr. George Gallup and Harold Rudolph has provided creative people with a backlog of facts as to the public's reading behavior as regards newspapers and magazines and their viewing behavior as regards television. Not opinion, but facts. News in a headline gets more readership than a headline without news. Sentences with more than twelve words are

hard to read. Photographs get more attention than drawings. Editorial layouts get more readership than gadgetry, designy layouts. . . . 90% of all persons who note an advertisement look only at the headline and the illustration. 90% never read the body copy. Research says, therefore, to any reasonable man that you must put the name of a product in the headline—or waste 90% of your client's money. The same sort of information is available on television. Problem-solution commercials sell more merchandise than stand-up commercials. Start selling in the first frame instead of trying to attract attention with irrelevant lead-ins. Photography works better than animation. And above all, demonstrate, demonstrate, demonstrate.

"Does this kind of research inhibit creativity? Let me show you a few advertisements and television commercials that are a product of our agency.

THE INCREDIBLE STORY OF THE ZIPPO LIGHTER
—and a man who believes a lighter should work forever

Hathaway revives the striped tartan

"This is the man in the Hathaway shirt. Pure creativity, they said when it appeared. Sure, it was, creativity applied to a thorough respect for research. Name of the product in the headline. Photograph, not a drawing. Body copy that dealt with the shirt and the shirt alone. And, after all, where did the patch come from? From the research finding of Dr. Rudolph that illustrations with story appeal get more readership than straight product illustrations. The patch injected story appeal and it was put in the advertisement for that reason.

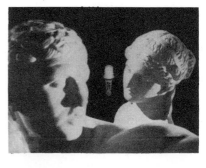

waterproofs lashes

"The Puerto Rico advertisements. The research rules are observed and creativity roars on—uninhibited.

"The Zippo campaign. The research rules are observed—and the copy writer and art director wriggle with joys of self-expression.

"The same pattern seems to hold in television. Here are three commercials for Pepperidge Farm, Ban, and Helena Rubinstein. All are created within the disciplines of research. They are concentrated on the product. All start selling in the first frame. All demonstrate. No tricks, no gimmicks, no animation. But who would say no creativity?

market research . . .

"1. It can define the market against which the advertising is directed. Market research proved that all housewives were not an equally receptive market for a dessert topping. Young housewives with small children are the prime market. This fact changed the character of the advertising.

"2. Market research defines the needs and desires of consumers as well as their attitudes. A study proved that consumers of stomach remedies recognize the fact that nervous tension is a leading cause of stomach upset. This allowed the agency to proceed with a campaign on this theme as we knew not only that nerves actually do cause stomach upset but that consumers know they do.

"3. Market research can pinpoint specific product advantages which can then be exploited in advertising. Coffee drinkers are primarily concerned with flavor and aroma, we learned, as opposed to stimulation. This fact dictated a fundamental campaign approach.

"4. Market research can measure the brand image and indicate need for a change or strengthening of that image. The Puerto Rico advertisements were created after a study which clearly defined American attitudes, revealing latent and overt prejudice against Puerto Rico and Puerto Ricans. This prejudice was based on ignorance and the Commonwealth

of Puerto Rico campaign has worked hard to correct this condition of ignorance. The research rather than inhibiting the writer, gave him the tools with which to make brilliant advertising.

basic promise research . . .

"Now, we come to the research that concerns itself with the selection and presentation of the basic promise. I would guess that 80% of the work in preparing a new campaign at Ogilvy, Benson and Mather is done before pencil is set to paper for the actual writing of a TV commercial or an advertisement. We have a specific procedure which is followed in the creation of all new campaigns.

The OBM Procedure for Creating a New Campaign

"1. **Educate yourself.** This includes immersing yourself in research reports, competitive advertising, the client's previous advertising. Call your account executive, your research director, your librarian, and above all, on yourself in gathering this material.

"2. **Visit the client,** if the account is new to the company. Try to find out what the spirit of the company is, as well as looking for specific copy information.

"3. **Conduct research.** Write as many promises as your studies have led you to believe have merit. Include the client's former promises and the leading competitive promises.

"4. **Consult the research.** If a clear winner has emerged—and judgment presents no overwhelming obstacles—use it. If the Research Department feels that further research is called for, prepare it.

"5. **Write the copy policy.**

"6. **Write the advertising.** If more than one technique of delivering the promise emerges, consult the research department. Techniques can be researched as well as content.

"It sounds inhibiting, doesn't it? But consider a case history in which this procedure was followed precisely.

"When General Foods gave our agency the Maxwell House Coffee account, first, the agency studied the precedents. Every piece of coffee research done for the Maxwell House brand over the past years was read and analyzed. The campaigns of the past 50 years were read and analyzed. All competitive advertising—and you

know what that means in the coffee business—was examined.

"The agency spent a considerable amount of time in Hoboken observing the complex process of manufacturing coffee and meeting the people who made Maxwell House the kind of operation it is. We were even allowed to enroll the account executive and copy writer in Maxwell House's green coffee school—a one-week course in the basics of the coffee business.

"The agency was now prepared to take step three. Conduct research. Thirty-two copy promises were prepared, including the promises of our leading competitors and previous Maxwell House promises. They were tested for relative selling strengths among a national sample.

"Point Four is **consult the research.** If a clear winner has emerged—and judgment presents no overwhelming obstacles—use it. If the Copy or Research Department feel that further research is called for, prepare it.

"In this piece of research, two promises finished far out in front. One was a generic promise which had no clear advertising usefulness and which had been used by several other coffees over the past years. The second was a much sharper and more individual promise which seemed to have good advertising execution inherent in it. It also was a promise that stemmed precisely from a genuine product advantage. This promise was "It tastes as good as it smells." The agency elected—**on a judgment basis**—to proceed with the second promise.

"This illustrates a vital point. Copy research must never be removed from the healing touch of common sense. It is a vital part of the creative process. But it is not, in itself, the creative process.

"The agency was now ready to write the copy policy for the brand. We had done our home work. We had the skeleton, the spine at any rate, of our advertising—the promise. As soon as the copy policy was prepared, creative work was begun. Mind you, not one word of copy had been written. Not one layout made. Not one rough storyboard had been executed. The question was how best to implement this story of the coffee that tastes as good as it smells. How could we get across to people the wonderful advantages of flavor and aroma that making a pot of regular

203

Maxwell House Coffee would give them. The creative process was on full blast. Many different translations of the basic promise were prepared. The creative process was not stifled by the research that had preceded it. It was channeled and there's a world of difference.

"On judgment, the agency picked one execution of the promise and made a rough television commercial. It was then researched against previous advertising for the brand. The results were good and indicated how the basic promise could be made stronger and more unique to the brand. At that point, the commercial was presented to the client.

"The agency did not present a number of different executions. It did not present a number of different promises. It presented one promise and one commercial—and it knew why. It knew why because research had told it so.

"The commercial was approved and ran. Judge for yourself whether research inhibited creativity. Or rather did research so channel creativity that it did a good, deep, penetrating job of finding a specific answer to a specific problem."

creativity and seven layers of criticism...

Two forces are at work that adversely affect the excellence of advertising. "Force number one is the sense of shame that has been artificially engendered in creative people for what we are doing," Bryan Houston told the 56th Annual Convention of the Advertising Federation of America. President of Fletcher Richards, Calkins & Holden, Mr. Houston was talking about creativity in a business oriented atmosphere. He said, "A sense of shame is the poorest possible soil from which to expect a good creative crop."

Force number two concerns today's multi-layered corporate advertising department and the passing of an advertisement from hand to hand up the line until its original freshness is thumbprinted to death and its lifeblood has leaked out through a thousand niggling, nibbling changes. He said it took only two people to write a great ad—"One to write it, the other to hit him over the head when it was done, before he ruined it by fiddling with it.... If we could vest the authority to edit in no more than

one knowledgeable advertising man and eliminate the troupe of midgets who crawl all over the creative product with their little red pencils and squeeze the life out of it before it can be born," it would raise the level of advertising by at least 50 per cent.

"It is not practical to get a great ad through seven layers of editorial criticism and it is completely impossible to keep good creative people at top productive levels if their work is to be constantly and repeatedly rehashed."

let creative people alone week...

Sounding a similar note was Herbert R. Mayes, editor of McCall's, when thanking the New York Art Directors Club for citing him for inspiration and encouragement given to the art directors of McCall's.

"As a token of appreciation to all of you, I would like to suggest to management everywhere, and more especially in the areas of advertising and publishing, the observance of an annual Let-Creative-People-Alone Week; a week in which creative men and women might be free to exercise their best talents, unimpeded by the traditional structures of advertising managers and account executives, unhindered by research departments and the statistics of Roper, Politz, Gallup, Robinson and Starch.

"In such a Week, it is not unlikely that more good copy would be written, more compelling layouts developed, more impelling typography designed, more challenging photography produced, and more sales of consumer merchandise and services engendered, than anybody so far has imagined possible.

"Our fierce affliction, it seems to me, is the averageness that is being imposed upon us; because we cannot be average without being as absolutely close to the bottom as to the top.... It's been said that man's mind stretched by an original idea never goes back to its original dimension..."

a house built upon sand?

One of the big controversies this year centered around Vance Packard's best-seller, "The Wastemakers." His theme is sounded in a quote from Dorothy L. Sayers "Creed or Chaos." She wrote, "A society in which consumption has to be artificially stimu-

lated in order to keep production going is a society founded on trash and waste, and such a society is a house built upon sand."

Mr. Packard says we live in such a society, asks what will we do about it, has some solutions to offer.

The economy is a mammon that can thrive only on ever increasing production. It is faced by a consumer loaded with goods and services. To make him unload and junk the old for the new is the role of marketing and advertising. And the whipping boy is often advertising. Mr. Packard recognizes three kinds of product obsolescence: replacement by product of significant superior function (this is progress and he does not quarrel here); outstyling, making things psychologically obsolete long before they functionally wear out; manufacturing products with built-in death dates so that a replacement market will be readily available. The last two techniques are the targets of Mr. Packard's wrath.

Advertising men have reacted variously. Printers' Ink attacks it in seven pages of a special report titled, "Is Waste Makers a hoax?" Here seven ad men charge him with flagrant misrepresentation, half-truths, extrapolations, phony moralism, false Malthusianisms, unproved innuendoes, of being guilty of the practices he condemns.

Other admen would prefer to sweep the book under the rug, hoping no one will notice it. But a best-seller cannot be ignored.

Every adman should read "The Wastemakers" for the same reason that every American should be informed about Communism. It is not sufficient to be emotionally against it.

You should read this book 1) to know what a good chunk of your market has read and been influenced by, 2) to stimulate thinking on moral issues underlying advertising. Mr. Packard's book, for all of the antagonism to it, cannot be written off as a pack of lies. If the evidence is selected and sometimes contradictory, much of it is correct and to the point. The questions it raises are big, and concern everyone of us both as citizens and as admen. To help balance your reading of it, see Printers' Ink, September 30, 1960. And also see Dr. Ernest Dichter's new book, "The Strategy of Desire."

the strategy of desire...

Dr. Dichter's book is intended as an

answer to Vance Packard's first attack on advertising, "The Hidden Persuaders," as well as the fears expressed by Edward R. Murrow in the mid-forties that the power of social scientists to influence people might get out of hand. The few with the power to change the minds of the many might make Orwell's 1984 a reality, and ahead of schedule.

Naturally, Dr. Dichter says no. Evil is not inherent in power, he argues, but in the goals to which it is aimed. (He does not deny the power of scientifically aimed persuasion although some have found it, at present, much less a force than feared), nor does he explain how men with undesirable goals can be kept from manipulating mass minds and desires.

He writes, "Persuasion is good if there is a correct goal." One such goal is "an invitation to new experiences, to a more creative and more fulfilled life." This would seem to justify the promotion and sale of new products to replace others not physically worn out. This would make Dr. Dichter a wastemaker. The school of thought that opposes Vance Packard's "wastemaking" argument doesn't deny the element of waste, does insist that it is more than counter balanced by economic growth for the benefit of all and by contributing to the more fulfilled life of which Dr. Dichter speaks.

What is the bad goal? "It is only when the goal of persuasion is to instill static and stale contentment that it results in eventual maladjustment and unhappiness and thus becomes clinically incorrect and morally undesirable."

Dr. Dichter's book explains the why and how of motivational research, the need to uncover hidden desires (often these are the key to the **real** reasons why people buy), the technique of finding out why people behave the way they do and then the prescribing of a method to motivate them.

It is this last consideration, re-motivating people, changing their minds and wants, that is currently under attack.

Dr. Dichter explains when MR is advisable and when it is not needed to help the marketer understand and control his market. He explains the major principles of persuasion: re-orientation, encouragement, insight, removal of mental blocks, setting of goals, identification and role playing, testimonials.

Diagnostic (motivational) research seeks to answer **why** something happened the way it did. This kind of research is valuable, says Dr. Dichter, when:

"1. The data being sought may not be present at the rational or conscious level.

"2. We are dealing with psychological mechanisms and with cause-and-effect relationships.

"3. The person questioned has a chance to produce interference, conscious or unconscious, between the time he understands the question and the time he answers it."

Of particular interest to art directors, artists, photographers, designers, is the section on verbal illusion. Dr. Dichter concludes that, "There is much evidence to show that it is the non-verbal, implied communication that is much more often the effective one than the pure logical verbal form of communication."

This viewpoint has also been emphasized by Chicago Tribune research director Pierre Martineau. If some art directors wonder whether researchers are friend or foe, they might remember that motivationalists consistently stress the power of the visual image, its ability to reach the emotion rather than the intellect and thus to reach the strongest but often hidden motive. Researchers only ask that the visual symbols be aimed with psychological accuracy.

visual communications international . . .
Peoples of the fast developing world markets, how to understand them and how to help them understand us, were the dominating subjects at Visual Communications International, two-day conference sponsored by the Art Directors Club of New York.

The conference started with "The differences in people are not as important as their samenesses." Not everyone agreed. Some speakers said that clear understanding of people's differences could be as important as an awareness of similarities.

speed plus understanding . . .
We can fly to London or Paris in little more than six hours, noted ADC President Garrett P. Orr. But now we must get our ideas as well as ourselves across the oceans with equal speed. Opening the conference, Mr.

Orr called for "speed and understanding" in communications to meet the challenge of international events.

taste, don't meet it, lead it . . .
Don't give the public what it wants, was Sylvester L. (Pat) Weaver's advice as he emphasized quality in communications. If we really gave the public what it wanted we'd live in a comic strip world. Communications media must lead rather than meet public taste. To Mr. Weaver, this is commercially feasible. Sadler's Wells ballet program reached 30,000,000 TViewers, he noted. A good way to set back the concept of quality is to put a good show on at a poor time, and then use the inevitable low rating as an excuse to eliminate other good programs.

Pat Weaver sees our society in its fourth explosive stage. Stage 1 was our 18th century struggle for equality. The industrial revolution and resultant economic equity for many comprise stage 2. We have lived through the beginning of an explosive scientific era and are now overlapping it with a communications explosion. In a world beset by the possibility of a nuclear war followed by a second stone age, Pat Weaver sees a new golden era if today's communications get the message of modern times around the world.

What is the message? We must elevate the condition of the common man the world over. Mr. Weaver sees moral and economic objectives reinforcing each other here.

there is no certainty . . .
The search for certainty is a sign of immaturity. We may never know the truth, the final truth, says Pat Weaver, perhaps with an eye on research and ratings. Shifting his glance to Hollywood, he finds we have primitives in power. The focus on attendance rather than on values inherent in the communications power of the medium is part of the give-them-what-they-want philosophy which is an irresponsible excuse for poor programming in any medium. He found magazines more responsible.

The public cannot want what it does not know. Mr. Weaver feels it is the responsibility of media to expose the public to new things, even at the risk of low Starches and Hoopers. He pointed to the more mature TV programming in both Europe and Canada.

the "all or nothing" fallacy...

"There is a need to break down the 'all or nothing' picture of an 'enemy,' which is one of the most pressing things in the world today," Dr. Margaret Mead advised the conference.

"If we can develop some way of remembering simultaneously that the members of another society love babies, love their husbands, love nature and want peace and have loving care in their schools and so forth—and, at the same time, that their governments are pursuing policies that, unless they are checked by our Government, may bring a holocaust on the world—this, it seems to me, is one of the most important and necessary tasks facing us."

pictures can express ideas...

Photographer-author Philippe Halsman at a luncheon session, left this clear idea: it has been thought that the limit of visual media was in its ability to express facts but not ideas. His aim, even in a single portrait, is to express an idea. Communications in the international arena will feature interchange of ideas as well as of fact.

and what about the USSR?...

If we will try to circulate ideas internationally, can we penetrate the iron curtain? Newsweek Soviet Affairs Editor Leon Volkov, Russian-born and educated, but in the U.S. since 1945, said:

• USSR leaders aren't as sure of themselves or of their own directions as we think they are.

• therefore we have a new opportunity to communicate into Russia.

• Russian leaders and cultural and scientific teams visiting the United States are returning home aware that we are **not** on the verge of a proletariat dictatorship, that our people are essentially content and live well.

• this knowledge must make them re-examine their thinking.

• our exhibitions, our exchange visits to Russia are getting through to the Russians.

• but perhaps the big fact of Russian life today is that a hard core of this generation is less naive than their parents. Stalin, by censorship, controlled education, and the basic ignorance of the people, painted any picture of the outside world that suited him. Today, about 15,000,000 Russians have been outside Russia, mostly soldiers in the last war. Their exposure to Western standards made them less gullible than were their parents. We now have a better chance to be heard in Russia, and to be believed.

the camera, penetrating or superficial...

It is not enough to capture the basic emotional story common to all peoples, as did the Family of Man, says Claudio Campuzano, New York correspondent of Visao. The photographer must make clear the true social relationships in a complex society. He must be sensitive to the similarities and dissimilarities among cultures to interpret one people to another.

"It is not enough that the audience be moved by the images captured by the photographer. These images should also convey comprehension and understanding.

"The photographer will find these images easy to come by when he portrays a primitive or semi-primitive society. The essential characteristics common to all men will be easily recognized.

"These characteristics will still be visible, coming up to the surface here and there, and the photographer—without distorting reality in any way—may abstract them in the form of emotionally charged images.

"He will only have to exercise a sensitive and wise selection.

"But what happens when the photographer's interest is focused on more complex societies?

"Latin America may offer a good example. Here is a human society that might first impress a foreign photographer—usually American or European—as being materially different from his own.

"If the photographer does not understand to what extent this difference is only material, his role as communicator will be seriously impaired.

"He will not realize that many of these different social relationships come, in effect, very close to the meaning of those he knows from his own environment.

"Not realizing this, he will emphasize the dissimilarities, the contrasts even, imposing through his selection of images his own preconceptions, his own standards.

"And he will finally fall upon recording the quaint, the picturesque, to the exception of almost anything else....

"When the photographer has been in contact with his subject long enough, the dialectical process between emotion and intellect urges him to dig deep into the surrounding reality and allows him to come up with a hard core of communicable substance.

"Such is the way that great photographic works of visual communications like David Duncan's "Private Life of Pablo Picasso," Eugene Smith's "Spanish Village" or Emil Schultess' "Africa" have taken shape."

when does humor sell?

It is possible that humor as an international characteristic may be a poor medium for international communications. Humor is often too local, too specialized. Margaret Sweeney (London) notes that even in England different admen see humor differently. One finds it based on the pun, visual and verbal. Another sees it stemming from literary tradition. Still another finds it non-existent.

In any event, Miss Sweeney finds humor used in special situations. Answering her own question, "How is humor used today?" she reports:

"...of the products the public has come to accept as of basically high standard, categories like beer, cigarettes, petrol, bread, any product advantage is marginal. Advertising on the basis of product plus has very little point, and runs the risk of selling the category as a whole rather than your brand. If you can step out front with humor, and the right kind of humor, you can really win."

IDC '60...

At Aspen you arrive with answers and leave with questions. 1960's questions were concerned with the role of the designer in the corporation and whether professional discipline is preferable to individual inspiration when the one must make room for the other. The 10th International Design Conference asked if there is room for innovators in our 20th century technology.

Some of the best unanswered questions were asked by Joseph McGarry toward the close of the final day. Reminding artists and designers that creativity was not exclusively theirs and attacking designers for their superficial attitudes, he asked: "What are you designers in business for? Are you in it for kicks? Are you serious about what you are doing? Where do you want to do? Can you get there from here?"

individuality vs professional discipline...

And C. Northcote Parkinson, whose chief role was to ask questions, asked:

"Are we in a position to seize opportunities when they arise? Do we have the prestige? Will people heed our advice? Are we high enough in the organization to make our view heard?" He had one answer, "No."

Why? "Because of a lack of discipline among ourselves." It was suggested that doctors, lawyers, engineers and other groups have greater prestige because "Behind the training and behind the professional discipline is a broad agreement on essentials. ...Generally speaking, the same question, although addressed to different members of a profession, will produce the same answer from each. And the public esteem in which the profession is held depends to a large extent upon this being so."

The clash with the subjective, personal-inspiration oriented artist was obvious. Parkinson's new law advises discipline. "On the one hand you have the claims of professional discipline. On the other hand you have the claims of the individual artist. The choice...the liklihood of being listened to as against the artist's freedom to express himself. My advice is to move rapidly towards the establishment of a professional discipline ...train their (designers) successors in an accepted tradition, set their professional standards and establish their professional examinations."

creativity vs innovation...

Program chairman George D. Culler (painter, printmaker, Associate Director San Francisco Museum of Art) distinguished between creativity and innovation. "The creative process is the ability of the human mind now and again to fuse aspects of experience into a new relationship, to achieve a new insight, an enlargement of understanding. Wherever it may occur...the idea is a force let loose, not thereafter to be recalled. ...It is perhaps fortunate that we are only very rarely creative. Society absorbs new ideas slowly. And it may be that for the purposes of this conference, we should save the word creative to name those rare and brilliant insights...that burst on the world from time to time, upset old notions and illuminate new vistas for man."

Mr. Culler suggested that for the more modest, and day to day mak-ing of new combinations to solve problems the word "innovator" be used. The big question he asked of the conference was: "What are the opportunities and limits of action for innovators in the 20th Century Technological Society?" Some of the answers, and some new questions developed at IDC follow.

what! no principles?

Joseph McGarry, like Parkinson, deplored the confused image designers have made of themselves and the lack of profession-wide principles. The designer, he says, "lives on his ability to change things, even though he knows that change is not always an improvement. The commercial requirement of styled obsolescence clashes with his professional pride."

To the designer who thinks he is misunderstood, Mr. McGarry thinks the shoe might be on the wrong foot. The designer complains he is working at too low a corporate level, that he should be a policy maker. But, "It is not an uncommon complaint among businessmen that the designer they hired to improve a package presented a proposal that would have obsoleted his whole warehousing and distribution system...it shows that he has not yet found his true place in business."

a fadist movement in design...

"With nearly one million active corporations in the United States, all of whom require some services from a designer, he has relatively few instances to show where his full influence was felt. Where once he had to prod and plug for change, he now finds himself caught up in a world changing so fast that it is using up his ideas faster than he can create them and is encouraging a faddist movement in design."

Joseph McGarry, Vice President, Public Affairs International Minerals & Chemical Corp.

a British Vance Packard?

With all the unanswered questions being bounced around under Aspen's tent, Leslie Julius answered some that weren't asked. Like Vance Packard, he deplored economic waste resulting from corporate greed. From London he saw both our coasts. "Large areas of Los Angeles are sinking into the sea because of the removal of oil from beneath its foundations...whilst the whole of the Eastern seaboard, which is becoming one vast industrial urbanized area, is being salinated because of the removal of its fresh water resources." Mr. Julius also deplored small businesses being squeezed out by the corporations.

Ultimately he sees industry demanding ever greater markets, encouraging population explosions and further depletion of our resources. This is akin to Packard's argument in "The Wastemakers" (McKay, 1960). Julius thinks architects, town planners, designers and thinkers must come to the rescue. He asks, and answers: "Will industry cooperate? I doubt it."

Leslie Julius, S. Hille & Co. Ltd. British furniture manufacturer

profits plus social obligation...

If Joseph McGarry seemed to be telling simply how the designer could help corporations make bigger profits, and Leslie Julius bluntly tagged corporations as social evils, Dr. Traugott Malzan suggested profit-making and social responsibility were compatible.

"We should be lenient toward large corporations...they have to make profits to continue to exist. If they produce products that won't sell, nobody profits, the designer included. ...Industry must serve both a civilizing and cultural purpose. It must acknowledge its sociological obligation."

How it could do all this while manufacturing genocidal weapons was wondered aloud in Aspen by John Meehan of the Martin Company.

Dr. Traugott Malzan, Heads Radio, Phono, TV Dept. in Communications and Design Div. of Max Braun, West German manufacturer of electrical appliances.

a corporation is like a painting...

After the representatives of large, medium and small corporations had had their say, one of the first to offer the viewpoint of the designer was Eliot Noyes. To Mr. Noyes a design program for a corporation is useful and valid only if it attempts to identify the character and meaning of the company in context with the more significant aspects of our society and economy. Most so-called 'corporate image' programs, he finds, deal in synthetic images and so are as superficial as wallpaper.

"A corporation should be like a good painting; everything visible should contribute to the correct total statement; nothing visible should detract ... such a program can help a corporation think more clearly about its goals."

designer's obstacle course ...
Some corporate blocks to design effectiveness listed by Noyes were:
* key executive exercising personal esthetic preferences irrelevant to the problem
* introduction of "other" designers into program destroying concept's single-mindedness
* committees (a camel is a greyhound designed by a committee).
* too much research reliance (you might get Edselled)
* budgets
* difficulty of contact with key people
* autonomous subdivisions

Eliot Noyes, architect, industrial designer, and Consultant Design Director for IBM

designers must know more ...
"We designers must know more, we must collect and formulate our knowledge so that we can take our place alongside economists and technicians as comrades and helpers and not as opponents. Economists and technicians have a decided advantage when it comes to factual arguments and results. They ... operate in a field in which values can be measured. But what are the measures for harmony and balance, fantasy and beauty? ... It is the designer's lack of knowledge of the function and results of his efforts that has hitherto confined him to the role of a creator of containers and outer dress."

Olle Eksell, a Swedish freelance artist (studied engineering for four years)

too much mediocrity ...
"Why is degenerative design sponsored, praised and propagated? There has been too much glorification of the commonplace. A seemingly relentless propulsion to make small accomplishments into essential and eternal verities. An urgency to render everything an act of genius. A compelling insistence to evert truth for the sake of merchandising. A deliberate aim to foster mass value as the criterion of our culture."

Craig Ellwood, architect

outside the corporation ...
Mr. Ellwood believes the corporation needs the designer more than vice versa, and that the designer's place is outside the organization to preserve his "identity, integrity, dignity." He must remain free from corporate poli-

tics. "I prefer to eat, sleep and drink design rather than to eat, sleep and drink corporation."

It was questioned whether Mr. Ellwood is able to practice his own beliefs. Dr. Malzan suggested that Mr. Ellwood is a corporation since he heads up a design organization of about 25.

the future ...
"When corporations come to recognize the importance of design and communications there will be a demand for designers such as there now is for scientists and engineers." That was Vernon Welsh's opinion. But he, too, had more questions than answers. He questioned the designer's readiness to serve the corporation.

"Designers seldom come to us with an integrated design proposal. ... Could it be that designers are not bold enough ... could it be that designers are not imaginative enough to challenge the corporation's present programs of advertising ... could it be they are not studious enough to read annual reports and other company publications ... or are they not well enough self-educated to understand the sociological importance of the problem?"

Vernon M. Welsh, communications consultant, former VP, General Dynamics Corp.

position gaining vs problem solving ...
One of the weaknesses of the corporation is the individual's greater concern with his own position than with the corporate objective. Stressing the "Organization Man" theory, Paul Fine sees little room for creativity and the creative man in the corporation, feels he must best work outside it. He believes that society will change and the future of creativity depends on such social changes. The corporation, even now, is changing to make room for individuality and creativity. (One of the other speakers had called attention to special rules for research scientists, such as no fixed hours). But for the moment, conformity pressures in the corporation often force the corporation to go outside for creative talent. Although Mr. Fine sees present corporate structure impeding creativity he seems to see pressures both from within the corporation and outside it that are bringing a little closer the day of corporation-creativity togetherness.

Paul A. Fine, Exec. VP, Center for Research in Marketing Inc.

a quantity of quality ...
Paul Reilly favors corporate bigness. "This seems to be the way of the world ... one may regret certain losses of individuality or of personal service ... but the advantages in universal availability greatly outweigh these handicaps. I agree with the English economist, Graham Hutton, that through mass production and the power of great corporations, we may be approaching for the first time in history the possibility of quantity of quality." Mr. Reilly also:
* suggested government patronage to encourage design innovators
* said the deciding classes have lost their cultural nerve, and that
* perhaps the designer has not sold himself properly
* reported that those in power are afraid to patronize innovators
* and suggested that therefore some kind of patronage must step in, perhaps governmental
* recommended that we isolate the key factor in our times that most significantly affects design and exploit it. This force, claims Mr. Reilly, is mobility.

Tokyo's Aspen ...
Design leaders from around the world gathered in Tokyo in May, 1960 to make the World Design Conference a cross-roads of ideas. The courtesy of the hosts almost became a fault. Designer Herbert Pinzke reports, "I found the Japanese people courteous and thoughtful in the welcome they extended to all of us. During the conference this became a slight drawback because it meant that we were not able to come to grips with problems on occasion simply because of a reluctance to disagree."

clogged roads ...
"Messages are not communication unless they are received and understood. If they become the basis for action, they have not only communicated, they have motivated. And that is the real goal of a message. Communication is like a two-way street ... or a busy intersection in the heart of any big city ... like those avenues of physical communication, so have the roads of aural and visual communication become clogged with a surfeit of traffic. If we are to purposefully fulfill our role as designers ... we must accept our share of responsibility for whatever we add to the

traffic snarl.... A vital part of our job is to ... simplify and clarify messages. Communication is the growing edge of understanding." (Herbert Pinzke)

individuality an illusion ...

"For centuries European art has turned its back on the fundamental conception of nature in art, and Western man has imagined himself and Nature as being in antithesis. In reality, his much-vaunted individuality is an illusion, and the truth which the Orient now reveals to him is that his identity is not separate from Nature and his fellow-beings, but is at one with her and them." (Christopher Tunnard, "Gardens in the Modern Landscape")

designing demand ...

"The producer ... regards design as one of the elements determining demand.... The designer is a builder who includes the man as part of a system. Arts and crafts activities do not make this consideration. They give the product its latest fashioned look by considerations of style. And here lies the danger of the present design-popularization. We all are extremely subjected to this danger when we are willing to work primarily ... for market stimulation.... The collaboration of the individual designer must contribute toward increased use-value of a product." (Hans Guelot) (Mr. Guelot does not oppose use of design to increase sales, suggests that sales value will derive from emphasis on use-value.)

undesigned design ...

"I am an industrial designer who doubts existing popular industrial design.... I have often thought that design would be much improved if there were no designer ... for example, airplane, baseball glove, experimental instruments such as a beaker or flask that are not designer designed but are anonymously designed with consideration only to function are very healthy." (Sori Yanagi)

impulse design ...

"Salesmen request the designer to design what may attract the consumer. This is so-called impulse design ... it is not a matter of value of product but of its surface ... such a product is wearied out as soon as it is bought. Again people begin to look for the next novel product. Here is a trap of salesmanship. It turns after

fashion and fans it by means of mass communications ... is not this a mere makeshift of short sight profit? What a loss it is for the factory if they are always to change the model.... Even for the consumer, isn't it wasteful?" (Sori Yanagi)

the same ... yet different

"Individuality creates the face and expression of the work of art, and of the two elements of design, the machine and beauty, it penetrates more deeply into the side of beauty. People have the desire to have the same thing as others, and at the same time they also have the desire to have different things ... if we were to equate the former with the essence and the latter with externals, the essence would be function and the external would be esthetic variation. ... Individuality exists in order to satisfy the desire for esthetic variation. Good design is something created by individuality." (Yusaku Kamekura)

individuality crushed ...

"The problem in Japan is: how to give individuality a place within enterprise. But in America, one has the feeling, the individuality, particularly of the graphic designer, is being crushed by the intense progress in technology and culture." (Bruno Munari)

a less pressurized economy ...

If Lawrence A. Mayer, Fortune Associate Editor, is correct, pressures on our economy due to World War II and the Korean War have been felt as a series of recessions of wrinkles rather than the customary post-war depression. Mr. Mayer told the 11th Atlanta Advertising Institute that the wrinkles are smoothing out, that advertising will soon be operating in a less pressurized economy. In such an economy. said Mr. Mayer. ". . . a dollar is going to be harder to earn and therefore it will be more carefully spent. So, prices, as well as cost of upkeep, will become more important to the consumer. For an example you need look no further than the nearest compact car. Consumers may be less diverted by novelties and more interested in the fundamental needs a product can fill. By the same token, the utility of a product will have to be more clearly demonstrated to the buyer. For examples of the foregoing think of the

simplified appliances now making their appearance. Business will be applying still more ingenuity and thought to its operations than at present, and that includes advertising and merchandising. Competition will be keener. More established market patterns, as in autos and in cigarettes, may be upset. And all this adds up, of course, to one thing—selling anything will be tougher."

pressureless growth ...

One of the chief advocates of the growth economy is Arno H. Johnson, Vice President and Senior Economist of J. Walter Thompson Co. Writing in Advertising Age, Mr. Johnson sees growth the answer to inflation by keeping productivity up and unit costs down. Aggressive marketing, not tight money, is the way to encourage production and stop inflation. He writes:

"Expansion of total consumption is an important key to our economic strength. In stimulating the continuing betterment of our standard of living, advertising is to become a factor of increasing influence in our economy.

"The past six years have demonstrated how essential it is to have a growing consumer demand—a consumption growth to keep pace with increases in production ability and capacity. Unfortunately, there once was wide acceptance of the old theory that demand and purchasing power must be curtailed to avoid inflation. This originally was based on the belief that inflation is caused by 'too much money chasing too few goods.'

"Actually our experience of the last six years—1953 to 1959—would indicate that when there is no real shortage of supply of goods, and when we have excess productive capacity, any slowdown in demand lowers productivity, increases unit costs, and creates pressures for price rises to protect profits. Thus, slowing demand can be inflationary.

". . . Our economy is so fundamentally sound, however, that any slowdown in consumer demand should be temporary and should not interfere with the opportunity for rapid growth in 1961 and over the next ten years. . . .

"So expansion of consumption to match our increased productive ability is the major task facing marketing, advertising, and selling today. Increasing total consumer demand by 10% by 1961 could be a powerful force in checking inflation through making possible increased productivity and lower costs per unit.

meeting consumer attitudes . . .

The companies that will ride the economic growth wave in the face of stiff competition will be those that best understand and appeal to new consumer attitudes. This was the conclusion of the Brand Image Symposium sponsored in 1960 by Walter Landor and Associates. Dr. Ernest Dichter summed up the changes in consumer attitudes.

"(1) **Today's consumer has a much higher aesthetic appreciation:** She responds to superior package design, wants attractive packages in her kitchen and on her table; she appreciates and demands many imported food items of gourmet quality.

"(2) **She has changed her attitude toward advertising:** Television scandals have left their scars—she is less easily led; she may tolerate brash advertising, but is no longer hypnotized by it.

"(3) **Customers want to feel they are 'in partnership'—psychologically—with a company whose products they buy:** Consumers want companies to 'take them into their confidence,' explain why a new product is being introduced, why a new package design is being launched; this is particularly important now that customers are fighting against the 'increased misery of choice.' A manufacturer may want to add an item "to complete its line," but that is not reason enough for its potential customers.

"(4) **Consumers are more sure of themselves:** Most Americans have a four-generation tutelage of advertising behind them—they are better educated, more sophisticated; they know what they want, and insist on relying on their own judgment.

"(5) **A hunger for quality in products and packaging can be seen everywhere:** The average consumer is ready to pay more—in some cases a great deal more—if the quality story is properly presented; she has shown, for instance, that she is more than willing to pay for convenience packaging.

"(6) **A strong desire exists at the consumer level for change:** There is a basic expectation that a manufacturer should not stand still—that he should move ahead, be it with an improved product or package; 'What have you done for me recently?' is a common consumer attitude. 'Operation Day-Dream,' then, should be on every company's agenda to keep bringing future products into the present.

"(7) **Increased individualism characterizes today's consumer:** A consumer will go out of her way to purchase a specific product if she feels that product or its package design is more 'her'; she will also buy several varieties of the same product group if she feels each fills a special need.

"(8) **Consumer markets are changing:** The usual type of socio-economic group indexing is on its way out— it is no longer as relevant with the vast re-distribution of income. ('A man who is making $10,000 this year for the first time should not be classified with the man who has been making this amount for a number of years.')"

bad art drives out good art . . .

The mass media "destroy both creativity and good taste . . . It seems to be a modern law that bad art drives out good art . . . A deluge of trashy material is flooding us. It is difficult for any man to keep his head above this bilge and his eye fixed on the good . . . It is a dreary prospect. I don't see any signs of increasing awareness of people to the importance of art."

Playwright, Elmer Rice, speaking at the University of Michigan

how to weaken creativity . . .

Cooperation aids creativity, competition hinders it, according to University of Michigan Professor of Design Arre K. Lahti.

"Competition brings forth expediency and not basic contributions."

He cited these factors which destroy or weaken creativity:

"Possessiveness stifles creativity, while sharing does not . . . secretiveness defeats but openness produces . . . evasiveness corrodes, while the willingness to make commitments refreshes . . . the rejection of group participation retards, while the awareness of the inseparable nature of the need for others accelerates . . . and finally, the fear of being wrong is the most insidiously debilitating of all these factors, since at best we are seldom more than partially right."

creativity attracts clients . . .

The co-founder of Y&R and president of John Orr Young Associates told the Association of National Advertisers workshop on advertising management that for attracting new clients, creativity beats presentations.

"I have always been attracted to the creative people in advertising— the creative writers, the versatile art directors and artists, the resourceful salesmen, the planners, the creative research and media men.

"One agency possessing the beforementioned characteristics is located in Chicago and the output of this agency is so interesting, seeable and convincing that the agency is establishing some brilliant new records in the agency field. It is what might be called a 'fun agency.'

"The boss' greatest fun is working and he has surrounded himself with employers and officers of the same sort. They work so joyously, early and late, that it is no wonder the agency is going places. If they develop a touch of indigestion, they merely need to take fewer of the many accounts offered them.

"There are seven smaller agencies and five larger ones in New York, each acquiring account after account and building enviable reputations for character, sound planning and creativity.

"Each of these agencies abhors mediocrity. Their dedication is to competitive creativity—a deep desire within the consciousness of each man to create something better today than yesterday's best.

"° ° ° Their creativity is not limited to copy and art, but includes all phases of modern marketing.

"They spend less time on presentations to prospective clients than most agencies I know, but they are attracting more new clients of a high order than the agencies who are making the greatest number of time-consuming solicitations of accounts."

point of no return . . .

While some ad men worried about the best climate for creativity and others were looking under couches for hidden motives, company executives were largely concerned with advertising's point of diminishing return.

As reflected by the Van Diver studies in Printers' Ink, fewer were asking if advertising paid, more were asking how to get the most out of it, at what point does its value becomes less than its cost. For example, General Foods Corp. executive vice president C. W. Cook told the annual meeting of the Advertising Research Foundation, " 'How much advertising' is the most outstanding challenge facing advertising and marketing research today . . . When a product becomes mature, advertising and promotion become more and more difficult." Mr. Cook agreed with the economic growth theories of Arno Johnson and others in calling for advertising progress "at a time when we need all the economic power we can muster."

media credibility . . .
In a time when management wants more effective advertising, consumer attitudes are becoming increasingly skeptical. But, wary of such generalizations, the ad and promotion planners ask what are the most effective appeals, the most believed in messages and media.

To help answer this, consumer attitudes toward media were studied by Louis Cheskin Associates, using motivation research techniques. Some of the findings:
• Television, of all the media, has the largest number of associations with such words as "pleasing" and "like best," but also with "false, irritating, insincere, in bad taste, not beneficial, deceptive and like least."
• Newspapers have the largest number of associations with "true, informative, sincere, in good taste, beneficial, honest, important."
• Radio, TV, magazines are considered more for women and newspapers and billboards are considered more for men.
• Favorable associations ranking: newspaper advertising 83% magazine advertising 76%, TV 49%, radio 34%, billboards 31%. This "favorable association" rating reveals a big switch in consumer attitudes toward media since 1957. At that time a similar study reported: TV 84%, newspapers 59%, magazines 53%, billboards 28%, radio 19%.

to make friends, don't outrage . . .
Outdoor advertising men are perhaps more sensitive to consumer attitudes toward their media than are most ad men. The government harrasses them with legislation or threats of legislative restrictions. At the International Congress of Outdoor Advertising, held in mid-1960 in Toronto, London's Ashley Havinden said, "After all, the job of advertising— in all its forms—for Big Business today is to 'make friends with the public.' This can never be done by outraging

them. This can only be done successfully when all the resources of art and design are mustered to the task."

Mr. Havinden recognizes that outdoor advertising is unpopular, feels that bad taste is at fault. His diagnosis and prescription:

"If outdoor advertising is not to become finally so unpopular that resentment will lead to its being legislated against—then the qualified artist and designer must be brought much more into the picture.

"The artist's advice must be sought early in the planning of outdoor campaigns—because he represents the public's point of view. He knows what shapes and colors, and in particular letter forms, will attract the eye of the public, and hold its interest.

"The artist must be treated by advertisers and their contractors as a planning equal—and not as a hack to be ordered about by businessmen.

the art of interruption . . .
"The good artist and designer specializing in the poster field knows that, in the same way that people don't buy newspapers and magazines in order just to look at the advertisements—so they don't walk down the streets of towns—or go into the countryside—in order only to see posters and 3-D spectaculars.

"(a) Outdoor advertising, therefore, to be successful in attracting the public's attention must practise what might be called 'The Art of Interruption'!

"(b) The only justification for interrupting people is to do them a service. In the case of outdoor advertising—it must be a 'visual' service. People must enjoy being interrupted!

"(c) To derive pleasure from viewing a piece of outdoor advertising, it **must be attractive to look at!** Only thus will its message be studied, and the product advertised be admired and remembered.

Ostentation . . .
"Outdoor advertising—if it is to succeed in interrupting people's vision— must, also by its nature, be ostentatious. Since we've all been brought up to regard ostentation as being synonymous with Bad Taste—the big problem, therefore, facing the advertiser and his advisors is how to 'interrupt' with Good Taste!

"(a) This is where brilliant artists and designers can help. With their

knowledge of form, color and typography, they know best how to make dramatic, and at the same time beautiful designs, which in terms of 'visual communication' will attract the eye and convey the message with the maximum speed.

"(b) The coming of the motorcar has made the old-fashioned academic techniques of pictorial expression obsolete! The modern poster and outdoor sign must act swiftly if it is to communicate successfully. The designer is now required to produce what might be called 'visual telegrams.'

"(c) To interrupt!—and attract people's attention!—to be ostentatious— and yet be in good taste—**and to do it swiftly—is a formidable task!**"

truth and taste . . .
With consumers and legislators reacting strongly to many advertising abuses, advertisers, agencies and media have been on the defensive for the past few years. Printers' Ink, which in 1959 and again in 1960 ran depth reports on truth and taste in advertising, reports some progress:
• "The Federal Trade Commission has been considerably more effective in eliminating illegal deception.
• "The local better business bureaus and the National Better Business Bureau are exerting considerably more influence in controlling deceptions before they require legal action.
• "The advertising associations are showing much more leadership in encouraging high standards of truth and taste in advertising."

an idea in action . . .
Amid the welter of talks, conferences, books on the importance of research and how, teamed with creativity, it can make for more successful advertising, just a few companies, agencies, advertisers practice what is widely preached. One of three few is McCurdy's department store in Rochester and agency Charles L. Rumrill. McCurdy's new ads are visually fresh and exciting. They grew out of research (as did the Hathaway eye patch). Here is the case history report on McCurdy's FFR (Favorable Feminine Reaction) technique.
When, where, how do women buy . . . and why? What makes a women prefer one department store to another? What makes identical merchandise more desirable in one store than in a competitive establishment?

How can a store win and hold customers?

These, and may more, were the questions in mind when The Rumrill Company, Advertising Agency of Rochester, New York, undertook a study of women and their shopping habits, preferences, motives, likes and dislikes when it came to department store shopping. The research paved the way for the mood-making, symbol-building, women-influencing advertising campaign which appeared weekly in 1960 in Rochester newspapers for McCurdy and Co. local department store.

The McCurdy effort has scored three department store "firsts." The first depth research of the customer herself. The first use of a new research technique—semantic differential. The first advertising campaign based wholly on beliefs and principles uncovered by the research findings. McCurdy's concern with the "sameness of department store advertising, with the lack of tangible results from a large proportion of daily newspaper space, and a conviction that retail advertising **could** do a better job were responsible for the investigation and their series of advertisements.

FR . . .

The effort has been labeled "FR." It stands for **feminine reaction.** The basic research undertook to determine feminine reaction to department stores, in general, and to McCurdy's in particular. A significant section of the depth-probing effort was conducted by Doctor Vincent Nowlis and Dr. Helen Nowlis of the Psychology Department of the University of Rochester. They set up criteria for an **ideal department store.** They measured the factors of youth, excitement, friendship, dependability, security, satisfaction, and more . . . and **emerged with a profile of McCurdy's,** a pattern of acceptance and rejection which established a firm feminine reaction. The pattern gave the store **an unprejudiced look** at its present and prospective market.

FFR . . .

Once "FR" was established the advertising agency set about supplying the principles that had been uncovered and incorporating them in a series of newspaper pages for the store. These pages sought to establish "FFR"—**favorable** feminine reaction for McCurdy's

Having determined that over 85% of the store's merchandise moved out because of "FFR" it became objective of the advertising to establish an "FFR" symbolism—in the case of McCurdy's—a helpful friend, a dependable neighbor, an understanding, benevolent, wise, witty, wordly, knowing champion of women. Not an organization, not an impersonal institution, not a commercial company —but a friend—a woman's **special** friend.

The investigation had established the fact that "FFR" endows goods with certain characteristics, bestows on the store a highly individual personality, creates a mood which makes identical merchandise more desirable in one store than in another.

The achieving of "FFR" for McCurdy's was a goal set up with full knowledge of strengths and shortcomings, a completely objective approach to (1) increasing McCurdy's share of the market (2) increasing dollar sales (3) establishing McCurdy's as a state-of-mind that would sell goods on a non-competitive basis. For research had proved that it was a state of mind, FFR—that brought a woman into a **specific department store** in spite of competitive price claims, competitive lures, a multitude of new and open doors.

Why does a woman visit department stores? Primarily to keep abreast. A store is her chief source of information. In a store she learns what is new, what is right, what is changing. She uses the store as a stage. It is a place where she day-dreams, acts out her hopes and desires.

What does she look for? She is constantly looking for the articles, the stories, the pictures, the stores, the advertising with which she can identify herself. She pictures herself as a certain type of person and she automatically allies herself with anything she sees, or reads, or experiences that is associated with the person she wants to be.

What stores did she prefer? Shopping is an expression of her personality. She prefers the store that reflects a view of life consistent with her own. A store that offers merchandise that fits in with her home, or her vision of what she wants her home to be. She looks first to the store that mirrors her own personality, her own hopes and dreams. She forms a mental and spiritual alliance with the store that reflects herself. She forms

a special rapport with one store above all others. That store becomes hers.

She judges stores in terms of herself. Her ideas and her attitudes are influenced chiefly by her conception, and her practice of **family life, religion, group activities, and suburban living.**

What was her attitude toward a price ticket? She has a new attitude toward a bargain. There is less and less economic reason for penny pinching. She is under no compulsion to buy the cheapest. To her a bargain is the better buy—not the lowest price in dollars and cents.

What is the dominant buying urge? A woman's basic urge to better her family is perhaps the single greatest factor in the growth of the economy for the next decade.

What is her greatest need? Recognition as an individual, commendation, approval, a secure and satisfying commercial womb, to which to return. In the maze of new products, the surge of new ideas, new manners, new philosophies . . . she looks for reassurance, for direction, for authority, for approval of her procedures. One of the most important things a department store can supply is a mature and parental approval, an authoritative guidance, a surety to fall back upon. A store must justify purchases, solve problems, provide security and comfort to which she may return.

Mr. Gilbert G. McCurdy, General Manager of McCurdy's sums up the attitude of the store management: "We at McCurdy's believe that a woman's concept of our whole store is just as important as her impressions of any item or any department. Her impressions of our standards, our policies, our service and our people make up, in her mind, an over-reaction which is symbolic of McCurdy's. We have endeavored by our series of newspaper messages to establish McCurdy's as the store that understands women. The results have been so tangible and specific that McCurdy's is following the pattern for the second year."

what's the big idea?

Perhaps the big idea is one that is successfully applied. Like the eyepatch, or the McCurdy's campaign.

what's new in typefaces?

Shown here are new typefaces introduced during the past year by leading American and European type founders. New sizes are reported for older faces.

Amsterdam Continental has added a 48 and 60 to Juliet and a 72 to Slogan. Intertype has added 6, 10, 11 Royal with bold; 8, 9, 10, Royal with italic and small caps; 36 Futura demibold; 7 Futura Book with oblique; 18 Futura medium condensed with bold condensed; 5½, 7, 11 News Gothic condensed with bold condensed; 7 Baskerville with italic and small caps; 9, 11 Bodoni Bold with italic and small caps; 8, 10 David Hebrew medium with bold; 7 Lambrakis Greek. New Ludlow sizes are: Record Gothic bold italic, 12; Record Gothic bold extended italic, 12, 14; Record Gothic extended, 6, 8, 10, 12; Record Gothic bold, 6, 8, 10; Condensed Gothic No. 2, 12, 14; Franklin Gothic, 84; Tempo Black extended, 60, 72; Tempo Bold condensed, 84; Tempo Bold extended, 12, 14. New Mergenthaler Linotype sizes include Trade Gothic extended with bold, 8, 12; Trade Gothic bold with light, 18; Spartan Extra Black, 30; Aurora with Bold Face No. 2, 8½. In addition to the data given here, both Intertype Corp. and Mergenthaler Linotype Co. have made additions to their news and teletypesetter faces.

For showings of typefaces, address the manufacturers or distributors as follows:

American Type Founders Co., Inc.
200 Elmora Avenue
Elizabeth, New Jersey
American Wood Type Mfg. Co.
42-25 9th St.
Long Island City, New York
Amsterdam Continental
276 Park Ave. S.
New York 10, New York
Bauer Alphabets, Inc.
235 E. 45th St.
New York 17, New York
Intertype Corp.
360 Furman Street
Brooklyn 1, New York
Lanston Monotype Co.
P.O. Box 4768
Philadelphia 34, Penna.
Ludlow Typograph Corp.
2032 Clybourn Ave.
Chicago 14, Illinois
Mergenthaler Linotype Co.
29 Ryerson St.
Brooklyn 5, New York

Craw Clarendon Con

ATF—14, 18, 24, 30, 36, 48, 60, 72, 84, 96

univers

ATF—Univers 55; 6, 8, 10, 12, 14, 18, 24 small, 24 large, 30, 36, 48

univers

ATF—Univers 56; 6, 8, 10, 12, 14, 18, 24 small, 24 large, 30, 36, 48

univers

ATF—Univers 65; 6, 8, 10, 12, 14, 18, 24 small, 24 large, 30, 36, 48

univers

ATF—Univers 66; 6, 8, 10, 12, 14, 18, 24 small, 24 large, 30, 36, 48

univers

ATF—Univers 75; 6, 8, 10, 12, 14, 18, 24 small, 24 large, 30, 36, 48

univers

ATF—Univers 76; 6, 8, 10, 12, 14, 18, 24 small, 24 large, 30, 36, 48

BRITANNIC

American Wood Type—8, 10, 12, 18, 24, 30, 36

BRITANNIC ITALIC

American Wood Type—8, 10, 12, 18, 24, 30, 36

BRITANNIC BOLD

American Wood Type—8, 10, 12, 14, 18, 24, 30, 36, 48

ABCDEFGHIJKLMN abcdefghijklmnopqr

Klang Bold
American Wood Type—18, 24, 30, 36, 48, 60, 72

ABCDEFGHIJKL abcdefghijklmnopqr

London Script
American Wood Type—14, 18, 24, 30, 36, 48

Mole' Foliate
American Wood Type—48, 60, 72

Allegro

Amsterdam Continental—12, 14, 16, 18, 24, 30#1, 30#2, 42, 54, 72

Amazone

Amsterdam Continental—14, 18, 24, 30, 36, 48, 60

LARGO LIGH

Amsterdam Continental—4/6, 6, 8, 10, 10/12, 12, 14, 16, 18, 24, 30#1, 30#2

LARGO BOI

Amsterdam Continental—4/6, 6, 8, 10, 10/12, 12, 14, 16, 18, 24, 30#1, 30#2

Standard Italic

Amsterdam Continental—8, 10, 12, 14, 18, 24 small, 24 large, 30, 36

Standard Medium Itali

Amsterdam Continental—8, 10, 12, 14, 18, 24 small, 24 large, 30, 42

Folio Medium Extended Italic

Bauer—16, 18, 30, 42

Laurel

Fotosetter

Laurel Italic

Fotosetter

Laurel Bold

Fotosetter

Times Bold

Fotosetter

News Gothic Italic 206

Lanston Monotype—6, 7, 8, 9, 10, 11, 12

News Gothic Bold Condensed 205

Lanston Monotype—6, 7, 8, 9, 10, 11, 12

Record Gothic Ex. It

Ludlow—12, 14, 18, 24, 30, 36, 48

Tempo Alternate Bc

Ludlow—10, 12, 14, 18, 24, 30, 36, 42, 48, 60, 72

Tempo Alternate Heavy

Ludlow—10, 12, 14, 18, 24, 30, 36, 42, 48, 60, 72

Tempo Black Ex.

Ludlow—12, 14, 18, 24, 30, 36, 48

what's new in production...

printing, platemaking, paper and typographic developments speed presswork, upgrade quality, offer new effects

LETTERPRESS

The big drive in recent years has been to cut production time and costs while maintaining or improving quality. Target has been a better competitive position with respect to lithography. Meaningful progress has been made in these areas:

- increased use of rotary press for greater speed, many with web feed
- wrap-around plates to cut original and duplicate plate costs, reduce press down time before actual running
- development of lightweight plates
- reduction of makeready time
- rapid, one-bite etching of photoengravings

A wrap-around printing plate is flexible enough to be wrapped around the printing cylinder. Offset plates and rubber plates have long used the wraparound principle. News today is being made by a thin etched direct printing letterpress plate. Some of its features:

> WRAP-AROUNDS . . .
> - plate costs reduced so as to be comparable to offset costs

- sharp, clean impression with full tone range
- ability to maintain color fidelity throughout a long run
- can use enough ink to achieve brilliance and full coverage
- elimination of makeup and lockup time
- great reduction in makeready time
- use of rotary press makes speed comparable to offset
- plates are good for long runs, can be chrome-plated for extra-long runs
- eliminates need for electros
- can utilize step-and-repeat method for multi-image printing
- plates can be metal (zinc, copper, magnesium) rapid- etched or one of the new plastic compositions such as Dycril
- presses have been specially built to use the thin wrap-arounds. They have a precision inking mechanism, necessary to cover the plate in one rolling without filling in the shallow etch (about ⅓ that of conventional plates).
- the press was developed by Harris Intertype Corp.
- a nylon wrap-around plate has been developed by Merganthaler Linotype Co. It is a long-life plate with automatic makeready features, is lightweight, flexible, requires no metal backing
- for book printing plastic printing surface has been bonded to a rubber plate. Developed by Cambridge University Press

Wrap-around plates are in commercial use in some plants, are being tested in others. The newspaper industry is particualrly interested in them. A breakthrough in their wide use is considered imminent.

PHOTOPOLYMERS, ETC. . . .

Materials that can be etched more rapidly, more successfully, more economically than metal also moved a step nearer wide commercial use this year. Best known of these is Du Pont's Dycril. It can be made for flat-bed or rotary printing, is suited to the new wrap-around press. At present, its cost is high, so that the plates are not economically suited to all jobs.

To get the best results from a Dycril plate the halftone negative must be "engineered" to a perfect balance of exposure and development.

The Dycril material is not chemically sensitive, like film, but, when exposed to ultra-violet light physically hardens and becomes insoluble. Exposed plate is washed out in a high-pressure alkaline spray. Total platemaking time is less

than 20 minutes. So far, platemaking economy compensates largely for high material cost. When and if Du Pont can get material cost down, Dycril plates will represent a real plate economy. Plates have excellent ink affinity, can run for over a million impressions, thus eliminating electros.

The nylon plate developed by Merganthaler Linotype is made from the negative in 8 minutes. The specially formulated nylon is sensitized in a fluid for 2 minutes, exposed under conventional arc lamp for another two minutes, then developed by rubbing for about 4 minutes on a solvent-damp pad. All that remains is mounting for the printing method desired. Commercial potential is now being studied.

RAPID ETCH . . .

Powderless (one bite) etching, commerically introduced a few years ago, is now used all over the world, the Dow-Etch process alone having more than 700 licensees in the United States and Canada. Once limited to magnesium or magnesium-zinc alloys, and not capable of handling combination plates, it is now used for zinc, magnesium, or copper. Experienced shops use it successfully for line or halftone or combination work. It speeds etching, cleans up the process by eliminating the dragons blood dusting between bites, gives more ideal dots without undercutting. At present powderless etched plates are the same cost as conventionally etched plates on the same metal. The chief customer advantage is in the superior molding and printing quality of the plate.

ELECTROTYPES . . .

One trend is toward level-impression printing. This implies precision platemaking (especially with respect to plate thickness) and more accurate press adjustments. The printing face of the electro is levelled to within .001" of a plane and plate thickness is controlled to within plus or minus .001". Precision platemaking is superseding the premadeready plate, developed in the '20s, which featured mechanically raising the plane in shadow areas, lowering highlight areas, so that some makeready was built into the plate, reducing press makeready.

Magazine printing has required lighter weight plates. To meet this need laminated plates were developed. A curved electro shell is adhesive bonded to a curved aluminum backing. In connection with the laminated curved press plates, a new system of locking the plates to the press offers quality control advantages. Instead of locking down by means of keys on bevelled edges, small areas are scarfed into plate backs. When tension is applied the plates are engaged by holdown clamps. This permits plate butting, thus wider use of bleeds, reduction of paper waste, more accurate register, higher press speeds.

Plastic, rather than aluminum backing, also lightens plate weight. Among the plastic backings used now are the PPR or Electroplastic Plate and the Bista plate. In both cases an adhesive is applied to the back of the electro shell and a plastic applied to it, in the proper thickness, is allowed to harden. The Bista plate is backed in a curved position. It is as durable as a conventional electro but weighs one-sixth as much.

The weight reduction of the aluminum and plastic backed plates cuts centrifugal force on the revolving cylinder, permits higher press speeds without throwing the plates, or flexing of plates on the cylinder. These plates also claim to cut makeready time.

Other new plates include the Plastalum and the E-Z Plate. The former is made by CSW Plastic Types Inc. The latter is made by other platemakers but the material is supplied by CSW. The plates are the same. E-Z is a duplicate plate composed of plastic and aluminum. It has dimensional stability, long press life, can be used on rotary or flat-bed presses. The plastic printing surface is molded; heat and pressure, form a mold of the original form.

Another plastic and aluminum plate is the Color-Line electro developed by Printing Plate Supply Co. of Chicago. Here a copper or copper-nickel shell is deposited in conventional electro procedure, on a mold from the original. Instead of tin-bonding the shell to lead backing, an adhesive bonds the shell to a laminated backing consisting of two rigid vinylite sheets with a perforated aluminum center sheet. Plates can be made to a range of thicknesses and curvatures or supplied flat. The plate claims superiority through surface levelness, true arc of face, light weight (1¼ lbs. vs conventional 7.8 lbs.), press durability, suitability for tension lockup system described above.

MAKEREADY REDUCTION . . .
Reducing makeready time without cutting quali-

ty control is a major objective of current letterpress research. Many of the products and methods described above contribute toward this end. Improvements have also been made in the development of lightweight but dimensionally stable plate blocks to replace wood. Printers are also raising standards on precision lockup of forms, use of cleaner, unpitted unbroken type. Greater efforts are being made to control precision of material (paper, plates, type,) coming in to the pressroom.

Other letterpress developments include heatset inks which offer better drying at higher speeds for web printing. Speeds have moved from 600 feet per minute to 1600 and will soon reach 2000. Improved electronic register devices, automatic press feeders, high-speed binding machines, trimmers attached to binders, better web tension controls, electronic scanning, powderless etching of photoengravings, and the tension lockup system have enabled printers to improve quality at higher speeds and lower costs.

Thus the big trend of the year may well be the turning of the tide in the offset-letterpress battle. The '40s and '50s saw new lithographic technical and equipment developments up litho quality and cut costs so as to take much business from letterpress. At the start of the '60s the biggest new developments in both quality and cost control are on the letterpress side.

LITHOGRAPHY

Web offset is becoming bigger commercially (10 presses operating in 1950; 200+ today). Its ability to run four colors at several times the speed of sheet-fed presses, to use high-fidelity conversion negatives made by the Brightype process (there is said to be less quality loss than takes place when an electro is made from a photoengraving) and the development of long-life plates such as the Lithure and Lithengrave put the process in the long-run, high-speed, good quality, competitive cost category. Publications can accept letterpress material and make Brightype conversions. The process takes advantage of the economy of buying paper in rolls. With the use of bi-metallic plates, dampening is minimized, bright, sharp printing is possible on many letterpress grades of machine coateds.

LITHOGRAPHY IN THE '60s . . .
What is lithography doing to meet the stepped up challenge from letterpress? In the past dec-

ade some of the major developments were:
- presensitized plates
- copperized aluminum deepetch plates
- paper dampeners
- LTF sensitivity Guide
- new plate surface treatments
- non-binding lacquers
- fast-setting and heat-set inks
- machine coated offset papers
- dimensionally stable film bases
- contact screens
- improved masking techniques
- electronic scanning and color correcting

These add up to better tone and color control, faster and more economical production. Each was the result of laboratory research to meet a commercial need. Today research labs, such as the Lithographic Technical Foundation, Battelle Memorial Institute and others are working on other problems which they expect to lick in the '60s. These are:

- dampening. Mullen and Dahlgren Dampening Systems are being tested as replacements for the parchment paper dampeners. Aim is to use less water and the ink-water balance can be more quickly established. Ultimately the hope is to eliminate the dampening system by incorporating dampening material in the ink. This could represent a major advance in quality control.

- inking. Dampening improvements will make possible new ink-distribution systems, facilitate more even distribution of ink, get better ink flow through softer inks and less water.

- non-absorptive offset blankets. Absorbency of present materials affects ink control.

- inks. Instant-setting, softer inks, bluer and cleaner magenta inks and cleaner cyans are being developed.

- paper. Opacity in lighter weights is being increased. Better binding of pigment to sheet surface is also being studied. It is hoped to eliminate linting, dusting, tinting and to make papers less sensitive to moisture conditions. Such dimensionally stable paper would reduce curl, improve press operations and register.

- pre-sensitizing. All plates of the future will be presensitized, making for more standardization and performance predictability.

- electrostatics. Researchers are studying application of Xerography and Electrofax techniques for putting the image on the plate.

Other offset developments now in the labs are increased applications of phototypesetting with lithographic platemaking, more camera color composing to eliminate much stripping, more web printing.

GRAVURE

LOOK-KROMATIC . . .

As of January 1961 Look magazine boosted its number of Look-Kromatic pages from 12 to 24. The process is a gravure variation offering higher quality through greater gloss, deeper tone and color hue saturation and white-ink printing. A special ink, a new machine-coated paper and 10-color presses are used.

In conventional gravure uncoated paper is used and ink is absorbed by the paper fiber. In Look-Kromatic a coated, non-absorbent paper is used, the ink is heat-dried on the paper surface as in letterpress.

Copy of art suitable for letterpress is suitable for Look-Kromatic.

The process also employs a new halftone screen that extends tonal range, and makes possible a 400% ink coverage compared to the 240% limit in wet-letterpress. The result is a richer appearance with more depth and naturalness in lower key areas.

A 150-line screen gives good detail reproduction. Single-etch, automatic equipment gives greater dot depth control. Use of trailblade coated paper adds to ink sheen. Press has five cylinders on each side of the web, the fifth cylinder being used for white inking. The white ink is whiter than the best white paper, improves reproduction of copy with white areas.

HI-FI COLOR . . .

This is a method of getting uniform color quality in a schedule of newscolor ads. Process is gravure. Instead of letting each paper print the ad in a regular run, the whole schedule is printed by Marathon division of American Can Co. and supplied to each paper as an insert. Paper not only collates it and binds it in, but backs it up. Printing is on rolls, to diameter, width and core size of each publication. Printing cylinders are furnished by the advertiser.

FLEXOGRAPHY

Flexography is a variation of letterpress—using rubber plates, different ink formulations and presses—to make possible high-speed printing on such hard-to-print materials as cellophane, polyethylene, saran, foil, mylar, vinyl, Christmas wrappings, Scotch tape, plastic tablecloths, drinking cups, linoleum, etc.

Toward the end of 1958 the industry established its own research organization which is concerned with stepping up the training of personnel, establishing a glossary of terms for the rapidly growing process, making possible better quality and finer screen halftone reproduction and increasing the versatility of available color combinations.

SCREEN PROCESS

One of the chief developments in silk screen printing is the improvement in fluorescent inks. They are more brilliant, smoother, no longer require underprinting with white on many jobs. Faster drying inks are also being developed and the use of mechanical presses has become widespread, making the process more economical for longer press runs.

ELECTRONIC SCANNING

Potentially, electronically produced color separations can improve shadow detail, produce full clarity of detail, alter tone scales as required by the process, inks and paper to be used, all without resort to hand finishing. The potential is for a better plate, made more rapidly and economically, and with a naturalness that excessive hand finishing sometimes destroys.

If the scanners did all this today, every shop would have one. But they are constantly being improved and their costs are being reduced. Today, several scanners are in limited commercial use, others are about to enter the market. The PDI Electronic Scanner, for example, is available at scanner studios in Chicago and Stamford, Conn., in London, Paris and The Netherlands. The studios serve advertisers, national magazines, offset, gravure and letterpress printers and platemakers.

What scanning means to the art director and the production man is clear from some of their testimonials.

Brendan Wood, Production Director of Esquire, who uses PDI scanned separations, finds they "give our process color reproductions a consistent naturalness never before obtained with conventional separation systems."

Charles Tudor, AD of Life, reports:

"Life was the first and still is the largest client of the PDI Scanner." (also known as the Time-Life Scanner) ". . . normally the resultant separations are the best both in terms of color rendition and 'drawing' in all of the colors that we have ever seen."

McCall Photoengraving plant manager Frank Cox reports, "The functions of compression of brightness range, color making and undercolor removal necessary for four-color wet letterpress printing are performed by the PDI Scanner as programmed."

And McCall's magazine AD Otto Storch finds such separations plus good photoengraving technique at the plant "assist me in creating a consistent naturalness . . . much desired photographic clarity in both our conversions of flat art and transparency reproductions."

Essentially the scanners work as follows:

1. Color copy is scanned by a light source, a line at a time.

2. At any given instant a beam of light that represents the color of the spot being scanned is sent into the color separator unit.

3. Filters break the beam into three paths with colors corresponding to the strength of each primary color in the spot.

4. Photo tubes convert light into electricity. Thus three circuits are set up. The strength of any circuit at any instant is controlled by the intensity of the light being converted which in turn is controlled by the intensity of the corresponding primary color at the spot being scanned.

5. Previous settings control the operation of the color computer section. Here two chief objectives are accomplished.

a) colors are "corrected" by altering voltages in each circuit. This is done to compensate in advance for the effect the inks, color rotation, paper etc. will have on the reproduction.

b) voltage is subtracted from each circuit in proper proportion so as to permit the setting up of a fourth circuit for the black printer negative.

6. Each circuit activates an exposure lamp which varies in brightness as the circuit's voltage fluctuates.

7. The exposure lamp acts on a rotating sensitized film, exposing it synchronously with the scanning at the copy end. Thus the four separations are simultaneously exposed. They are then developed, put into the platemaking process much as any other separations except that little or no additional color correcting is required.

The PDI Scanner works from transparencies up to 8x10. Scanner Studios convert flat copy to transparencies when required. Scanned separations can be enlarged up to 300% for 500-lines per inch scanning, to 600% for 1000-lines per inch scanning. Normal delivery services for a set of color corrected separations is three days from receipt at studios.

The above description is based on the PDI Scanner. It is true in principal for most other scanners, although each has its own mechanical variations. The chief other scanners are:

• The Fairchild Scan-A-Color. Output is continuous tone, color corrected separations on film, three or four color, same size as original copy up to 8x10. Negatives or positives can be produced. Works equally well for any printing process. Scans 500 or 1000 lines to the inch. Scans an 8x10 of 500 lines per inch in 50 minutes. Can be adjusted to compensate for ink characteristics, customer copy changes, to improve weak copy, to accentuate highlight detail, shadow detail, to construct black printer for full value or for accent. Can produce halftone positives or negatives directly from the original. Works from transparencies or reflection copy that can be wrapped around a cylinder.

• The Colorgraph Scanner. This scanner is in operation in New York at the Collier Photoengraving Co. It is also known as the Hell Colorgraph, after its inventor, Dr. Rudolf Hell.

This scanner works from a photographically separated set of negatives rather than from original copy. It claims the advantage of being able to work more readily from a wider variety of copy, transparency or opaque, and to enlarge or reduce when making the photographic separations.

From three-color photo separations the Colorgraph can produce three or four fully color corrected continuous tone negatives or positives. These can be used for gravure, offset or letterpress. Maximum plate size is 12" x 15". Scanning time for a full-size set of plates is one hour and forty minutes. Undercolor removal and contrast range can be regulated within wide limits, as can color correction.

Other scanners being watched with interest in the American market are:

The Crosfield Scanatron (British); The Hell Vario-Klischograph (German); Hunter-Penrose H.P.K. Autoscan (British); Belin Belinograver (French) and the Miehle Color Scanner (U.S.A.).

The Scanatron, like the Colorgraph, corrects a set of photographically pre-separated negatives. The Vario-Klischograph scans original copy and produces color printing plates . . . screened, relief plates. It can enlarge or reduce, make plates up to 12¼" x 17".

PHOTOGRAPHY

If the trend toward more location photography has been impelled by the creative photographer's desire for the real thing it has been made possible by developments in film and equipment. The great improvement in picture quality in both b/w and color films makes possible better reproductions today from a 2¼ x 2¼ blowup than were possible 10 years ago with sheet film. Improved film quality encouraged manufacture and wider professional use of smaller commercial cameras, such as the Hasselblad. Coupled with portable electronic flash units the small camera enabled the photographer to shoot around his object, to vary angles, to shoot under much less favorable lighting conditions. It made possible more variety in composition, more on-location realism.

The big technical news in recent years has been in films, rather than equipment. Some of the key developments:

• faster b/w film: such as Agfa Isopan Record, 16 times as fast as the fastest pre-war film.

• faster finer grain developers, cutting developing time from 16-20 minutes to 2-3 minutes.

• variable contrast papers. Polycontrast, Varigam, Multigrade make it unnecessary for the photographers to stock four or five contrast grades.

• faster color films. Here's how some of today's films compare to 1940 Kodachrome's rating of 10. Anscochrome, 32; Ektachrome E3,50; Super Anscochrome, 100; and Highspeed Ektachrome, 160. And these are the "normal" ratings. The films can be forced. This makes possible more color action photography, shooting under lighting conditions with natural light that a few years ago would have yielded a poor picture or none at all.

• negative color materials (Ektacolor, Agfacolor) yield transparencies, opaque color prints, or b/w prints. They eliminate one processing step in making color prints or copies, don't sacrifice film speed since the compensating filter is eliminated, permits changing filtration in printing, eliminates reshooting for b/w since b/w print can be made from the color negative. System gives the photographer greater control over colors.

Process also is used to speed platemaking. The Denver Post has reported printing four-color pictures in its Sunday edition of the previous day's local football game. Negative color also makes it easier to get good color shots with a wider range of cameras.

• a new camera and film size may be in the making, 70mm. Film would not have paper backing. Air Force is experimenting with this camera, takes 400 pictures in 15 minutes.

• wider use of Polaroid Land Camera for test shooting.

• and, in the offing, Polaroid Land color film.

• increased use of dimensionally stable film bases

in graphic arts platemaking, replacing glass for critical register work. Du Pont's Cronar, Ansco's Plestar, EK's Estar are examples.

PAPER

Four major printing paper trends are:
- increased use of the bright white (fluorescent pigmented) papers and more grades being made bright white
- increased use of colored and textured papers
- more printing from rolls. As letterpress printers swing toward more rotary press equipment, many are adding web feeders. Even though sheets are delivered and backup must be sheet-fed, roll buying saves from 10% to 20%, speeds presswork.

What's being roll printed? Almost everything, and in letterpress, flexography, gravure and off-set. Labels and magazines, packaging materials and newspapers, books, snap-out forms, tags, mail-order catalogs, direct-mail advertising, trade publications, even long-run letters.

Not only are web-feeds being attached to sheet-printing rotaries, but more web-fed presses are being installed. Web presses process paper three times as fast as sheet-fed presses.
- more and more mills are using trailing-blade coating instead of conventional roller coating, thus more papers show higher printing impression tolerance (more printability with less impression). Increased surface levelness reduces required amount of supercalendering, lessens makeready time, makes makeready more effective. Of greatest value in letterpress, also good for offset and gravure (see Look-Kromatic, above).

The process actually trowels the coating onto the base sheet, tending to fill in low areas. This levelling action makes for a more uniformly level surface. Less pressure is used in super-calendering such papers, thus a less dense, more dimensionally stable sheet results. Also, thanks to less severe calendering, brightness and opacity are improved.

TYPOGRAPHY

The three major directions of type composing are:
- increased use of photographic composing (See Advertising Directions Vol. 1 for data on Mono-photo, Brightype, ATF Typesetter).

Other photographic typesetting machines are the Linofilm, Photon, and the Fotosetter. No major advances were made in this field during the past year although refinements and improvements on existing equipment took place. For example, the Fotosetter now has a model cap-able of setting all sizes from 3 to 72-point, making it possible to handle 99% of all news-paper display copy without the need for additional units or multiple photographic exposures. While photographic composing is being increasingly used, the big commercial break-through awaits the wide commercial use of wrap-around letterpress plates.
- fewer new faces introduced by American foundries with a greater number of new or revived designs coming in from Europe (see showings of new typefaces in this book).
- increased automated, high-speed equipment

AUTOMATED CASTING . . .

To cut composing costs new equipment features high-speed automatic composition. Some of the leading machines introduced:
- Intertype Corporation's keyboardless Monarch works 25% faster than standard tape-operated machines. To increase operating speed, new machine design eliminates vibration problems, new mechanism speeds matrice assembly distribution. Keyboardless, since it is operated by perforated tape, many conventional operating parts of the Intertype are eliminated. A variable speed control ranges casting from 8 to 14 lines per minute.

Merganthaler Linotype's Comet line was the first adapted to automation and other Linotype models now also handle tape.

Late in 1959 Lanston Industries introduced the Monomatic keyboard and Monomatic caster. They use basic Monotype typesetting principles. In place of the standard double keyboard there is a single keyboard with standard typewriter arrangement and two alphabets, caps and lower case. Monotype system has always involved perforating tape and feeding the tape to activate a caster. The Monomatic equipment is simply a refinement and speed-up, to handle all kinds of composition at reduced cost.

As composing machines swing over to the two-step system of perforating and casting, tele-typesetting equipment of the Fairchild Graphic Equipment Co. is coming into wider commercial use. Present big demand is in newspaper and publishing plants, but it is being increasingly used in book and job shops. By separating the single complex machine operation into two operations, perforating and casting, the latter can be made fully automatic, thus speeding up production. The system also frees the keyboard operator from many time-consuming non-productive machine operations. It is claimed that the tape operator can produce from 75% to

100% more by this system than conventionally. TTS is not new. It was first commercially installed in 1932. But it is news today in that it is being widely employed by job as well as publication shops.

Also introduced during the past year was the Nebitype. This is a type casting system similar to the Ludlow. In fact, it can use Ludlow matrices as well as Nebimats. It is for high-speed line casting of hand composition in display sizes. Equipment is distributed by Lanston Monotype Co.

Typewriter composing machines are also coming out in high-speed tape-operated models. An example is the Friden Justowriter. A Recorder unit has a built-in tape punching mechanism. Speed is limited only by typist's ability. As copy is typed, tape is punched.

Completed tape is fed through tape reading unit on the Reproducer which justifies copy at the rate of 100 words per minute. Copy is set on reproduction paper from which pasteups are prepared for negatives and platemaking. Copy can be set directly on paper plates.

art business news roundup

studio billings, profits

1960 was a year of billings and profits down. After running ahead of 1959 billings for the first seven months, billings tapered off for many studios. But even when running at a record pace in the beginning of the year, there were signs that studio profits were down from the 6-7% pace of three years ago to about 4¼%, although many studios had profits of 10-15%.

Different sections of the country fared differently. According to CAM Report, NYC and Eastern studios were billing at 160% of their 1957 pace toward year's end. The midwest studios were billing 126% and Southern California studios were moving at a 105% pace.

studio costs

The National Association of Art Services Inc. and CAM Report studied studio operating costs, compared them to a 1958 CAM survey. The average studio spends its incoming dollar as follows:

cost factor	average	median	high
Salaried artists	23.69	27.0	54.0
Inside free lances	7.03	11.3	45.0
Outside free lances	6.82	3.0	40.0
All artists	37.54		
Typography	5.31	5.43	33.0
Printing, engraving	5.07	3.0	46.0
Photostats	2.77	2.45	8.7
Photography	2.59	2.0	15.6
Art supplies	3.24	2.43	25.0
All outside purchases	18.98		
Salesmen	6.51	8.0	20.89
Officers, owners	15.09	12.9	36.00
Office personnel	3.65	2.95	12.00
All non-art salaries	25.25		

General expenses: The above items account for 81.77% of the average studio's incoming dollar. Another 14% is spent as follows:

Rent	3.22
Office supplies	3.38
Advertising	.76
Entertainment	1.81
Insurance	.72
Legal counsel	.58
Contributions	.42
Petty cash	.50
Taxes	2.61
Total	14.00

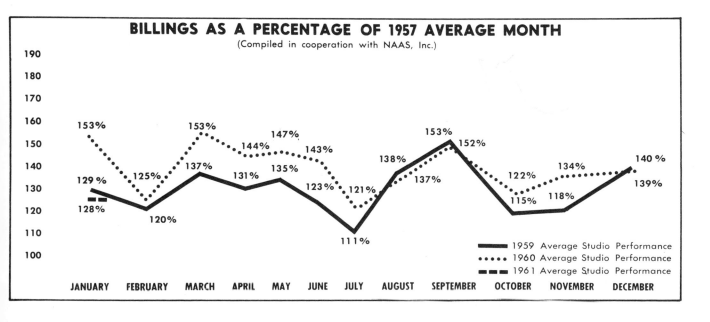

BILLINGS AS A PERCENTAGE OF 1957 AVERAGE MONTH
(Compiled in cooperation with NAAS, Inc.)

—— 1959 Average Studio Performance
•••• 1960 Average Studio Performance
▬ ▬ ▬ 1961 Average Studio Performance

This leaves an average studio profit of 4.23%, down from the 6.64% reported in a study made three years ago. Highest profit reported in the 1960 CAM study was 17.25%. One studio had a 22% loss. Half the studios reported profits of better than 6.45%.

In another study, CAM Report noted that 41 of 64 studios were expecting bigger billings in 1960 over 1959, only 32 were expecting better profits.

Two trends in studio costs were evident during 1960: the higher billing with lower profit trend and a shift toward more outside purchases, such as for typography and printing.

salaries

The trend was up through 1960, with talent shortage keeping pressure on salaries in many job categories. For much of 1960, top mechanicals men were in such demand that many quit staff jobs to freelance. This situation appeared to be stabilizing at year's end.

A study by the Art Unit of the New York State Employment Service shows salaries rose across the board. 600 applicants were checked for 1960 vs 1959 salaries, with the following results:

	May 1959	May 1960
Median salary	$85	$100
Average salary	$91.82	100.76
Under $75 per week	22%	15%
$75-100 per week	41%	32%
$100 per week or over	37%	53%

Income brackets of commercial artists were checked by the Art Directors Club of Washington. Results of the national study:

Income	Number	Percent
$25-40,000	50	8
15-25,000	130	21
9-15,000	276	44
5-9,000	149	24
2-5,000	22	3
	627	100%

High and low salaries reported to CAM during 1960 were:

	High	Low
ADs	20,000	5,200
Ass't AD	8,000	6,000
Ass't AD, publ.	10,000	7,500
Comp letterer	10,000	7,800
Comp renderer	10,000	
Display designer	10,000	8,000
Jr. Designer	7,800	6,500
Layout artist	10,000	4,420
Mechanicals men	6,500	3,120
Package designer	7,800	5,200
Retail artist	6,500	
Studio designer	20,000	6,000
Trainees	85 wk	45 wk

employment trends

Through most of 1960 the talent demand, especially in New York where for the first half studios ran at a record pace, ran well ahead of supply, pushing salaries up. However agencies, studios, advertising departments offering high art salaries were not quick to fill them, wanting top and versatile talent in return.

The pendulum began a return swing toward year's end. In October, CAM Report noted, active files for job applicants were comparatively heavy and for the first time there was some falloff in employer requests for personnel. Also, there was some boomeranging in the freelance setup. Employers were resisting high rates and at the same time freelancers, such as mechanicals men who had only recently quit staff jobs, were not anxious to go back on staff.

Although no national artists organization took shape, reports from San Francisco, Des Moines, and Westport, Conn., showed much thought being given to such a possibility.

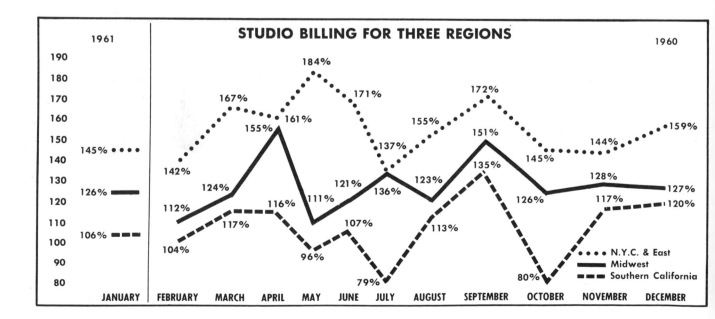

STUDIO BILLING FOR THREE REGIONS

club
exhibition
directory

American Institute of Graphic Arts, 5 E. 40th St., N.Y.C. 17.
50 Best Books of the Year
Design and Printing for Commerce and 50 Best Aids of the Year.
Textbooks
Children's Books
Packages
Record Album Covers.

American Management Assn., 1515 Broadway, N.Y.C.
Annual Packaging Exhibition.

Art Directors Clubs listed separately, below.

Associated Business Publications, Inc., 205 E. 42nd St., N.Y.C. 17.

Direct Mail Advertisers Assn., Inc., 3 E. 57th St., N.Y.C. 22.

Fibre Box Assn., 1145 19th St. N.W., Washington 6, D.C.

Financial World Magazine, 17 Battery Place, N.Y.C. 4.
Best Annual Reports.

Folding Paper Box Assn. of America, 222 W. Adams St.,
Chicago 6, Ill.

Lithographers & Printers National Assn., Inc., 597 5th Ave., N.Y.C. 17.
Annual Awards Competition.

National Assn. of Travel Organizations, 1322 K St. N.W., Washington 5, D.C.
Awards for best travel posters, brochures, folders.

National Industrial Advertisers Assn., 271 Madison Ave., N.Y.C.

National Paper Box Mfrs., Philadelphia 7.

Annual Set-up Paper Box Competition.

National Visual Presentation Assn., 19 W. 44th St., N.Y.C. 36.

New York Employing Printers Assn., 461 8th Ave., N.Y.C. 1.

Outdoor Advertising Assn. of America, 24 W. Erie St., Chicago 10.

Package Designers Council, 331 Madison Ave., N.Y.C. 17.

Point of Purchase Advertising Institute, Inc., 11 W. 42nd St., N.Y. 36.

Printing Industry of America, Inc., 5728 Connecticut Ave., N.W., Washington 15, D.C.
Advertising for printing and lithography firms.

Professional Photographers of America, 152 W. Wisconsin Ave., Milwaukee 3.

ROP Newspaper Advertising Award Competition, c/o Editor and Publisher, 1475 Broadway, N.Y.C. 36.

Screen Process Printers Assn., 549 W. Randolph St., Chicago 6.

Society of Illustrators, 128 E. 63rd St., N.Y.C. 21.

Society of Typographic Arts, 6 E. Lake St., Chicago 11.

Society of Typographic Designers of Canada, 208 Adelaide St. W., Toronto 1, Ontario.

Technical Illustrators Management Assn., Box 1021, Hollywood 28, Calif.

Type Directors Club, Box 1607, Grand Central Station, N.Y.C. 17.

National Society of Art Directors, 115 E. 40th St., N.Y.C. 16.

(NSAD Clubs—unless otherwise noted, the address is that of the current president).

Atlanta—Robert W. Bragg, Pres., c/o Burke, Dowling, Adams, Inc., 992 W. Peachtree St. N.W., Atlanta, Ga.

Baltimore—Frank C. Mirabile, Pres., c/o Welch, Collins & Mirabile, Inc., 13 W. 25th St., Baltimore 18, Md. Club headquarters—13 W. 25th St., Baltimore 18.

Birmingham—Rocky Stovall, Pres., c/o Birmingham Publishing Co., 130 S. 19th St. Club headquarters—1130 Del Ray Dr.

Boston—Lee Le Blanc, Pres., c/o Arnold & Co., Inc., 262 Washington St., Boston 8.

Buffalo—Robert J. Witzel, Pres., c/o Robert J. Witzel Studio, 40 Ledge Lane, Williamsville, N.Y. Club headquarters—291 Delaware Ave, Buffalo 2.

Charlotte—Robert F. Alford, Pres., c/o Alford Studios, 109 W. 3rd St., Charlotte 2, N.C.

Chicago—Herbert S. Bull, Pres., c/o J. Walter Thompson Co., 410 N. Michigan Ave., Chicago 11. Club headquarters—6 E. Lake St., Chicago 1.

Cincinnati—Fred C. Pottschmidt, Pres., c/o Sales Production Corp., 1617 Reading Rd., Cincinnati 2.

Cleveland—Dan Gallagher, Pres., c/o McCann-Erickson, 355 Second Federal Bldg., Cleveland 4.

Columbus—J. Richard Lewis, Pres., c/o Harry M. Miller, Inc. 595 E. Broad St., Columbus 15, O.

Dallas-Fort Worth—William Neale, Pres., c/o Tracy-Locke Co., Inc., 2501 Cedar Springs, Dallas 1.

Denver—Harold F. Smith, Pres., 2222 S. Raleigh, Denver 19.

Detroit—C. Bruce Unwin, Pres., c/o MacMunus, John & Adams, Inc., Bloomfield Hills, Mich.

Des Moines (Art Directors Assn. of Iowa, Box 265, Des Moines)—Robert La Casse, Pres., c/o Townsend Direct Mail, 427 E. Walnut St.

Jacksonville—Joseph F. Mikulas, Pres., 1633 San Marco Blvd., Jacksonville 7, Fla.

Kansas City—George Moyer, Pres., c/o Moyer-Crandall Studios, VFW Bldg., 406 W. 34th St., Kansas City 11, Mo.

Los Angeles—E. W. Poyser, Pres., c/o Gaynor & Ducas, Inc., 291 S. La Cienega Blvd., Beverly Hills, Calif. Club headquarters—4315 W. 2nd St., Los Angeles 4.

Memphis—Leonard Crook, Pres., c/o Lake-Spiro-Shurman, Inc., Radio Center Bldg., Memphis 5.

Miami (Art Directors Club of Greater Miami, Box 1062, Miami 6)—Sam Willig, Pres., c/o Art & Design for Industry, 623 Brickell Ave., Miami 32.

Milwaukee—Gardner Meyst, Pres., c/o Gardner Meyst Studios, 757 N. Broadway, Milwaukee 2.

Minneapolis-St. Paul—Norman Hamilton, Pres., c/o Studio One, Inc., 612 2nd Ave. S., Minneapolis.

Montreal—Adolphe Leduc, Pres., c/o The T. Eaton Co., 677 St. Catherine St. W., Montreal 2, Quebec Province, Canada.

Nashville—Haskell Richardson, c/o Baptist Sunday School Board, 127 9th Ave. N., Nashville 3, Tenn.

New York—Robert H. Blattner, Pres., c/o The Reader's Digest, 230 Park Ave., N.Y.C. 17. Club headquarters—115 E. 40th St., N.Y.C. 16.

Omaha—Walter LaHue, Pres., 319 Barker Bldg., Omaha 2.

Philadelphia—Warren Blair, Pres., c/o Smith, Kline — French Laboratories,

1500 Spring Garden St., Philadelphia. Club headquarters—Poor Richard Club, 1319 Locust St., Philadelphia 7.

Pittsburgh (Art Direction Society of Pittsburgh)—A. H. Kiefer, Pres., c/o Fuller & Smith & Ross, Inc., 211 Oliver Ave., Pittsburgh 22.

Portland—Peter Teel, Jr., Pres., 1015 S. W. Yamhill, Portland, Ore.

Richmond—George P. Riddick, Jr., Pres., 1310 Vassar Rd., Richmond, Va.

Rochester (Rochester Art Directors Club, Box 941, Rochester 3, N.Y.) —John W. Jordan, Pres., c/o Williamson Associates, Inc., 580 Jefferson Rd.

St. Louis—Carl F. Klinghammer, Pres., c/o D'Arcy Advertising Co., 14th & Olive Sts., St. Louis 3, Mo. Club headquarters—122 N. 7th St., St. Louis 1.

San Diego—Ken Kitson, Pres., 8865 Robin Hood Lane, La Jolla, Calif.

San Francisco (Art Directors & Artists Club of San Francisco, 609 Sutter St., San Francisco 2)—Wayne Mayfield, Pres., c/o L. C. Cole Co., 406 Sutter St., San Francisco 2.

Seattle—Robert Morgan, Pres., 203 14th Ave. N., Seattle 2. Club headquarters—1217 2nd Ave.

Spokane (Spokane Society of Art Directors, W. 325 Riverside Ave., Spokane, Wash.)—Jack Rogers, Pres., c/o Rogers Art Studios, S. 118 Lincoln St.

Toledo—Bert Strand, Pres., c/o Techway Hall Studio, 225 Michigan St., Toledo.

Toronto—Frank Davies, Pres., c/o MacLean-Hunter Industrial Publications, 481 University Ave., Toronto 2, Ontario, Canada. Club headquarters—64 Avenue Rd.

Washington, D.C. (Art Directors Club of Metropolitan Washington)—Thomas Huestis, Pres., c/o Nation's Business, 1615 H. St. N.W., Washington 6, D.C. Club headquarters—500 Walker Bldg., 734 15th St. N.W.

new books

Advertising Layout & Art Direction. Stephen Baker. McGraw-Hill. $13.50. Not how-to but how-it-was-done commentary on art direction as a business, by Cunningham & Walsh's senior AD.

The Advertising Truth Book. Morton Simon. Advertising Federation of America. Free 56-page manual details AFA's "local self-regulation program" & discusses governmental agencies' functions.

American Advertising 1800-1900. Myron Johnson. George O'Donnell Agency, Beacon, N. Y. $2.

Animation Art in the Commercial Film. Eli L. Levitan. Reinhold. $6.95. Illustrated planning-production-filming text includes commercial production details.

Art Directing. Edited by Nathaniel PousetteDart. Hastings House. $15. What the AD does & how he does it—a detailed account.

The Art Director at Work. Edited by Arthur Hawkins. Hastings House. $6.-50. Conception-to-finish study of winners in the 37th Annual Exhibition of the N. Y. Art Directors Club.

Barriers to Creativity. Deutsch & Shea. Industrial Relations News. $1.-50. 32-page booklet, third in series, analyzes creative-process helps & blocks.

Basic Design: Principles & Practice. Kenneth F. Bates. World. $4.95. Concepts for all art styles & media, from simplest spot, line & shape to subtle sophistications.

Casebook of Successful Ideas for Advertising & Selling. Samm Sinclair Baker. Hanover House (Doubleday). $3.95.

Design for Point of Sale. Ladislav Sutnar. Farrar Strauss & Cudahy. $8.50. 344 illustrations.

Developing the Corporate Image. Edited by Lee H. Bristol, Jr., Scribner's. $5.95. 30 specialists evaluate use of tools, techniques & media.

Exhibition & Display. James Gardner, Caroline Heller. F. W. Dodge. $13.75.

Motivation in Advertising: Motives That Make People Buy. Pierre Martineau. McGraw-Hill. $6. Analysis of advertising factors influencing consumers' buying behavior.

The New Anatomy of Advertising. Mark Wiseman. Harper. $5.95. Methodized approach to the advertising arts.

The 100 Greatest Advertisements. Julian L. Watkins. Dover. $2.25. Paperback revise of the classic, up-dated through 1958.

1,001 Advertising & Selling Books, Pamphlets & Articles Published in the Last Year. Business Methods Index, Box 453, Ottawa, Canada. A bibliography.

On the Writing of Advertising. Walter Weir. McGraw-Hill. $5. A high-level how-to: ad types, communication problems, research, writing discipline & ideals.

The Package. Mildred Constantine. Doubleday. $1.25. The Museum of Modern Art's show, plus discussion of packaging methods, designs & materials.

Packaging: An International Survey of Packaging Design. Edited by Walter Herdeg. Hastings House. $18. 1022 package illustrations in 15 categories, complete with technical & materials data, plus planning checklist & competitions roster.

Point of Sales Display. R. H. Talmadge. Viking. $6.50. A complete course, with European display examples, by the English designer.

The Powerful Consumer. George Katona. McGraw-Hill. $6.50. Psychological studies of the American economy.

The Preparation of the Annual Report. Vol. 1. Edited by Don A. Talucci. Research Bureau, Inc. $15.

The Search for Certainty in Advertising. Donald B. Gooch, Editor, Bureau of Business Research, University of Michigan. $4. Paperback report of the 1959 ad conference at Ann Arbor.

The Self-Conscious Society. Eric Larabee. Doubleday. $3.50. Exploration of America's tendency to self-judgment.

The Status Seekers. Vance Packard. McKay. $4.50. An exploration of class behavior in America & the drive for status symbols.

The Strategy of Desire. Ernest Dichter. Doubleday. $3.95. The whys & hows of applied psychology for mass communication.

Symbology. Edited by Elwood Whitney. Hastings House. $6.95. How to use symbols in visual communication. A Visual Communications Conference report.

Taken at the Flood. John Gunther. Harper. $5. The late Albert D. Lasker's biography—the story of advertising & its famous practitioners.

They Laughed When I Sat Down. Frank Rowsome, Jr., McGraw-Hill. $7.50. Laughs, information & 200-plus illustrations—an informal history of advertising.

The Wastemakers. Vance Packard. David McKay Co. $4.50. Consumption for consumption's sake & planned, psychological & product obsolescence are indicted by the author of The Status Seekers.

Why People Buy. Louis Cheskin. Liveright. $5. People's, mostly women's, behavior in the market place.

annuals

Advertising Directions—Trends in Visual Advertising. Art Direction Book Co. $10. Visual interpretive presentation of ideas, opinions & tenets of 30 leaders in creative advertising, showing product promotion, media, graphics, materials-services & creativity trends.

Graphic Annual 60/61. Edited by Walter Herdeg. Praeger. $15. 9th edition shows work of more than 500 artists & designers from 22 countries.

Illustrators '59. Editor in Chief, Arthur Hawkins. Hastings House. $12.-50. Permanent record of the Society of Illustrators' first annual show & exhibit analyses.

Illustrators '60. Edited by Howard Munce. Hastings House. $12.95. Lester Beall-designed record of the best of current American illustrations.

International Poster Annual 1960/61. Edited by Arthur Niggli. Hastings House. $12. Outstanding posters from 25 countries.

Modern Publicity. 1960/61. Edited by Wilfred Walter. Hastings House. $9.-95. 30th Anniversary edition includes ad examples in various media from 28 countries.

1960 Outdoor Annual. Outdoor Advertising, Inc. Spiral-bound record of the Art Directors Club of Chicago's 28th National Competition & Exhibit of Outdoor Advertising Art.

The Penrose Annual. Vol. 54. Edited by Allan Delafons. Hastings House. $12.50.

39th Art Directors Annual. Farrar Strauss & Cudahy. $15. Year's best examples of advertising & editorial art & design in all media; special feature commemorates Art Directors Club of N. Y.'s 40th anniversary.

art

Art & the Creative Unconscious. 4 essays by Erich Neumann. Bollingen Series LXI. Pantheon. $3.50. Psychological analysis of the artist's relationship to his culture & himself.

Canadian Art. Alan Jarvis, Editor. $2. Special issue on graphic design, with 261 illustrations.

Comic Art in America. Stephen Becker. Simon & Schuster. $7.50. An interpretive history, from political cartoons & comic strips to magazine, TV & film humor.

Commercial Art As a Business. Fred C. Rodewald & Edward M. Gottschall. Viking Press. $4.95. Enlarged edition of Rodewald's 1954 book, newly revised & updated by Art Direction's editor Gottschall, contains latest markets, prices, practices, media needs & contract data.

Creativity. Edited by Paul Smith. Hastings House. $6.50. A Visual Communications Conference Report covering process, method, individual attitude & other aspects of creativity.

Creativity & Its Cultivation. Harold H. Anderson, Editor. Harper. $5.15. Authorities, from many different fields, discuss creativity from their respective viewpoints.

Introduction to 20th Century Design. (From the Museum of Modern Art collection). Arthur Drexler & Gretna Daniel. Doubleday. $2.95. Design evolution, recorded in George Barrow's photos, from 1900 to now.

The New Graphic Art. Karl Gerstner & Markus Kutter. Hastings House. $15. Visually interpretive review of world-wide graphic design, principally from the early '20s through today.

The Non-Objective World. Kasimir Malevich, translated by Howard Dearstyne. Paul Theobald. $4.50. The first & only English translation of the theories of the Russian suprematist.

A Pictorial History of Music. Paul Henry Lang & Otto Bettmann. Norton. $10. B/W pictures (over 600 paintings, sculptures, prints, drawings & photos), plus text abridgment of Lang's Music in Western Civilization.

Paul Rand. Edited by Yusaku Kamekura. Knopf. $13.50. Examples of his work up to 1956 & appreciative estimates by author & contributors.

The Styles of Ornament. Alexander Speltz. Dover. $2.25. The entire range of ornament, in chronological sequence, from prehistoric to mid-19th Century.

The Visual Arts Today. Edited by Gyorgy Kepes. Wesleyan University Press. $6. A discussion of the arts, from esthetical, psychological and sociological viewpoints, by 52 contributors.

color

Bychrome 2-Color Charts. ByChrome

Co., Inc. $22.50. A joint research project by publisher, the Byrum Lithographing Co. & Byrum-Jones Advertising pinpointing 1 & 2 color choice, prediction & control, from artist's color selection through lithographic production.

The Color Planning Guide. Colortone Press. $25. A 2-volume presentation of 11,000 yellow-red-blue-black colortones in 4-color process printing.

Color Swatch Book. Color Swatch, Inc. $47.50. Offers over 24,000 easily-removed (& replaced) swatches for expediting color matching.

Duo-Color Guide. Graphic Publishing Co. $45. 4200 different color patches & the most effective colors in every practical 2-color combination.

4-Color Process Guide. Graphic Publishing Co. $110. Every possible 2-, 3- & 4-color process ink combination. 5632 different color patches.

The Grand 3-Color Blending Book. Hans Gaensslen. Graphic Publishing Co. $45. Screenless, overprinted & screened color printing, plus 50 letterpress-offset specimens.

New Horizons in Color. Faber Birren. Reinhold. $10. An examination of all known color-color harmony systems.

photography

Directory of Professional Photography 1960/61. Professional Photographers of America. $5. A 144-page listing, arranged alphabetically by states, cities, studios, individuals & services.

Color Separation Photography. Lithographic Technical Foundation. $8. Technical manual of copy-preparation, separation, masking & other procedures.

Moments Preserved. Irving Penn. Simon & Schuster. $17.50. Penn's photographs reflect his sensitive mind's eye or second image reaction to the exterior world—a composite picture of his creativity.

Observations. Photographs by Richard Avedon. Comments by Truman Capote. Simon & Schuster. $15. People, in seemingly unguarded poses, delineated in striking photography & prose.

The Picture Universe, U.S. Camera 1961. Edited by Tom Maloney. Holt, Rinehart & Winston. $10. 25th Anniversary issue of U.S. Camera.

Portraits of Greatness. Yousuf Karsh. Thomas Nelson & Sons. $17.50. 96 of Karsh's most memorable portraits, documented with conversational, incidental & biographical text.

Posing for the Camera. Harriet Shepard & Lenore Meyer. Hastings House. $6.95. Manual treats posing from a creative viewpoint: roles of director-photographer & camera as a working team.

The World of Werner Bischof. E. P. Dutton & Co. $7.95. Universal similarities of man in 74 large gravure reproductions.

production
Advertising Agency & Studio Skills: A Guide to the Preparation of Art & Mechanicals for Reproduction. Tom Cardamone. Watson-Guptill Publications. $4.75. Explains procedures involved in publishing books, manuals, brochures or fold-outs.

Exploring the Graphic Arts. Anthony Marinaccio. Van Nostrand. $6. A guide to printing processes.

Line, Halftone & Color. American Photoengravers Assn. Letterpress platemaking explained & illustrated.

Planning for Better Imposition. H. Wayne Warner. Judd & Detweiler. $10. Money & time-saving ideas for booklets, folders, inserts, etc.

Rendering Techniques for Commercial Art & Advertising. Charles R. Kinghan. Reinhold. $13.50. The author (BBDO & in the field for over 37 years) discusses demonstrations, visual aids, professional samples, comps, etc.

television
ABC of Film & TV Working Terms. Oswald Skilbeck. Hastings House. $3.95. British "vocabulary" & cinematographic bibliography.

Designing for TV. Robert J. Wade. Farrar Strauss & Cudahy. $8.50. A complete art-TV design reference work.

The Handbook of TV & Film Technique. Charles W. Curran. Farrar Strauss & Cudahy. $3. Executives' non-technical production guide.

A Pictorial History of Television. Daniel Blum. Chilton. $10. 278 pages of b/w clips from 22 TV categories.

The Television Manual. William Hodapp. Farrar Strauss & Cudahy. $4.75. Practical TV production-programming guide.

TV Advertising. Arthur Bellaire. Harper. $6.50. Production methods, corporate TV ad examples & top U.S. TV markets.

TV Tape Commercials. Harry Wayne McMahan. Hastings House. $4.50. 9 illustrated lesson-chapters on tape production & creation.

typography and lettering
Alphabet Thesaurus. Edward Rondthaler. Reinhold. $10. 740-page compilation of more than 3,000 style-classified alphabets & derivatives & their work.

The Book of Borders. A. A. Archbold, Publisher, Box 332, Burbank, Calif. $6. 81 different 6 to 12 pt. conventional art borders designed for offset reproduction.

Borders Unlimited. Harry Bigelow Coffin. $5.50. Classical, medieval, oriental, early American & contemporary border patterns & 30 corner-formed patterns.

Decorative Alphabets & Initials. Edited by Alexander Nesbitt. Dover. $2.25. 91 complete alphabets, 3824 initials, in 123 page plates, with history of manuscript & printed initials.

Lee Streamlined Copy-Fitting Handbook. Arthur B. Lee. $4.95. 32 pages of Linotype & Intertype faces with lowercase, caps & small caps alphabet showings of all available sizes up to 18 pt. (With Lee Streamlined Copy-Fitting Gauge).

Lettera. Armin Haab & Alex Stocker. Hastings House. 3rd Ed. $8.50. Classical & modern type faces, chosen for form, originality & usefulness.

Letter Design in the Graphic Arts. Mortimer Leach. Reinhold. $12. Current designs & concepts, including type & lettering in ads, outdoor & packaging, plus examples of lettering techniques.

A Psychological Study of Typography. Sir Cyril Burt. Cambridge University Press. $3. A study of the mind's capacity to absorb a printed message.

Typography 60, Typography in Canada. Society of Typographic Designers of Canada. Paperback presents in 153 b/w reproductions the best Canadian designs in books, magazines, newspapers & commercial printing.

miscellaneous
A Diderot Pictorial Encyclopedia of Trades & Industry. Vols. 1 & 2. Dover. $10 each, $18.50 set. The first comprehensive illustrated survey of industrial knowledge — reprinted for the first time in two centuries.

The Importance of Wearing Clothes. Lawrence Langner. Hastings House. $7.50. Significance of styles in projecting culture images.

The Madison Avenue Handbook, 1961. Peter Glenn. $4. Diary-directory contains 80-page list of ad agency ADs art supply houses, illustrators, photographers, etc., tailored for N.Y., Chicago, Los Angeles, San Francisco & Miami ADs.

A Picture History of English Costume. C. Willett — Phyllis Cunnington. MacMillan. $7. Summaries, captions & 428 illustrations (many early works of art) highlight fashion history.

Who's Who in Commercial Art & Photography. Director's Art Institute. $15. Complete name-address-phone reference list covers artists, photographers, studios, reps & agency-magazine-book publishers-business art buyers.

film, slide sources
Beginning in its December 1960 issue, Art Direction Magazine is printing a list of films, slide sets and filmstrips available for ADs' club programs. The list covers 16 different categories, as follows:

Advertising, architecture, art, art films around the world, calligraphy, experimental-inspirational cinema, film techniques, industrial arts, lettering, packaging, paper, photography, printing, production, sculpture and typography.

Following is a key identifying distributors of these films—some 80-odd sources altogether which art directors can contact for films and catalogs: AC: American Can Co., 100 Park Ave., N.Y. 17. ADCM: Art Directors Club of Milwaukee; George Heim, c/o Wells Badger Corp., 225 W. Capitol Drive, Milwaukee, Wisc. ADCNY: Art Directors Club of New York, 115 E. 40th St., N.Y. 16. AF: Association Films, 1816 N St. N.W., Washington, D.C. ANPA-BA: American Newspaper Publishers Assn., Bureau of Advertising, 485 Lexington Ave., N.Y. 17. ANPA-RI: American Newspaper Publishers Assn., Research Institute, Box 598, Easton Pa. AS: Abitibi Service, Inc., 131 N. Ludlow St., Dayton 2, O. ATAA: Advertising Typographers Assn. of America, 461 8th Ave., N.Y. 1. BBB: Bemis Bro. Bag Co., 408 Pine St., St. Louis, Mo. BIS: British Information Service, 45 Rockefeller Plaza, N.Y. 20. BP: Bowster Paper Co., Inc., 250 Park Ave., N.Y. 17. CB: Chase Bag Co., 309 W. Jackson Blvd., Chicago, Ill. CC: Continental Can Co., Community Relations, 100 E. 42nd St., N.Y. 17. CCA: Container Corp. of America, Display Division, 900 Ogden Ave., Chicago 22, Ill. CCNY: City College of New York, Audio-Visual Center, 17 Lexington Ave., N.Y. 10. CF: Coronet Films, Coronet Bldg., Chicago Ill. CFI: Contemporary Films, Inc., 267 W. 25th St., N.Y. 1; Midwest Office: 614 Davis St., Evanston, Ill. CIES: Consolidated International Equipment & Supply Co., Martin A. Rose, Dept. G, 330 W. 26th St., N.Y. 1. CP: Copley Productions, Union-Tribune Bldg., San Diego, Calif. CPC: Continental Paper Co., Ridge Park, N.J. C16:

Cinema 16, 175 Lexington Ave., N.Y. 16. CT: The Chicago Tribune, Chicago, Ill. CTFL: Canadian Travel Film Library, 630 5th Ave., N.Y.C.; Midwest Office: 111 N. Wabash Ave., Chicago 2, Ill. CW: Colonial Williamsburg, Film Distribution Service, Williamsburg, Va.

DMAA: Direct Mail Advertising Assn. 3 E. 57th St., N.Y. 22. DP-PR: E. 1. du Pont de Nemours & Co., Public Relations Dept., both Wilmington, Del.

EBF: Encyclopedia Britannica Films, 1150 Wilmette Ave., Wilmette, Ill. EKP: Eastman Kodak Co., Audio-Visual Service, Rochester 4, N.Y. ESANY: Electrotypers & Stereotypers Assn. of New York, Inc., 110 E. 42nd St., N.Y. 17.

FI: Film Images, Inc., 1860 Broadway, N.Y. 23. FBA: Fibre Box Assn., 1145 18th N.W., Washington, D.C. FCHS: F C. Hyok & Sons, Rensselaer, N.Y. FPBA: Folding Paper Box Assn., 337 W. Madison St., Chicago, Ill. FWC: Floyd W. Cocking, 4747 Constance Drive, San Diego, Calif.

GPP: Goss Printing Press Co., 501 W. 31st St., Chicago 50, Ill. GTA: Gravure Technical Assn., Inc., Edward St. John, 30 Rockefeller Plaza, N.Y.C. GTR: Goodyear Tire & Rubber Co., 1144 E. Market St., Akron 16. Ohio.

H: Hankscraft Co., Booster Bldg., Reedsburg, Wisc. HE: Horan Engraving Co., Inc. 44 W. 28th St., N.Y. 1. HHH: H H. Heinrich, Inc., Port of Authority Bldg., 8th Ave. at 15th St., N.Y. 11. HP: Hercules Powder Co., Cellulose Products Dept., Wilmington, Del. HPP: Hudson Pulp & Paper Corp., Film Lending Library, 505 Park Ave., N.Y. 22. HS: Harris-

Seybold Co., 4510 E. 71st St., Cleveland 5, O.; Eastern Office: 380 2nd Ave., N.Y. 10; Western Office: 460 Battery St., San Francisco 11, Calif. IC: Intertype Corp., 360 Furman St., Brooklyn 1, N.Y.C. IFB: International Film Bureau, Inc., 57 E. Jackson Blvd., Chicago 4, Ill. IP: International Paper Co., 22 E. 42nd St., N.Y. 17. IPI: International Corp., Printing Ink Div., 67 W. 44th St., N.Y. 36.

KC: Kimberly-Clark Corp., E. J. Levendowski, 250 Park Ave., N.Y. 17.

MAB: Magazine Advertising Bureau (Magazine Publishers Assn., Inc.) 444 Madison Ave., N.Y. 22. MB: M. Brombacher, Inc., Film Library, 460 W. 34th St., N.Y. 1. ML: Mergenthaler Linotype Co., Park & Ryerson Sts., Brooklyn 5, N.Y.C. MCL: McCandish Lithograph Corp., Roberts Ave. & Stokely St., Philadelphia 29, Pa. MMA: Museum of Modern Art Film Library, 11 W. 53rd St., N.Y. 19. MP: Mead Packaging, Inc., 230 Park Ave., N.Y. 22. MPPM: Miehle Printing Press & Mfg. Co., 2011 Hasting St., Chicago, Ill. MTPS: Modern Talking Picture Service, Inc., 3 E. 54th St., N.Y. 22.

NAEA: National Advertising Executives Assn., Robert C. Pace, Box 147, Danville, Ill. NCA: National Canners Assn., 1739 H St. N.W., Washington 6, D.C. NJM: New Jersey Machine Corp., Willow Ave. at 11th St., Hoboken, N.J. NFBC: National Film Board of Canada, 630 5th Ave., N.Y. 20. NYDN: New York Daily News, 220 E. 42nd St., N.Y. 17. NYU: New York University Film Library, 26 Washington Place, N.Y. 3.

OI: Owens-Illinois Glass Co., Toledo 1, Ohio.

PHG: P. H. Glatfelter Co., Spring Grove, Pa. POPAI: Point-of-Purchase Advertising Institute, Inc., Dorothy A. May, Director, Member Service, 11 W. 42nd St., N.Y. 36. PP: Peerless Processing Corp., 165 W. 46th St., N.Y.C. PRS: Powell River Sales Corp., 10 E. 40th St., N.Y. 16. RD: Reader's Digest, 270 Park Ave., N.Y. 17. RFL: Rembrandt Film Library, 267 W. 25th St., N.Y. 1. RH: Rohm & Haas Co., Plastics Dept., Washington Sq., Philadelphia 5, Pa. RM: Reynolds Metals Co., 19 E. 47th St., N.Y. 17. SB: Stephen Baker, Vice-President & Senior AD, Cunningham & Walsh, Inc., 260 Madison Ave., N.Y.C. SBST: San Bernardino Sun & Telegram, San Bernardino, Calif. SD: South Dakota State College, Photo-Lab College Station, Brookings, S.D. SF: Sanford Museum, Cherokee, Ia. SFMA: San Francisco Museum of Art, Civic Center, San Francisco 2, Calif. SS: Stokes & Smith Co., 4900 Summerdale Ave., Philadelphia 24, Pa. STA: Society of Typographic Arts, Luke Wasserman, Education Chairman, c/o Klein-Wasserman Design, 11 E. Walton, Chicago 11, Ill. SV: Sinclair and Valentine Co., 611 W. 129th St., N.Y. 27. TBA: Television Bureau of Advertising, Inc., 1 Rockefeller Plaza, N.Y. 20. UP: Ulano Products Co., 610 Dean St., Brooklyn 38, N.Y.

USC: Dept. of Cinema, University of Southern California, University Park, Los Angeles 7, Calif. UK: University of Kansas University Extension, Bureau of Visual Information, Lawrence, Kans. USMC: United Shoe Machinery Corp., 140 Federal St., Boston 7, Mass.

WMDF: W. M. Dennis Films, 2506½ W. 7th St., Los Angeles 57, Calif.

about the authors...

HARRY CARTER
Harry Carter is a freelance illustrator and designer and a past-president of the Society of Illustrators. He was chairman of Illustrators '60, the 2nd National Exhibition of Illustrators sponsored by the SI. In the early 30's he studied at California School of Fine Arts. His latest important work is the new illustrated edition of Baron Munchausen, published by Devin-Adair in 1960.

MAHLON A. CLINE
Treasurer of The Art Directors Club of New York since 1954, he heads his own organization in mid-Manhattan, serving clients as AD, designer and typographic consultant. Affiliations include the AIGA and the Type Directors and Salmagundi clubs. A frequent lecturer, for many years he taught typographic design and layout at Pratt Institute, his alma mater.

JOHN P. CUNNINGHAM
One of the most quoted men in advertising — constructive, provocative, often controversial. A Harvard grad, he joined Newell-Emmett (1919) as an artist, following World War I experience as a naval ensign, moving (1921) to the copy department and advancing (1930) to V-P over all creative production. He became Executive V-P (1949, when the agency changed to Cunningham & Walsh), president (1954) and board chairman, his current post (1958). He originated The Man From C&W promotion, having done much retail selling himself. He chairmanned the 4A's board (1952-53) and is currently on its Advisory Council. He is also AFA vice-chairman and a member of its board and executive committees.

WILLIAM R. DUFFY
Senior AD, in charge of TV and motion pictures, McCann-Erickson Advertising (U.S.A.), he has won 14 distinctive merit awards and/or exhibition acceptances from the Art Directors Club of New York. A pioneer in the creation of TV shows and commercials, he has lectured widely. Currently an instructor at New York University, he has also taught and conducted seminars at Television Workshop, Columbia University and Pratt Institute.

GENE FEDERICO
Born in Greenwich Village in 1918, he studied at Pratt Institute and the Art Students' League, then did layouts for L. Bamberger & Co. After spending 4½ years—2½ overseas—in the Camouflage Corps and the 84th Engineers (in charge of plans-operations graphics), he AD'd at Abbott Kimball, Grey Advertising, Doyle Dane Bernbach and Douglas D. Simon. He is now vice-president and art group head at Benton & Bowles. Extra-curricula activities include design instruction at The Workshop School, panelist and judge for the American Society of Magazine Photographers, participant in the Typography U.S.A. Forum, and juror for many ADC exhibits. He is a member of AIGA and the Type Directors Club and has exhibited at Galerie Colline, Oran, Algiers, the N.Y. AD Club, the AD Gallery and AIGA shows. His work has been discussed in U.S. and foreign graphic arts publications.

DAVID FLASTERSTEIN
The editor of Spot Magazine, covering point-of-purchase advertising exclusively, broke into publishing with Collier's Magazine. He has worked in public relations, has authored short stories and plays.

JAMES K. FOGLEMAN
Administrative Design Director, CIBA Design Center (Summit, N.J.), he collaborates with CIBA American dyes-plastics-pharmaceutical-chemical divisions in all visual presentations. In 9 years his programs have won over 100 awards. Born in Indianapolis in 1919, he was an aircraft-engineer (4 years of installation engineering with GM's Allison Division), simultaneously attending Purdue and Alabama U's for more engineering and Indiana U for liberal arts. Postwar, he studied art at Yale, where he became associated with George Paton Studio, Indianapolis, working on Eli Lilly promotions, eventually becoming, in N.Y., a pharmaceutical promotion specialist. He has practiced industrial design, taught at Southern Methodist, and done special products engineering at Chance Vought Aircraft. After a year-plus at L.W. Frohlich & Co. as creative design director, he joined CIBA in 1951 as a pharmaceutical advertising AD. His constant objective: Winning management's acceptance of design as a major business tool. He is vice-president, Yale Arts Assn. and Yale School of Architecture & Design, a member of the American Society of Industrial Design, the Aspen Institute, the ADCNY and AIGA.

GEORGE GIUSTI
Born (1908) in Milan, where he graduated from the Reale Accademia di Belle Art di Brera. He became an AD in Lugano, Switzerland, and had his own studio in Zurich for 7 years. Coming to the U.S., aged 30, he began a new career as freelance ad and publication designer. His campaigns for chemical firms and his Fortune covers won widespread attention. In addition to many AD clubs and AIGA honors, he won the 11th NSAD award in 1958.

WALTER P. GLENN
A Virginian and graduate of West Virginia University, he grew up in Pittsburgh where he held numerous art posts while studying art at Carnegie Tech night school. He joined Young & Rubicam as an AD in 1937 and has been there ever since (except for a brief sojourn in Washington, D.C.), becoming manager (1951), then director (1959) of the art department. He is active in various civic organizations in Rye, N.Y., his home town.

GEORGE GUIDO
New York City-educated, he skipped formal art school training because of military service and learned the business through on-the-job experience—first (1946) with various N.Y. art studios, then with: Anderson, Davis & Platt (assistant to AD Robert Pliskin); Wm. Weintraub (hired by Paul Rand), Anderson & Cairns & Grey. He was also a freelance designer for Time. In 1954, he joined Campbell-Ewald, Detroit, as assistant AD on the Chevrolet newspaper account and today is head AD for Chevvy passenger cars and trucks. Detroit AD Club 12th Annual Exhibit winner of 3 gold and 5 silver medals, 1 Umbrella Award and the Best-of-Show Award and the Club's 1960 "Art Director of the Year" nominee. He has also won awards at the Chicago AD Club shows and has exhibited in N.Y., San Francisco and Los Angeles AD shows and at the Michigan Fine Artists Show and the Detroit Institute of Fine Arts.

KEN LAVEY
A graduate of Pratt Institute and the California College of Arts & Crafts, he hails from California. Entering the employ of L. W. Frohlich & Co., N.Y., as a designer in 1949, he is now a member of the creative team directing the agency's work.

ROBERT M. JONES
Recipient of over 40 certificates from major graphic arts groups, his professional experience has been wide: Photographer (The Deseret News), Assistant State Director (Utah Art Project), editorial-sales promotion art (Life), AD (Columbia Records and Park East Magazine), and instructor (Cooper Union). Established Glad Hand Press (1953) and has had one-man exhibits at the STA, Princeton University, Gallery 303, Cooper and Beatty (Toronto), and the Vancouver and New York AD clubs. Has lectured extensively on photography and album cover art. His work has been reviewed by American publications and Gebrauschsgrafik.

GEORGE LOIS
29 years old, he (and Julian Koenig) left Doyle Dane Bernbach to form Papert, Koenig, Lois, Inc. During his year at DDB (1959), he won three gold medals and a distinctive merit award in the Art Directors Club of N.Y. show. A native New Yorker, he attended the High School of Music and Art and Pratt Institute, where he teaches an evening class. His first job was at Reba Sochis Advertising. Following a 2-year Army hitch during the Korean War, he joined CBS as a designer, later becoming Sudler & Hennessey consumer division AD. He was a co-designer of the 37th Art Directors Annual.

RUSSELL LYNES
A clergyman's son, he was born in the St. James Episcopal Church rectory, Great Barrington, Mass., where he attended public school. Further schooling followed in Jersey City, New York (the Cathedral School Choir), Sheffield, Mass. (the Berkshire School), and Yale. He joined Harper & Brothers following graduation from college, later switching to Vassar College, in charge of publications, and the Shipley School, Bryn Mawr, where he and his wife were assistant principals and subsequently principals. In 1944, he joined Harper's Magazine as assistant editor and is now managing editor. He is affiliated with the John Hay Whitney and McDowell foundations and the Greenwood Fund. A popular lecturer and contributor to magazines, he has authored "The Tastemakers" and other books.

HOWARD MUNCE
Vice-President and Senior Art Director of Foote, Cone & Belding and AD for its Rheingold (Liebmann Breweries) account. A past president of the Society of Illustrators, he is editor of Illustrators '60 and a Sunday painter and sculptor.

ANDREW NELSON
First V-P of the AD Club of New York and art supervisor for J. Walter Thompson Co. on the Pan American World Airways, Panagra Airways and Ford accounts. Before joining JWT, he was AD at 3 N.Y. agencies and (1942-45) was a combat engineers company commander. A leisure-time painter, he has exhibited in N.Y.-N.J. galleries and museums, private collections and has won 2 gold medals and 2 distinctive merit awards in the ADCNY Members Painting Show.

ONOFRIO PACCIONE
After graduating with honors (Tau Phi Sigma) from Community College, he became—at 22 —the youngest AD of the then $5,000,000 Revlon account at the Wm. H. Weintraub agency under Paul Rand. He is now head director and a v-p at Grey Advertising Agency. He has lectured at art schools, written for art publications and books, has judged New York and out-of-town AD club shows. His ads have won awards from the New York AD Club, the Type Directors Club and the AIGA—and have also been chosen for the 50 Best Ads of the Year and for discussions in the advertising trade press.

DONALD R. RUTHER
Modern Packaging Magazine AD for the last 22 years (excepting 2½ years of Army service during World War II) and a member of the New York AD Club for over 25 years, his first art jobs were in the department-store and advertising agency fields. Graduated from Pratt Institute in his native Brooklyn.

ART SCHLOSSER
Head of Monogram Art Studio. After graduating from Rutgers, he joined The New York Times' ad department. He opened his studio in 1946. From a one-man operation it's now manned by more than 50 staff and free-lance designers, illustrators and production technicians. It has won more than 25 major awards. His current operation includes Monogram-Gordon Associates (retouching), Monogram Presentations (films, slides, recordings and other production requirements), and Syracuse and Baltimore affiliates.

ORVILLE SHELDON
A native Chicagoan, attending the Academy of Art there, he has been AD at Foote, Cone & Belding for the last 11 years. He is a past president of the Art Directors Club of Chicago and is currently a member of the advisory board. He has lectured at Northwestern University and has exhibited his paintings. Campaigns have included Hallmark Cards, Armour Canned Meats, Dash Dog Food and Imperial and Walker's Whiskies.

PAUL R. SMITH
Executive vice-president, in charge of creative services, Grant Advertising, he attended the University of Minnesota. Originally an electrical engineer, he switched in the '30s to advertising, first as copywriter, then as an AD. One of the few ADs to fill the top executive post in a major ad agency (he was president as well as creative director at Calkins & Holden), he twice headed The Art Directors Club of N. Y. and has won every important art direction award, including the AAA Medal (twice in one year). He has consistently advocated layout functionalism—a philosophy he attributes to his early mathematical and scientic training. His water colors and other works have been widely exhibited. He edited **Creativity**, recently published, a record of a 2-day symposium sponsored by the ADC-NY and held under his direction.

OTTO STORCH
Otto Storch gave art direction a new dimension in 1959-60-61. His dramatic, strongly communicative layouts for McCall's have made other ADs, in magazines, agencies, companies, studios, perk up their notions of how to win and influence readers. Otto studied at Pratt Institute, Art Students League, Art Associates, and The New School for Social Research. Before coming to McCall's he was Art Editor at Better Living Magazine and AD for Jens Risom Design Inc. He had also freelanced both as an AD and an artist. He has won two ADC gold medals and four awards of Distinctive Merit plus numerous Certicates of Merit in addition to a special citation for "His outstanding Art Direction of McCall's Magazine." He is a member of the New York ADC, the TD and the SI.

ROBERT WEST
He is V-P and Executive AD of Sullivan, Stauffer, Colwell and Bayles, secretary-treasurer of the NSAD, and a past 1st V-P of the Art Directors Club of N.Y. A native New Yorker.

IRVING TRABICH
Previously head AD at two N.Y. agencies, he is now Executive AD, Raymond Spector Co., and director of product-packaging design development for its Hazel Bishop cosmetics account. Agency creative co-ordinator for over 25 TV shows. Originally studied business and accounting. Deciding on a career in art, he attended Pratt Institute, Art Students League and the National Academy of Design. He teaches at the Queens College Youth Center for Art. His paintings have won three N.Y. Art Directors Club awards.

ARNOLD VARGA
Creative Art Supervisor, BBDO, Pittsburgh. The NSAD named him Art Director of the Year in 1959. The State Dept. has exhibited his ads abroad. He has had one-man shows in Chicago and Pittsburgh. His work also appears in the Carnegie Institute of Fine Arts' and the Museum of Modern Arts' permanent collections, and his designs are used at national universities. He began his professional career 15 years ago at the Cox Specialty Store, McKeesport, Pa., and still services that account. He also worked in Pittsburgh and Cleveland retail advertising circles and for the Pittsburgh agency, Ketchum, MacLeod & Grove, before joining BBDO.

ELWOOD WHITNEY
Veteran adman of more than 35 years, the last 17 with Foote, Cone & Belding. There, as Senior V-P and Director, he is an International Div. management supervisor and advisor and New Business Dept. head. Educated in Brooklyn's public schools, he attended Cooper Union 5 nights weekly. He started businesswise as a part-time AD for Doremus, leaving after 5 years to become an AD at JWT where he became V-P, Senior Ad and Plans Board Chairman. He has consistently expounded an "art in industry" philosophy and advocated fine art illustration. He initiated the International Hallmark Art Awards, directed yearly by the Wildenstein Galleries. He is an authority on the advertising and marketing of perfumes (his classic Chanel ad format has remained unchanged for 15 years), watches (he has directed The Watchmakers of Switzerland advertising-marketing strategy in 28 countries for 13 years), tires, pharmaceuticals, soaps, beauty products, silverware, the Smith-Corona portable, company trademarks and symbols, and the language-symbols aspects of communications.

ROBERT WHEELER
A Tennessean who grew up in Texas, he spent the '30s in Chicago and New York as a free-lancing AD. Joining Young & Rubicam in 1940, he served a 3-year Army stint, then returned to Y&R late in '45. Six months later he was transferred by Y&R from New York to the Los Angeles office, where he has been stationed since.

FREDERICK WIDLICKA
Born into a family of artists, he studied drawing and fine arts at the Art Students League of New York and illustration with Pruett Carter and Harvey Dunn. After two years of illustration in New York, he became a printing house AD. "Possibly the youngest AD in the business," he recalls, "I had the signal honor of designing and painting the cover and format of the first full-scale 4-color high-speed rotogravure Sunday supplement." He started his agency career with Storm & Klein, where he became versed in liquor advertising. After free-lancing with other agencies, he joined Lawrence Fertig & Co., where he ADs major liquor accounts.

index to advertisers

Ames Assoc., Archer, 247

Art Direction, 251

Bebell & Bebell Color Lab., 246

Bookshelf, 239

CAM Report, 253

Cicero, Ray, 250

Galloway, Ewing, 248

Graber Art Assoc., Norman, 248

Koste & Assoc., Inc., Frank, 245

Langen & Wind Color Labs, Inc., 252

Lawrence Studios, Paul, 252

Mask-O-Neg, 250

McCall Photoengraving, 238

Monogram Art Studios, 237

North Studios, Inc., Charles W., 246

Price, Henry, 250

Stearns Assoc., Inc., Philip, 238

Ward Color Service, Jack, 248

Whitaker-Guernsey Studios, 240

Expect more from Monogram... No matter what you put in our hands, expect creative flow, the likes of which you've never seen. In the past fifteen years Monogram has helped clients win awards in every art category. You can put this professional quality to work for you, too, simply by calling PL 3-8974. Or write: Monogram Art Studio, Inc., 515 Madison Ave., N.Y. 22

Philip Stearns
Stanley Mangione
Charles Kerlee
Charles Weise
Tom Milson Rep.
Walter Keely Rep.

149 W. 54th St.
N.Y. 19, N.Y.
CO. 5-7605

PHILIP O. STEARNS ASSOCIATES INC. is a new photographic group that can help you creatively. Their vast experience in setting up and lighting huge sets . . . extensive photographic travel here and abroad . . . fashion . . . still life and industrial work add up to one important thing for you **KNOW HOW!**

bookshelf

*The bookshelf makes it easy for readers
to buy, at list price, the best books of current interest
to the art professional and advertising manager.*

NEW BOOKS

229. Haberule Visual Copy-Caster. 6th Edition. Quick character counter, 2 colors, plastic bound, 4-48 pt., over 800 faces, alphabetized, manufacturer-grouped—plus 29 caps-l.c. most popular face specimens. 53 precision pica unit character scales expedite counts of over 4,000 fonts. Plastic type gauge has 6-11 agate and 12-pt. scales, Elite-Pica typewriter character counts and 6" rule. $10.

230. Creative Color. Faber Birren. Psychological concepts in color manipulations, dominant harmonies, law of field size, chromatic light, color systems, iridescent-luminous effects. "Rarely achieved effects" finish each chapter. $10.

ANNUALS

225. New York Art Directors' 39th Annual of Advertising and Editorial Art and Design. Edited by Howard C. Jensen. Designed by George Elliott, senior AD McCann-Erickson, the book's 400 pp. 8x11¼, illustrate the show's 474 pieces in b/w but brilliant color is used for slipcase, bindings, endpapers. Different second colors are used in various sections, colored dividers separate the sections. Editorial features include a program summary of the Fifth Visual Communications Conference, by Frank Baker, conference director. $15. Also available, 38th Annual, $15, No. 197; the 37th, $12.50, No. 182; 36th, $12.50, No. 165; 35th, $12.50, No. 146.

214. International Poster Annual. Edited by Arthur Niggli. 505 outstanding current posters, 20 shown in full color, from 25 countries. Indexed. American selections number 37, take up 9 pages. Noted: continuation of international style trend observed in the last annual, emergence of large and important group of Japanese artists, "concrete" group in Switzerland. $12.

215. The Penrose Annual, Vol. 54. Edited by Allan Delafons. The new edition of the British classic international source-book on the graphic arts has 120 pages of articles reviewing and copious b/w and color plates and inserts illustrating trends and developments in esthetics, economics, techniques, and industry. $12.50.

220. The Picture Universe. U.S. Camera 1961. Edited by Tom Maloney. Includes a full color 4 ft. pullout view of Switzerland by Emil Schulthess, portfolios by Alexander Liberman (from his book The Artist in the Studio), Alfred Eisenstaedt, Roy Stryker (The Lean Thirties), William Klein (Rome), Harper's Bazaar (March 1960), Evelyn Hofer (The Stones of Florence), Vogue feature editor Allene Talmey on Penn, Irving Penn (Moments Preserved, from his book of the same title). Photography in Space. $10.

222. Modern Publicity 1960/61. Edited by Wilfrid Walter. Examples from 28 countries, including some in eastern Europe. Most, from Germany, Japan, Sweden and the U.S. No separation according to origin, so interesting juxtaposition of varied concepts and styles in same category. More than 400 b/w illustrations, 70 in color. $9.95.

223. Illustrators '60. Edited by Howard Munce. Best of current American illustration, in a book designed by Lester Beall and published for the Society of Illustrators of New York. More than 350 selections by about 300 artists from around the country, for the SI 1960 show. Judges discuss their categories. Articles by Harry Carter, George Shealy, Arthur William Brown. $12.95.

PRODUCTION

204. Advertising Agency & Studio Skills. Tom Cardamone. How to prepare art and mechanicals for repro. Detailed, illustrated. $4.75.

208. The 4 Color Process Guide. Sure to become standard reference work for 4 color process reproduction. This 11x14 200 page book showing full range obtainable in print using the four process colors was ADed and designed by Louis Dorfsman, in collaboration with Harry and Marion Zelenko. Scientific, accurate, objective and orderly system for determining precise color wanted. Over 5600 large color patches, each almost two square inches. 3 and 2 color sections are included. Plastic viewer isolates patches for exclusive examination of one color against black, white, and process colors. Special introductory price, $110 prepaid. 10-day trial period.

216. The Grand Three-Color Blending Book. Hans Gaensslen. Unique guide. 50 12x12 pp. letterpress and 50 pp. offset, in 1 edition, show 2-color combinations with black, and 3 colors in various combinations—more than 10,000 shades of color. With each 3-color table are 4 design examples comparing effects a design has in different color combinations and repro methods. Examples also show effects of overprinting and screening. Book includes information on printing inks, production of posters in tempera, choosing most suitable paper and screen, etc. $45.

218. Color Swatch Book. Contains 500 pages of printing ink colors, with over 24,000 perforated color swatches for easy removal. One section is printed on coated, another on uncoated, to facilitate exact matching. Designed for artists, designers, buyers and sellers of printing. Now you can avoid using silk screen, pastel, watercolor samples which printers and lithographers have difficulty in matching. Individual color sections can be reordered and inserted in this specially bound book. $47.50 prepaid, 10 day money back guarantee.

219. Lee Streamlined Copy-Fitting Handbook. Arthur B. Lee. Comes with the Lee Streamlined Copy-Fitting Gauge, made of Vinylite, which fits into a pocket inside 2nd cover. The book has 32 pp. of Linotype and Intertype faces with complete alphabets of all available sizes up to 18 pt. The gauge scale to be used for linear character count is indicated next to each alphabet showing. Many other aids included. Printed in 2 colors, 6x9 pp. $4.95.

227. A Book of Type & Design. Oldrich Hlavsa. 498-page, 2-color indexed Czechoslovakian compendium of 250 various-size Roman faces most popular in Europe and America is a cross-section from the foremost foundries and a practical manual and working specimen book of available book, periodical and jobbing types. $12.50.

228. The Styles of Ornament. Alexander Speltz. Paperback edition of Dover's '59 book (David O'Conor's translation of 2nd German edition) presents 3,766 illustrations, representing ornaments' entire range from prehistoric to mid-19th Century times—all reproducable without permission or payment. $2.25.

GENERAL

211. The Madison Avenue Handbook 1961. Paperback annual diary/directory lists corporate names, addresses, phone numbers and art-staff key buying factors among New York commercial art practitioners and consumers. Additional listings for Chicago, Detroit, Los Angeles, Miami and San Francisco. In all, 24 categories are covered—from ad agencies and art supply houses, photographers and publications to TV-film producers, TV studios and stage-TV union affiliates. Each diary spread has room for write-ins and features a column of 22 expense items. $4.

212. Commercial Art as a Business. Fred C. Rodewald and Edward M. Gottschall. Revised and enlarged edition of the book by the late Rodewald, himself a commercial artist, originally pubished in 1954. Brought up to date—incuding statistics not available before—by Art Direction editor Gottschall. Contains latest information on markets, prices, practices, media needs, contracts. $4.95.

224. Who's Who in Commercial Art and Photography. Director's Art Institute. Collection of lists of artists, photographers, agents, studios, representatives, art buyers. The last category is broken down into ad agency, book publisher, magazine, business. Name, address, phone, and specialty category listed for producers, buyers. $15.

226. Posing for the Camera. Harriett Shepard & Lenore Meyer. Excellently written and illustrated "professional guide" presents know-how needed by creative models and director-photographers to function as working team. $6.95.

James Bingham
Dolli Brackett
Robert Bugg
Roy Cragnolin
Robert Fawcett
Hector Garrido
Jack Hearne
Harold Johns
Richard Kalkman
Raul Mina Mora
Rick Schreiter
Arthur Shilstone
Kenneth Thompson
Thornton Utz

Frank H. Koste & Associates, Inc./ PHONE: PLAZA 1-1706

FRESHNESS

...is a quality strived for in every phase of daily living.

You'll find that desired freshness in the art work created at North Studios. A staff of designers and illustrators is directed to bring forth the best talent to handle any job from spots to 30-sheet posters.

Put freshness in your next job.

Call our representative, Jack McLoughlin, at MU 6-5740, and he will be glad to show you our portfolio.

CHARLES W. NORTH STUDIOS INC.
79 MADISON AVENUE NEW YORK 16

Creative thinking and careful production planning on every illustration, layout and mechanical.

artist: DAVID K. STONE	NORMAN GRABER	DON MILLER	BILL STEINEL
client: Lennen & Newell	Columbia Record Club	True Magazine	AMF/R & D Division
art dir: BOB FELS	LES KLEMES	ED CERULLO	ROBERT DEMOUGEOT

GRABER ART ASSOCIATES
37 WEST 57 STREET ▪ NY ▪ PLAZA 3-3251
Send requests for printed portfolio of samples to Dept. L.

JACK WARD

DYNAMIC SOURCE FOR CREATIVE IDEAS...

FREE! BRAND NEW STOCK PHOTO CATALOG

Speed up ad production with our spanking new catalog. Our wide variety of creative photos in every category are sure to give your artwork a big assist. Write today for your copy of this helpful, new catalog—it's yours free.

EWING GALLOWAY
420 Lexington Avenue, New York 17, N. Y.

ADVERTISING DIRECTIONS:

Trends in Visual Advertising

RaY CICERO

YUKON 6 8930

DESIGN PHOTOGRAPHY

If you buy art,

photography,

typography,

design,

you can buy

better with . .

AD Art Direction

ART DIRECTION,
the only monthly news magazine
reporting advertising art,
photography &
typography exclusively.
Each issue presents
pictorial coverage of the best ad art,
visual analysis of campaign
redesigns,
sources of supply of products
and services,
how-to data on copy preparation,
new and upcoming artists,
photographers, designers,
monthly report of new trends
and techniques in pace setting
advertising.
All this data is packed, with
maximum facts and minimum of
words, into every issue of Art
Direction magazine,
the official publication of the
National Society of Art Directors.
Only $6.00 for 12 news-packed
issues. It's your best business buy.

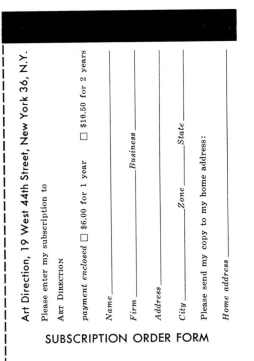

Art Direction, 19 West 44th Street, New York 36, N.Y.

Please enter my subscription to

ART DIRECTION

payment enclosed □ $6.00 for 1 year   □ $10.50 for 2 years

Name _____

Firm _____ *Business* _____

Address _____

City _____ Zone _____ State _____

Please send my copy to my home address:

Home address _____

SUBSCRIPTION ORDER FORM

251

SUBSCRIBE NOW TO
CAMreport
CREATIVE ADVERTISING MANAGEMENT

a new newsletter service for all art and photographic executives who must know prices / salaries / business volume / buying trends tax developments / legal data / ethical problems

If you make decisions — about ad art/photography/design — CAM Reports is for you. Whether you buy or sell, you'll want this twice-a-month crisp reading report. For the first time, art and photographic executives will have facts where there have been no facts. Now you can be in-the-know on what's happening in your city and around the country in art and advertising.

CAM REPORT WILL:

save you time. Its lightning fast readability gives you basic data, unavailable up to now, in a few minutes reading.

save you money. By familiarizing you with industry trends in salaries and prices, it sharpens your factual background for buying and selling supplies and services.

give you factual bases of comparison. Data tables on studio billings will reveal broad trends against which you can measure your performance. Data on percentages of costs for studio operation factors (selling expense, rent, talent, etc.) will enable you to see where your breakdown fits into the general practice.

give you up-to-date data. Published twice-a-month with data as new as the day before mailing, information is rushed to

you at the peak of its significance.

alert you to buying trends. Accurate, prompt reportage of trends, fads, swings in art, photography and business practice can mean the difference of hundreds of dollars to you.

prevent headaches. Just one item on taxes, accounting or law may save you — in dollars, time and aggravation — many, many times the value of the year's subscription.

Fortify your decisions with never-before available facts. Subscribe now.

CAM Report, written exclusively for you, is $20.00 per year for 24 issues. Each issue contains a wealth of material edited to help you save money, conduct your business affairs better. UNCONDITIONAL GUARANTEE: if not fully satisfied with your first four issues, the balance of your subscription will be refunded.

Subscribers to CAM Report are enthusiastic about it

Many CAM subscribers have written us to say how important the semi-monthly newsletters have become to them already. Many subscribers, too, have ordered extra copies for their executive staff. (One studio alone has 8 subscriptions.) Only two subscribers have requested a refund—a remarkable record when you consider that many subscribers bought their subscriptions sight unseen, before publication. Obviously, CAM Report has done what its publisher said it would do.

If you buy or sell art and photography, CAM Report is for you

Subscribe now to the new business newsletter, written exclusively for you twice a month with exactly the news you want and need.

TO BE MONEY AHEAD, TIME AHEAD, ON TOP OF THE FACTS, SUBSCRIBE NOW.

CAM REPORT 19 WEST 44th ST., ROOM 509 NEW YORK 36, N. Y.

☐ Yes. Send me CAM Report now, 24 issues for $20.00.

☐ Enclosed is prepayment in full. Please send me four bonus copies so that my subscription will run for 14 months.

SUBSCRIPTION BLANK

NAME

TITLE

ADDRESS

CITY **ZONE** **STATE**

CAM Report is published by the publishers of ART DIRECTION

A

**trends,
illustration,
subject
index**

Abbot, Jon 182
Advertising
    Believability 201
    Major challenge 209
    Point of no return 210
    Selling power 201
    Truth & taste 201
    Testing 201
Advertising, viewed by
    Art critic 12-13
    Social critic 11-12
    Social historian 13-14
    Historian of taste 14-16
Agfacolor 220
Agfa Isopan Record film 220
Agnew, Clark 138
Airline ad formats
    Air France 123
    Alitalia 124
    El Al 120, 123, 124
    Japan Air Lines 125
    Pan Am 122, 123, 124
    Panagra 121
    Qantas 125
    Sabena 122
Allen, Tom 75
Amana ad 84
American Home, The...66-67
American Type Founders 213
American Wood Type
    Mfg. Co. 213
Ames, Stacy, fashion ad 178
Amsterdam Continental
    Types & Graphic
    Equipment, Inc. 213
Andreozzi, Jerry 102
Annual reports
    Abbott Laboratories 59
    American Machine &
        Foundry Co. 61
    Corn Products Co. 61
    McCall Publishing
        Corp. 62
    New Jersey Bell
        Telephone Co. 60
    Chas. Pfizer & Co.,
        Inc. 62
    Sylvania 58

Annual reports, design
    checklist 56
    Early efforts 57
    Trends
    Charts 62
    Covers 58-60
    General make-up 61
    Illustrations 61
    Type treatment 62
Anscochrome 220
Ansco's Plestar film bases 221
Apostal, Jeannine 102
Appliance ad design problems
    The appliance
        syndrome 79
    Ad similarity 80
Appliance ad
    campaigns 79-86
    Amana 84
    Frigidaire 85
    General Electric 82, 85, 86
    Hotpoint 82
    Kelvinator 80
    Maytag 83
    Norge 81, 84
    Philco 80
    Puritron 84
    RCA 83
    RCA Victor 81
    Tappan 86
    Thor 81
    Westinghouse ... 80, 83, 86
    Whirlpool 83
Arbus, Allan & Diane 64
Arrow Display Associates 165
Art business salaries 224
Art Direction Magazine.. 35
Art direction trends 63-64
Art Directors Club of
    Washington 224
Art employment trends .. 224
Art studio
    Billings, profits 223
    Costs, general expenses 223
Aspen 207
Assn. for a World
    Language 191
Attebery, Charles 102
Authors' biographical
    data 231-235
Auto ad formats
    Corvair 186

Jaguar 186
Renault 186
Rolls-Royce 186
Rover 3-Litre 186
Volkswagen 186
Automatic type casting
Units
  Intertype Corp.'s key-
    boardless Monarch,
    Mergenthaler Lino-
    type's Comet,
    Lanston Industries'
    Monomatic keyboard
    caster, Lanston
    Monotype's Nebitype
    system, Fairchild's
    TT perforating-
    casting teletypesetter
    & Friden Justowriter
    typewriter composer
    221-222
Avedon, Richard 30, 78, 118

B

Bacon, Paul 175
Bahrt, Irv 102
Basic promise, the 203
Bass, Saul 138
Bates, Mercedes 181
Bauer Alphabets, Inc. 213
Bauman, Marty 116
Beall, Lester 102, 143
Beckman, Ronald 146
Beer ad formats
  Ballantine 117
  Budweiser 115
  Carling 116
  Carlsberg 114
  Falstaff 114
  Genesee 115
  Hamm's 116
  Hampden 116
  Holsten-Lager 115
  Lowenbrau 115
  Miller 116
  Narragansett 117
  Pabst 117
  Piels 117
  Rheingold 112
  Ruppert 118
  Schlitz 118
  Utica Club 114
Belin Belingraver 220
Benton, Robert ...19, 74, 75
Berger, Lawrence 138
Bergeron, Richard 102
Bernstein, Cal 71
Binder, Joseph 156, 158
Bista plate 217
Blossom, Dave 124
Blumenfeld 104
Blumenthal, Sidney 178
Books, new 227-229
Boots, Henri 102
Borgana fashion ad 178
Bouche, R. 105
Bowman, William R. ...66-67
Bradford, Ronald 22
Bramson, Hershel 185
Brand-image building 201

Brand Image Symposium,
  1960 210
Briggs, Austin 19
Briggs, Don 110
Brightype negatives 217
Broadhurst, Frank 138
Brolio ad 13
Brorby, Melvin 194
Brownjohn, Chermayeff
  & Geismar 175
Bruehl, Anton 27
Brussel-Smith, Bernard.... 185
Bryson, John 185
Budin, Elbert 65
Bull, Herbert 138
Bursk, Edward C. 202
Burtin, Will 102
Business Week article:
  How to Sell Your
  Profit Story 193
Butte, Mary Ellen 138

C

Cadge, William 64-65
Calograph (Hell Color-
  graph) scanner 220
Camera & film size, new 220
Camera color composing 218
Campazuno, Claudio 206
CAM Report 223
Capellupo, Vic 183
Carle, Eric 102
Carpenter, Mia 129
Cartier-Bresson, Henri .. 30
Caruso, Bruno 78
Cassandre, A. M. 12, 156, 158
Castellon, Federico 173
Cato, Robert 174
Challenge of sameness.... 200
Chicago Show Printing
  Co. 166
Chirico 13
Chwast, Seymour 114
Cigarette ad formats
  Camel 183
  Chesterfield 183
  Lucky Strike 183
  Pall Mall 182
  Salem 183
  Winston 183
Club exhibits
  directory 225-226
Coiner, Charles T. 180
Color correcting 218
Colored & textured
  papers 221
Color-Line electro 217
Communications
  Aural-visual 208
  Communicating
    advertising 187, 188
  Confusion, the one
    traceable trend 186
  International
    communications 204, 205
  Message 208
  Non-verbal vs. verbal 205
  Our most important
    problem 189
  Transacting business.... 187

Two-way street 208
Understanding 209
Consumers
  Consumerism 200
  Hostility to advertising 201
  Meeting & changing
    consumer attitudes .. 210
  Consumer waste 200
Condak, Cliff 72, 73
Conlon, Bill 20
Contact screens 218
Container Corp. of
  America 167
Cook, C. W. 210
Copy policy 203
Corporate image programs
  Ansul 46
  Braun 54
  Connecticut General... 48
  General Dynamics 47
  Neiman-Marcus 49
  Pan American 53
  Swissair 50
  Torrington Mfg. Co. .. 51
  Volkswagen 52
Corporation
  Bigness 208
  Blocks to corporate
    design effectiveness. 208
  Creativity
    "togetherness" 208
  Image program 207
  Profits vs. social
    obligation 207
Cosmetic ad formats
  Avon 110
  Bonwit Teller 107
  Breck 105
  Casaque Parfum 109
  Charles of the Ritz .. 110
  Clairol 108
  Coty 105
  Dorothy Gray 106
  D'Orsay 108
  Elizabeth Arden...105, 107
  Hazel Bishop 109
  Helena Rubenstein ... 108
  Houbigant 109
  Juliette Marglen 107
  Max Factor 108, 110
  Parfums Christian Dior 107
  Ponds 106, 110
  Revlon 109
  Tussy Eye Cream 107
  Yardley 106
Cox, Frank 219
Craft House Plastics
  Corp. 170
Creativity
  Attracts clients 210
  Competition & other
    hindering factors ... 210
  Cooperation aids it .. 210
  Creative process 207
  Creativity vs.
    innovation 207
  Creativity re-hashed.. 204
  Discipline 201, 202
  Future of creativity .. 208
  Innovation differences 200
  Research-inhibited
    creativity 202

Crosfield Scanatron 220
Culler, George D. 207

D

Dahlgren dampening
  system 218
Dali 13
D'Amato, George 102
Damron, Jack 117
Daniels, Draper 181
"Daphne Knows" fashion
  ad 178
David, Donald K. 197
Dechar Corp. 168
Decker, H. P. 142
Deitch, Gene 138
DeKooning, William 72
Del Sorbo, Joseph 125
de Narde, Florian 115
Derujinsky 31
Design
  Demand 209
  Impulse design, a
    salesmanship trap.... 209
  Japanese design
    problem 209
  Mediocrity 208
  Undesigned design 209
Designers
  Professional
    development 208
  Future demand for 208
Dichter, Dr. Ernest 204, 210
Dimensionally stable
  film bases 218
Di Paolo, Lou 102
Dimitri, Peter 67
Direct mail formats
  Alcoa 150
  CIBA 149
  Circulation Associates 152
  DMAA '60 Florida
    Convention 151
  Eaton Laboratories 153
  Eli Lilly 153
  General Electric 150
  Harris-Intertype 154
  Lehigh Furniture 154
  Life 149, 151
  Modess 150
  Robertshaw-Fulton
    Controls 151
  Saturday Evening Post 148
  Upjohn 152
  Westvaco Inspirations 154
  W. Va. Pulp & Paper
    Co. 154
Disciplined thinking ... 9-10
Doisneau, Robert 30
Dome, Paul 65
Dow-Etch process 216
Dows, Hal 129
Douglas, Lester 33
Drawing-painting school 19
Duffy, William 138
Duncan, David 206
Du Pont's Cronar film
  bases 221
Du Pont's Dycril plates 216
Duval, Francis 102

E

Eastman Kodak Estar
  film bases 221
Economy
  Less pressurized 209
  Growth, answer to
    inflation 209
Editorial design
  Cosmetics 104
  Magazines 63-78
  Pharmaceutical 98
Ektachrome
  E3 220
  Highspeed 220
Ektacolor 220
Eisenstaadt, Alfred 30
Electrofax 218
Electric scanning 218, 219
Electroplastic (PPR) plate 217
Electrostatics 218
Electrotypes 216
Ellwood, Craig 208
English, the common
  language 191
Eric 105
Ertegun, Nesuhi 173
Eskell, Olle 208
Esquire 74-75
Eutemy, Loring 23
Evan-Picone fashion ad.. 178
Evo, Charles 20
Expressionism 18
E-Z plate 217

F

Fabian, Robert 128
Faddist movement in
  design 207
Fairchild Graphic
  Equipment Co.
    TT perforating-casting
    tele-typesetter 221
  Scan-A-Color 220
Family of Man, The....... 206
Films, faster color 220
  finer grain developers 220
Financial ad designs
  Bank of America 90, 91, 92
  Bank of New York 91
  Bankers Trust Co. 92
  Chase Manhattan
    Bank 89, 90
  Chemical Bank New
    York Trust Co. 92, 93, 94
  Industrial Bank of
    Commerce 93
  Insured Savings &
    Loan Assn. 91
  Irving Trust Co. 91
  New York Stock
    Exchange 88, 94
  Savings Banks Assn. of
    State of N.Y. 94
Fine, Paul 208
Fink, Sam 180
Fink, William 19
Fiore, Robert 102
Fischer, Carl 102

Flack, John 125
Flexography 218-219
Flora, James 172
Fontaine, Alan 182
Food Additives
  Amendment 141
Ford Foundation symbol-
  ogy study 188
"Form follows function" 200
Fotosetter photographic
  typesetter 221
Friden Justowriter type-
  writer composing
  machine 222
Fox, Barbara 19
Frank, Robert 30
Frankfurt, Stephan 138
Frasconi, Antonio 24, 173
Freedman, Arnold A. 183
Frigidaire ad 84
Fuchs, Bernie 20, 185
Fusco, Paul 71

G

Gage, Robert 110, 138
Gallup, Dr. George ..202, 204
Geissman, Robert 23
General Electric ad
  formats 80, 81, 82, 84,
                    85, 86
Gentlemen's Quarterly ..76-77
Gertner, Richard 177
Gill, Frances McGlaughlin 116
Gill, Leslie 30
Gimmicks, direct mail 148-149
Girltown fashion ad 178
Glaser, Milton 20
Glusker, Irwin 22
Gnoli, Domenico 22
Goals, good & bad 205
Goodford, Jack 138
Gorbaty, Norman 102
Gorey, Tom 24
Government patronage
  suggestions 208
Graficon, Inc. 168
Graham, Ed Jr. 138
Graham, Robert M. 201
Great Lakes Press Corp. 174
Greco, Robert 102
Greenberg, Al 76-77
Grossman, Alvin 66, 67
Grossman, William 66
Grothkopft, Chad 138
Guelot, Hans 209
Guild, Rollins 138
Guild, Walter 201

H

Haas, Ernst 30, 78
Halfant, Jules 172, 173
Hall, Chadd 76
Hall, Emma Gene 77
Hallock, Robert 20
Halsman, Philippe 206
Halverson, Janet 20
Hampton, Blake 175
Harder, Rolf 142

Hard-to-print materials
  Cellophane, polyethy-
    lene, saran, foil,
    mylar, vinyl, Xmas
    wrappings, Scotch
    tape, plastic table-
    cloths, drinking
    cups, linoleum 218
Harper's Bazaar 30, 78
Hasselblad camera 220
Hathaway shirt man 202
Havinden, Ashley 211
Hays, Phil 24
Hawkins, Arthur III 115
Hecht, David B. 173
Helburn, William 110, 184
Hell Colorgraph
  scanner 220
Hell Vario-Klischograph 220
Herman, Elliott 102
Hesse, Paul 26, 111
Hesse Studios 117
Hester, Hal 146
Hidden Persuaders, The 205
Hi-Fi color 218
Hill, John 183
Hochman, Gerald 107
Hofer, Evelyn 128
Hohlwein, Ludwig 156
Hooker, Eugene 117, 183
Horn-Griner 115
Horowitz, Irwin 66, 67
Hotpoint ad 82
Houston, Bryan 204
Hoyt, Palmer 189
Hubley, John 138
Humanities-Science
  relationship 194
Humor in advertising 200, 206
Hunter-Penrose H.P.K.
  Autoscan 220
Hurd, Richard 20
Hurlburt, Allen F. 70
Hutton, Graham 208
Hyde, Scott 102

I

Iapalucci, John 183
Ideas 9-10
Illiteracy 191
Image 8
  Corporate image 43-54
  Corporate purpose 44
  Communication 44-45
  Corporate image
    programs 46-54
Improved masking
  techniques 218
Individuality
  Individuality vs. pro-
    fessional discipline .. 207
  Individuality an
    illusion 209
Inks, fast-setting &
  heat-set 218
  fluorescent inks 219
Innovators 206
  20th Century techno-
    logical society op-
    portunities & limits
    of action 207

International Design
  Conference, 1960 200, 206
International visual
  language 200
Interstate-Boochever
  Corp. 168
Investment Bankers Assn.
  of America 197
Ishii, Chris 117, 138

J

Jacobson, Joe 23
Johnson, Arno H. 209
Johnson, Luther 117
Johnson, Roy H. 146
Johnston, Myrna 181
Jones, Caroll 184
Jones, Dick 102
Jones, Robert M. 23, 172, 173
Jonson, Vance 143
Josephs, Devereux C. ... 196
Julius, Leslie 207

K

Kagy, Edmund 116
Kane, Art 31, 64
Kamekura, Yusaku 209
Kauffer, E. McKnight 12, 156
Kaye, Paul 200
Kelley, Tom 114
Kellman, Ray 177
Kelvinator ad 80
Keppler, Victor 26
Kim, Paul 138
Klein, W. 31
Kodachrome 220
Koehler, Henry 19
Koons, Irv 142
Korby-Cogeshall-Steinau
  Co., Inc. 170
Kowall, Gene 115
Kraus, Sigmund 31
Kreiger 31
Krein, Martin A. 185
Kuhle, Jerry 153
Kushner, Arnold 24

L

L'Aiglon fashion ad 178
Lacquers, non-binding ... 218
Lahti, Arre K. 210
Laubach, Dr. Frank C. .. 191
Lavey, Kenneth 102
Lax, Michael 146
Layout research
  Copy 202
  Editorial 202
  Gadgetry, design 202
  Headline 202
  Illustration 202
  TV commercials 202
Lehman, Acy R. 175
Leiter, Saul 31, 74

Leonian, Phillip 102
Let-Creative-People-
Alone Week 204
Letterpress 215-216
Leyendecker, J. C. 156
Liberty Corrugated
Container Corp. 169
Life 27, 30, 80
Life Insurance Assn. of
America 196
Lightweight plates 215-216
Linofilm photographic
typsesetter 221
Lind, Raymond 138
Lippincott & Margulies 169
Liquor ad formats
Hermitage 184
Imperial 184
Old Crow 184, 185
PM 184
Seagram's 7 & VO 184
Smirnoff Vodka 185
Liss, Abe 138
Lithengrave plates 217
Lithographic
platemaking 218
Lithography 217-218
Lithure plates 217
Livoti 114
Locomobile ad 13
Lois, George 176
Look 27, 30, 70-71
Look-Kromatic gravure .. 218
Low, Joseph 23, 172
Lownds, Hans 27
LTF sensitivity guide 218
Lubalin, Herb 102
Ludekens, Fred 181

M

Macomber, John D. 201
Maddalone, Andrew 183
Maddocks, Joe 143
Magazines 211
Editorial design 63-78
Image 63
Presentation 63
Magazines' editorial
formats
American Home 66-67
Esquire 74-75
Gentlemen's
Quarterly 76-77
Harper's Bazaar 78
Look 70-71
McCall's 64-65
Nugget 72-73
Playboy 68-69
Maisel, Jay 102
Makeready
reduction 215, 216, 217
Malzan, Dr. Traugott 207
Mandarino, Tony 24
Mandel, Saul 23
Manley, Ray 183
Market research 203
Marketing vs. inflation .. 201
Martin, Jerome 73, 102, 174
Martin, Noel 174
Martineau, Pierre 205

Mason, Joseph E. 165
Mathisson, C. A. 116
Matson, Richard 102
Matter, Herbert 104
Mayer, Lawrence A. 209
Mayes, Herbert R. 204
McCall, David 202
McCaffery, Bill 117
McCall's 64-65, 176, 204, 219
McCurdy, Gilbert G. 212
McGarry, Joseph 206
McKinney & Co. 201
McMahon, Franklin ..20, 102
McNally, Kevin 126
Mead Containers—
Gibralter Display Div. 167
Mead, Dr. Margaret 206
Medal-winning creative
agencies 201
Media
Mass media destroy
creativity and good
taste 210
Media credibility 211
Media responsibility.... 205
Meehan, John 207
Meek, Dwaine 166
Melahn, Tom 117
Meltzoff, Stanley 20
Merrill Lynch Pierce
Fenner & Smith 89
Metzl, Ervine 156, 157
Meyers, Arnold 175
Miehle Color Scanner 220
Mili, Gjon 27
Mobility 208
Mondrian influence in
direct mail 154
Monogram Art Studios.... 148
Monroe, Robert 117
Morrow 107
Moses, Eugene 102
Muench, Jos. 117
Muhfield, Otto 185
Mullen dampening
system 218
Multigrade variable
contrast papers 220
Munari, Bruno 209
Murello, John 174
Murray, Donald 102
Murrow, Edward R. 205
National Assn. of Art
Services, Inc. 223

N

National Better Business
Bureau 211
Nation's Business article:
Why You & Your Boss
Disagree 193
Negative color materials 220
Nelson, Andrew 121, 122,
123, 125
Nelson Co., George 146
Nepo, Arik 183
Nesbitt, Esta 22
Newspapers 211
New York Art Directors
Club 204, 205

Annuals 26
N.Y.S. Employment
Service Art Unit 224
New York Times 193
New York World
Telegram 193
Nodell, Martin 138
Nolan, Pat 116
Norge ad formats 81, 84
Nowlis, Dr. Helen &
Vincent 212
Noyes, Eliot 207
Nugget 72-73
Nylon plate 216

O

Obsolescence
Styled obsolescence 200
Product obsolescence.. 204
Off-beat, on-beat &
dead-beat advertising.. 201
Ogilvy, Benson &
Mather, Inc. 202
New campaign
procedure 203, 204
Old Print 175
Operation Day-Dream 210
"Organization Man"
theory 208
Orr, Garret P. 205
Outdoor advertising
Art of interruption 211
Ostentation-bad taste
problem 211
Poster's golden decade 156
Remembrance
ingredient 156
Simplicity essential 156
Too many cooks today 157
Trend setters 156
Outdoor poster designs
Blue Cheer .... 161•
Chicago Sunday
Tribune 161
Coca Cola 158
Ford 159, 160
Holsum Bread 162
Kool-Aid 160
Life 160
Life Savers 161
Marco-Polo-Tee 157
Meinl-Tee 158
New York City 162
Peristyle, The 157
Uneeda Baker 158
U. S. Navy 156
Wrigley's Gum 159

P

Packaging
Challenges 140
Consumer demands 140-141
New legislation impact 141
Supermarket 140
Packaging designs
Aerosol can 140
Aluminum can 144
Carton pouches 146

Chalk 142
Children's drops 142
Cutlery 142
Eggs 143
Electric tools 143
Flip-top box 140
Foil pans 145
High-density polyethy-
lene bottle 144
Light-weight glass 144
Molded foams 146
Pet foods 143
Polyethylene wrap 145
Polyethylene squeeze
bottle 144
Pump-type fiber can.... 140
Roll-on applicator 140
Sponges 142
Stereo tonearm 143
Tetrahedral cartons 145
Thermaform packs 146
Packard, Vance 204, 205
Pagano, Inc. 115
Page, Bill 72, 73
Paine, Wingate 114, 138
Paper innovations 221
Brightwhite (fluores-
cent pigmented)
papers 221
Colored & textured
papers 221
Dampeners 218
Machine coated offset
papers 218
Paper rolls 221
Trailing blade coating 221
Palazzo, Peter 19
Parker, Al 19
Parkinson, C. Northcote 207
Parks, Gordon 31
Paul, Arthur 68-69
Paulson, Carl 116
Payne, Harry 20
PDI Electronic Scanner 219
Peak, Bob 19, 117
Penfield, Edward 156
Penn, Irving 27, 30, 138
People's sameness &
differences 200, 205
Personal-inspiration
oriented artist 207
Personality 8
Store personality a
must 128
Persuasion 205
Pertchik, Harriet 118
Pharmaceutical ad
designs
Chlor-Trimeton Syrup 97
Elipten 97
Ethicon 96
Hesper-C Prenatal 97
McNeil Laboratories,
Inc. 96
A. H. Robins Co., Inc. 96
Philco ad 80
Philip Morris 182
Philips, Gerard 102
Phillips, Cole 156
Photography 202, 206
Dominance in record
album field 171

Editorial 27, 30
Innovations 220-221
Photographer's
responsibility 206
Reportorial 97
Trends, general 29
Food ad trends 180
Location trend 220
Photographic composing 221
Photographic typesetters
Linofilm, Photon &
Fotosetter 221
Photon photographic
typesetter 221
Photopolymers, etc. 216
Phototypesetting 218
Piel, Bert & Harry 112
Pinzke, Herbert 208
Plastalum plate 217
Plate surface treatments,
new 218
Playboy 68-69
Polaroid Land Camera... 220
For test shooting 220
Color film 220
Politz, Alfred 204
Polycontrast variable
contrast papers 220
P-o-P display designs
Bulova Co. 165
Coca-Cola Co. 170
Du Pont de Nemours
& Co. 165
DX Sunray Oil Co. 169
Early Times Bourbon 167
Enna Jettick 167
General Electric Co.... 168
Hiram Walker & Sons 170
Ideal Toy Corp. 165
Jantzen, Inc. 170
Julius Kayser & Co. 166
Longines-Wittnauer
Co. 169
Merck, Sharpe &
Dohme 166
National Distillers 167
Nestle Co. 168
Pet Milk Co. 166
Revlon, Inc. 168
Sherwin-Williams Co. 168
Schmidt's of
Philadelphia 169
Stahl-Meyer, Inc. 166
Possony, Stefan T. 189
Powderless (one bite)
etching 216
PPR (Electroplastic plate) 217
Presensitized plates 218
Product Presentations,
Inc. 165
Production innovations.... 215
Letterpress 215, 216
Lithography 217, 218
Photography 220, 221
Paper 218, 221
Typography 221
Inks 218, 221
Professional design
principle 200
Programming, European
& Canadian 205
Puritron ad 84

Q

Quantity of quality 208

R

Rapid etch 216
RCA Victor 81, 83
Reader's Digest, The 89
Record album designs
Atlantic 173
Columbia 174
Kapp 175
MGM 175
RCA Camden 174
RCA Victor 172, 173
Riverside 175
Roulette 175
Vanguard 172, 173
Recorder typewriter
composing machine 222
Regehr, Carl 102
Reilly, Paul 208
Reinsel, Walter 20
Renfro 161
Renning, David 130
Retail stores' ad formats
Cox's 130
Franklin Simon 129
Miller's 128
Neiman-Marcus 130
Revlon 106, 109
Rice, Edward 20
Rice, Elmer 210
Richards, Ray 138
Riley, Ken 20
Research
Readership research .. 202
Motivational research.. 205
Robinson, Dr. Claude .. 204
Rogers, Richard 143
Rolls-Royce 201
Roper, Elmo 204
Rose, Ben 104, 183
Rosen, Ben 142
Ross, Alexander 102
Rotary press, increased
use of 215
Rothberg, Sidney 184, 185
Roy, Pierre 13
Rudolph, Harold 202
Ruffins, Reynold 173

S

Saffir, Robert 102
Sanders, George 117
Sales Promotion 201
SP Mgr. coming man
in management? 201
SP sells better than
advertising 201
Sales Promotion
Executives Assn. 201
San Francisco Museum
of Art 207

Saturday Evening Post
article: Words that
Divide the World ... 189
Savage, Lee 138
Savignac 160, 161
Sayers, Dorothy L. 204
Scanner Studios 219
Schatzberg, Jerry 65
Scheck, Henry 118
Schiffer, Richard 146
Schmidt, Harvey 19
Schulteis, Emil 206
Schutz Co., Inc.,
Thomas A. 169
Screen process 219
Sculptural Promotions,
Inc. 167
Search for certainty, The 205
Selling statement 8
Seltzer, Abe 153
Semantics
Communication
confusion 193
Direct mail 148
Financial advertising.. 88
Semantics deception 191
Seminar for Management 202
Shaw, Robert 114
Shipman, Art 130
Shustak, Larry 72
Sidebotham, Jack 138
Siegel, Leo Dink 20
Silvas, Leslie 184
Simms, Bill 185
Simpson, Bernard 23
Simson, Jacques 115
Skippy Peanut Butter .. 201
Slade, Mark 102
Smith, Don 146
Smith, Eugene 206
Smith, Paul 181
Smiton, David 116
Snyder, Jerome 19
Snyder & Black &
Schlegel 170
Society, 4 explosive
development stages .. 205
Sokolsky, Melvin 175
Sophistication 7, 8, 103,
131, 164, 172
Sorel, Edward 23
Sources of films, slides,
etc., for club
showings 229-230
Spewak, William 114
Springmaid fashion ad 178
Standards, high 211
Starch, Daniel 204
Steichen 26
Steinau, Jack 23
Steinberg 78
Steiner, Ralph 26
Stensgaard, W. L. &
Associates 168
Stern, Bert 27, 65, 185
Sternglass, Arno 73
Stevens, Martin 123
Stoehrer, John 115
Storch, Otto 64-65, 181, 219
Strategy of Desire, The 204
Stuart, Ken 20
Super Anscochrome 220

Supermarket 140
Sweeney, Margaret 206
Swift, Philip 102

T

Tappan ad format 86
Tara, Bill 200
Taste
Don't meet it, lead it 205
Taste in advertising 201
Tate, Norman 138
Taubin, William 114, 120,
123, 124, 126
Taylor, Robert J. 118
Television 211
Yesterday, Today,
Tomorrow 132
Textured & colored
papers 221
Tesse, La 71
Textile Labeling Act 141
Third Annual Institute in
Technical & Industrial
Communications 188
Thollander, Earl 24
Thomas-Leeds Co., Inc. 166
Thompson, Bradbury 154
Thompson Co., J. Walter 209
Thompson, Richard 22
Thor ad 81
Time-Life scanner (PDI) 219
Toulouse Lautrec,
H. de 12, 156
Trailing blade coating ... 221
Tudor, Charles 219
Tunnard, Christopher 209
Tyler, William 181
Type faces, new
American Type
Founders, American
Wood Type Mfg.
Co., Amsterdam
Continental, Bauer
Alphabets, Intertype
Corp., Lanston
Monotype, Ludlow
Typograph Corp. &
Mergenthaler
Linotype Co. 213
Typography
Dynamic borders 38
Fun with type 41
Formal school 33
Informal school 33
Minor surgery 42
Non-integrated type.... 41
Trends 70
Type face mixing 39
Type-picture fusing ...36-37
Typography
innovations 221
Visual onomatopoeia.. 40
Word-picture ads 35

U

Understanding 200, 206
In communications 209
Ungerer, Tomi 23

University of Michigan 210
University of Rochester 212
Using visual media to
   express ideas 200, 205

V

Vachon, John 70
Van Diver Reports 201, 210
Varga, Arnold 130
Varigam variable contrast
   papers 220
Venti, Tony 115
Visual drama 200
Vogue 30
Volkov, Leon 206
Volkswagen 82, 186, 201

Vuckovic, Ched 110

W

Wall, Bob 126
Wastemakers, The 200, 204
Weaver, Sylvester L. 205
Web-fed presses 220
Web-offset printing
   growth 217
Weiner, Richard 23
Welsh, Vernon 208
Werbin, Irving 175
Westinghouse ad
   formats 80, 81, 82, 83, 86
Wheaton, Ned 185

Whirlpool ad 83
Whitmore, Coby 19
Wickersham, Robert 138
Widlicka, Fred 184, 185
Winogrand, Gary 102
Wohl, Jack 138
Wolf, Henry 78
Women's department
   store buying
   motivations 212
Wood, Brendan 219
Wood, Leona 20
Woodward, James 115
Woolite 201
Wooten, Rector 181
World Design Conference 208
Wrap-around plates 215, 216
Wynn, Dan 31

X

Xerography 218

Y

Yanagi, Sori 209
Young, John Orr 210
Young, Stan 66
Young & Rubicam 210
   House ad slogan 82

Z

Zieff, Howard 138